REPRESENTATIVE
MODERN PREACHERS

REPRESENTATIVE
MODERN PREACHERS

BY

LEWIS O. BRASTOW, D.D.
PROFESSOR OF PRACTICAL THEOLOGY IN YALE UNIVERSITY

Essay Index Reprint Series

BOOKS FOR LIBRARIES PRESS
FREEPORT, NEW YORK

First Published 1904
Reprinted 1968

LIBRARY OF CONGRESS CATALOG CARD NUMBER:
68-57306

PRINTED IN THE UNITED STATES OF AMERICA

To the Graduates of Yale Divinity School,
who have participated with me in the study of the
Great Preachers of the Christian Church, and with
whom I have passed pleasant class-room hours that
will never be forgotten,

   I Dedicate this Volume.

PREFACE

THE chapters of this volume were originally lectures to divinity students. I have ventured to present them in revised and expanded form to the general public, because I think that the preachers of whose personalities and products I have here attempted a critical estimate have, by their skill and force in presenting the truth, won the right to a special hearing. I have been a careful student of them for many years, and confess a special personal interest in most of them. Some of them are well known. A good deal has been said about them and they have been widely read. It may seem, therefore, to be bringing "coals to Newcastle" to discuss them anew. But some of them are not well known. A volume of Schleiermacher's selected and translated sermons was presented a few years ago to the American public. But I venture the surmise that but few, even among preachers, know this great representative of the German pulpit, either as preacher or as theologian. Newman and Mozley have still a limited circle of readers and admirers, but it might well be enlarged. The "up-to-date" man is not interested in Guthrie or Spurgeon. They have contributed little or nothing to the thought of the church. But each according to his type was a great preacher, and it would be a mistake to minimize their significance for

the practical life of the church. It is doubtless something of a venture to ask fresh attention to the more
widely known and read preachers of our group, who
bear most distinctively the modern mark. But I have
cherished the hope that by directing attention to the
influences that wrought upon all of these preachers,
by analyzing their characteristics of personality and
their homiletic methods and products, by indicating
what they represent as preachers, and by setting them
somewhat in comparison or contrast, I may have succeeded in a measure in getting them into fresh light,
and may have made some additional contribution, however slight, to the knowledge of them. Contemporary
with the preachers we are considering there were, of
course, others of great skill and effectiveness who
might well have been grouped with them. But personal preference is a factor in the selection; the plan
of discussion would not admit of enlargement of the
group, and it may at least be claimed that none of
their contemporaries surpassed them in their own lines.
There are living preachers who are their worthy successors, but the author does not wish to engage in
vivisection.

The preachers before us differ widely from each
other as representatives of the preaching of the last
century. Each in his own way represents some important interest, meets some real want, and is the
product of some movement of thought or life, or some
combination of movements, measurably manifest in
the last century. Some of them are theologically and
ecclesiastically reactionary, but not one of them is a
complete anachronism, and there is none that fails to

bring an important message for his age and for ours as well. No effort has been made to differentiate them formally by groups, or to classify them according to the schools they may be supposed to represent. But they represent different tendencies and they belong to different types. Ecclesiastically the first five may be called Broad churchmen, the two following High churchmen, and the last two Low churchmen, using these terms comprehensively. Theologically the first group represent measurably modern catholicity and liberality, the second church confessionalism, and the third an ardent evangelicalism. With respect to points of view or prevailing tendencies of homiletic thought and method, they may be called respectively humanistic, dogmatic, and Biblical. But these are only general terms, not exhaustive of either group, and much less of individual peculiarities and tendencies. They represent the diversities and varieties that characterize the modern pulpit, and, on the other hand, they share much that is common, and all disclose in some measure the influences that are everywhere at work in modern life.

We need to get back to the best. The great preacher is a gift from God, and the church and its ministers need incentive from their princes. If I may but succeed in securing from intelligent laymen, theological students, and preachers new interest in the men to whom I have ventured to direct their attention, my object will have been secured and I shall have my reward.

CONTENTS

CHAPTER I

FRIEDRICH DANIEL ERNST SCHLEIERMACHER

CHAPTER II

FREDERICK WILLIAM ROBERTSON

CHAPTER III

HENRY WARD BEECHER

CHAPTER IV

HORACE BUSHNELL

CHAPTER V

PHILLIPS BROOKS

CHAPTER VI

JOHN HENRY NEWMAN

CHAPTER VII

JAMES BOWLING MOZLEY

CHAPTER VIII

THOMAS GUTHRIE

CONTENTS

CHAPTER IX

CHARLES HADDON SPURGEON

CHAPTER I

FRIEDRICH DANIEL ERNST SCHLEIERMACHER

I

SCHLEIERMACHER'S SPIRITUAL AND INTELLECTUAL DEVELOPMENT

IT seems almost presumptuous to undertake, within the limits permitted, to investigate so complex a personality as that of Schleiermacher, even from the restricted point of view of the preacher. But when we consider that he is the representative and the organ of those complex influences that have so powerfully affected the religious life of the modern world, and when we recall his vast significance for the modern evangelical church, the undertaking may be sanctioned, however inadequate its success. And because of the representative character of his preaching, of its influence upon the German pulpit, and of its own intrinsic excellencies, perhaps no better selection from among German preachers, for our study, could have been made. In the realm of religion he was the representative man of his century, a man of most capacious susceptibilities and of most comprehensive genius. Perhaps no man of his time was so responsive to those intellectual, æsthetic, religious, ethical, ecclesiastical, and political influences that were at work in

B 1

the ferment of the latter part of the eighteenth and in the first part of the nineteenth century, and which are still evolving their results in the most characteristic tendencies and movements of our day. He can hardly be classified. He seems not so much an individual, limited personality as a vast and varied influence. He founded no school, but has influenced all schools. It was this universality and versatility that made him an object of misapprehension. He was himself conscious of it, and lamented its consequences. He was contemporary with most of the great men of Germany who have made themselves felt upon the modern world. In philosophy, Schelling and Leibnitz preceded him but by a few years, and Hegel was his colleague at the Berlin University. In literature, there were Lessing, Goethe, Herder, Schiller, Novalis, Jean Paul Richter, and the Schlegels, with the younger of whom he at one time lived in closest personal friendship. He was himself a philosopher of whom Schelling, in commendation of his " Discourses on Religion," in substance said that they were the product of the profoundest philosophical investigation, or else they must have been written under blind inspiration. By a competent authority, he has been called " the greatest theologian of the Protestant church since the Reformation," and at his death, Neander characterized him as "the man from whom will be dated henceforth a new era in the history of theology." He was a literary humanist, gifted with rare artistic sense, a teacher with rare gifts of exposition and of stimulation, a statesman whose voice was heard in troublous times in the councils of the nation, a church leader of catholic, tolerant spirit and of wide practical initiative, and he has been correctly designated by a French writer as the "most eminent Christian preacher in Germany," in his day. His industry was commensurate with his ability. From early years and up to the very last, he was an earnest and diligent student, rising at an early hour in the morning and sitting late into the night, detesting laziness in all men, and especially intolerant of it in himself, as one of the worst of vices. From this world of thought and of experience he won the most multifarious resources, perhaps, of any man of his time, all of which he assimilated with amazing facility and made tributary to his work.

The speculative side of Schleiermacher's development does not concern us, save as it is tributary to its practical aspect. It is with him as a preacher that we have to deal, and in tracing the course of his development, which seems necessary to our purpose, we shall have reference to its bearings on his work as a preacher. In his career there are four distinctly marked periods, in which four classes of influence wrought determinatively upon him. There was the early period of dominating religious influence; then followed the period of his student life, in which philosophic influences shaped his thinking; then came the literary influences of a still later period; and finally the influences that originated in the ecclesiastical and political conditions of his age and nation.

1. Schleiermacher was nurtured from early years in the school of mystical Moravian piety. He was himself constitutionally and most delicately responsive to religious influences, a man with a genius for religion, perhaps, beyond any prominent man of his age.

"Piety," he says in his discourses,[1] "was the mother's womb in whose sacred darkness my young life was nourished and was prepared for a world still sealed for it. In it my spirit breathed ere it had yet found its own place in knowledge and experience. It helped me as I began to sift the faith of my fathers and to cleanse thought and feeling from the rubbish of antiquity." His paternal grandfather was a man of religious visions. His father, a man of varied intellectual activities and of multifarious knowledge, at one time a sceptical preacher of the accommodating Kantian school, became an ardent dogmatic devotee of the evangelical faith, and of a mystical piety after the Moravian type. This early religious influence the son, in one of his letters in later life, acknowledged: "The first element that developed itself spontaneously was the religious. I can remember its first movements in me, during a walk with my father. He never allowed me to lose sight of it again, after it had developed itself." His mother was his only earliest teacher, a woman of sound judgment, of loving heart, and of pedagogic tact, who nourished in him a love of knowledge, inculcated the necessity of thoroughness in his intellectual tasks, corrected his youthful conceit of superiority, while she stimulated the sentiment of gratitude and cherished his earliest religious emotion. In this atmosphere of devout and earnest piety he spent the first fifteen years of his life, and was then sent to the Moravian school at Niesky. This school, with its local isolation, its attractive natural environment, its simplicity and unworldliness, and its devout piety, was chosen by the son himself, no less than by his parents,

[1] Schleiermacher's "Werke," Vol. I, Die Reden, p. 152.

as a defence for his soul against the possible corruptions of the more distinctively scientific schools. In the two schools of Niesky and Barby he remained for four years, or until he was nineteen years old; here the religious influences of his home are intensified, and here, although his intellectual life develops somewhat independently in association with two of his schoolfellows, his religious character is more deeply rooted, more richly nourished, more fully developed, and here it is permanently fixed. A vast blessing to the world were those schools of Moravian piety. Schleiermacher's letters to his parents during this school period indicate the strength of this religious influence upon his imagination and upon his religious feeling and affection; and it is easy to see that here there was in constant process of development that rare character which was so notable for its intensity and tenderness of affection. All of his correspondence, even to the latest years of his life in Berlin, is a continuous outflowing of a great loving heart. If in early years these affectionate utterances bear the mark of a diction common among the Brethren, and which was somewhat stereotyped and over-effusive, it is not the less genuine and real. If, in later life, these utterances are more simple and measured and humanistic, less distinctively religious in the formal sense, and are more specifically the utterances of human friendship and devotion, they indicate, nevertheless, their nurturing source in the early culture of the religious affections. The "moved heart," an expression that occurs frequently in his letters as in his sermons, is everywhere regulative for all forms of his activity. It is the emotional and affectional qualities that he values supremely, not only for himself, but in others.   This is the basis for his estimate of friends.   " For his intellect alone," he writes, " I love no man.   Schiller and Goethe are two mighty intellects, — but I shall never be tempted to love them."   It is this that accounts for his love of friendly association with women.   " It is through the knowledge of the feminine heart and mind," he says, " that I have learned to know what real human worth is."   His letters illustrate most impressively the possibilities of religion for the culture of the human heart, and are of great value to any one who will know the primal inspirations of this great character.   All through his life, subsequent to his departure from the Moravian school, he was indirectly connected with the Brethren through his sister, who was a member of the Community, and we are not surprised that he should freely acknowledge their influence.   Fifteen years after his separation from them, in 1802, during the period of his most intense intellectual activity as well as of free association with men of culture who did not share his spirit, he thus refers to this influence in a letter recalling a visit to his sister:[1] " There is no other place which could call forth such lively reminiscences of the entire onward movement of my mind, from its first awakening to a higher life, up to the point which I have at present attained.   Here it was that, for the first time, I awoke to the consciousness of a higher world. . . .   Here it was that that mystic tendency developed itself which has been of so much importance to me, and has supported me and carried me through all the storms of

[1] " Life and Letters of Schleiermacher," translated by Frederica Rowan, Vol. I, p. 283.

scepticism. Then it was germinating, now it has attained its full development; and I may say that, after all I have passed through, I have become a Herrnhuter again, only of a higher order." He always cherished and revered the simple, ardent piety of the Herrnhuters, and their worship became his ideal of what all elevating and edifying Christian worship should be. Indeed, their influence is seen in his fundamental conceptions of religion, of theology, and of the church. A Herrnhuter indeed he always was, only of a higher order, — a mystic, but more than a mystic. He was a man of too large a personality to remain only such, especially in an age like that.

On the intellectual side of his development, as we shall see, he came under the influence of the philosophical movements of his time, or rather of movements that passed more comprehensively under the name of Illuminism. But his religious culture stood by him. He only sought to strike below these movements, and to secure a position that should enable him to comprehend what was true in them, but that should also comprehend much more. On the speculative side he developed as a sceptic. But on the religious side, he was a mystic to the end, and it contributed to his rescue, not only from the old Rationalism that Kant had fought down, but from the new Rationalism of the Illumination itself, of which Kant was one of the chief promoters, against which Schleiermacher subsequently reacted, and ultimately it saved him from other influences of the Illumination. But his immense speculative and dialectical ability modified his mystical tendencies, giving us a higher type of mysticism, free

from the intellectual crudeness which he found so prevalent in the Moravian church.

2. What called itself the Illumination in Schleiermacher's day was an effort to emancipate the human
mind, in different departments of its activity, from the
bondage of tradition. In philosophy it was represented
by Kant, in literature by Goethe, in pedagogy by Rous-
seau, in politics by the French Revolution, which in
Germany found no counterpart, but with which many
who were animated by the new spirit, Schleiermacher
among them, to a degree sympathized; in theology it
was represented, with essential modifications, by Schleiermacher himself. In early life he had disclosed a sceptical attitude with respect to alleged historic facts and
had passed sleepless nights over the dark problem of
eternal punishment. Although profoundly religious,
he was always in a high degree intellectually inquisitive
and was conscientious in seeking to secure for his faith
a solid foundation. While connected with the school
at Barby, at the age of nineteen, his speculative difficulties reached the crisis point. He challenged the doctrine of eternal punishment, of the atonement, of the
deity of Christ, of the supernatural character of Christianity in general as then taught, and he regarded the
arguments of his teachers on moot questions as inconsequential and inconclusive. He charged that they were
silent about objections brought by its critics against the
Christianity of tradition, that they endeavored to conceal
sceptical opinions from him, and gave him no adequate
opportunity to know them or to investigate their validity. This naturally only stimulated him to know the
utmost. All this mental activity and independence,

although lingering still in the realm of scepticism, or
rather perhaps because of it, shows his gift for theology
and his vocation to it. He lays his mental difficulties
before his father and his maternal uncle, a professor at
Halle University. He receives judicious counsel from
his uncle, but evokes a storm of indignant, yet not the
less pathetic, reproach from his dogmatic and pietistic
father, and then follows a temporary strain in the relations of parent and son, although happily without permanent bad results. The correspondence that follows
is profoundly interesting, as illustrating the strength of
paternal and of filial affection in the German houschold.
The very extreme of filial devotion is manifest in the
son's willingness to leave the whole question of his procedure to the decision of the father and the school
authorities. But his intellectual and moral independence and the strong individuality of his character are
seen in the tenacity with which he maintains the right
of free inquiry, while a trace of the early dogmatic influence is evident in a certain semi-apologetic attitude
toward his father, as though he was doing the father
a wrong in thus wounding his feelings, and as if somehow the necessity of changing his opinions involved a
personal fault. The upshot of the matter is a break
with the school authorities, but with mutual good will
and respect. In 1787, therefore, at the age of nineteen,
without knowledge of the world, a diminutive, shy,
awkward, somewhat unkempt youth, but self-reliant
and awake to the vast significance of human life, he is
sent to the University of Halle and enters upon a new
sphere of intellectual activity. He was fortunate in
coming under the influence of his uncle, a man of toler-

ant spirit and well-balanced judgment, whose shaping hand in Schleiermacher's development is abundantly acknowledged. For two years he led a desultory student life, foraging widely and gathering only that for which at the time he hungered. What he says of himself, the year after leaving the university, is also true of his university course: "Although there are certain branches of knowledge for which I have a kind of repugnance, there is not one for which I have an exclusive predilection. . . . Everything that I do is done with a certain degree of impetuosity. . . . I do not, therefore, prosecute any occupation according to a fixed hour or day, but fitfully and during irregular periods."

From this it would seem that there was no unity in his work, and no reference to anything beyond the immediate present. He had no definite objective point, but followed the impulse that led him to satisfy the immediate hunger of the mind. Semler, the pioneer in Biblical criticism, and Knapp, the dogmatician, are teachers in the university, but there is no evidence that he got much from them. He was awakened, however, to the study of history, he continued his classical studies; and his uncle and Eberhard, the latter a teacher of philosophy, led him to the study of Kant, and under this influence he laid his foundation in philosophic knowledge. His father, who had a great admiration for the moral earnestness and austerity of Kant, and who had been a student and once a disciple of his, had already recommended the study, and early in his university course he writes his father as follows,[1] "As for the Kantian philosophy, which you recommend me to

[1] "Life and Letters," Vol. I, p. 68.

study, I have always had a very favorable opinion of it, because it brings back the reason from the desert wastes of metaphysics into its true, appropriate sphere." This sphere is, of course, the individual moral consciousness, and here we see the beginnings of the influence of philosophic Illuminism upon him.   Obliged to leave the university at the end of two years, at the age of twenty-one, he spends the following year, 1790, in the home and under the guidance of his uncle, who also had left the university and had taken a pastorate at Drossen. Here he undertakes to gather up the results of his previous studies and to unify his knowledge.   He reads Kant once more.   During the six or seven subsequent years he is an almost constant student of Kant and becomes gradually able clearly to differentiate his own philosophical position.   He dips into Aristotle's ethics, into Greek history, and is in preparation for the subsequent translation of Plato's works, a very laborious task which he began with Friedrich Schlegel, but completed alone.   At this time he became a candidate for the ministry and took his examination for licensure.   During these three formative years, he, in his own independent way, had passed under the influence of philosophic Illuminism.   The three subsequent years he spent in Schlobitten, as tutor in the household of a nobleman, with whose family he always held most friendly and advantageous relations, and here opens a new era in his life. Here for the first time he is called to the exercise of his preaching gifts.   He adopts the Scottish preacher Blair as his model, striving for his clearness of thought, in comparison with which he regards his own style as obscure. Coöperating with a clergyman of Berlin, a family rela-

tive, he subsequently translates a volume of Blair's sermons.   Resigning his tutorship, he enters the pastorate
at Landsberg in 1794, where he remains two years.   This
closes the period of his tutelage in philosophic Illuminism.   He is beginning to break away from it, and is
soon to come under the influence of another phase of
Illuminism.   During the next six years we find him in
Berlin, and the period of eight years, from 1796 to 1804,
six years in Berlin and two in the pastorate at Stolpe,
was the most important, as it was the most intense, period of his intellectual life, supremely significant for his
entire future.   He has passed through the mystical and
the philosophical phases of his development; we now
come to what may be called its artistic phase.

3.   At Berlin Schleiermacher was brought into intimate relations with the so-called Romantic school in
literature, of which Goethe and the Schlegels were
prominent representatives.   Romanticism, although it
involved a break with Illuminism in its return to the
past, was yet closely connected with it and may be called
a literary or artistic phase of it.   It was characterized
by great rhetorical enthusiasm, patriotic enterprise, and
especially by the diligent study and semi-poetic interpretation of history in the light of modern ideas.   Its influence upon Schleiermacher in a social, literary, and in
general artistic, way was great.   Under its inspiration he
enters the field of authorship.   During the period of his
tutorship we find already the stirring and the culture of
new artistic impulses and aspirations.   Then for the first
time apparently he is brought into relation with refined
and cultivated women of the world.   With strong, manly
traits, there was still much in his constitution that was

feminine, and he coveted the society and the friendship of such women. He understood the heart of
woman as few did, and association with this cultivated
nobleman's family was fit preparation for his Berlin life
of social and literary activity, in which he became prominent as member of a club composed of some of the
most cultivated men and women of his day. Here in
this family life he finds his latent gift for music. Here
he begins to cultivate his literary tastes, and they have
influence in modifying his philosophic conceptions.
And all this began to make itself manifest in his preaching. He had carried from the university his native individualism that had been intensified by the spirit of free
inquiry which characterized the Illumination. We find
him in sympathy with the French Revolution. In the
social circle of the Romanticists in which he moved in
Berlin during these six years he finds lax views of
family life. It was an age of revolutionary opinion, even
with respect to domestic relations, and prudery and
devotion to conventional standards were not among the
virtues of Berlin social life. Schleiermacher was himself a man of spotless purity of personal character and
life, but under the influence of the free thought of this
Romanticist circle and of his own individualistic and
unconventional standards, we find him complicated with
respect to domestic questions in ways that he subsequently did not approve, and which cannot be approved
in any age, however revolutionary, by any lover of
social order. But they are after all a testimony to the
lofty idealism of the man and to the purity of his spirit,
even if they show a lack of practical wisdom and of respect for the conventionalities of life. These complica-

tions, with which it is not important to linger, resulted
in his retirement from Berlin for two years to a pastorate in Stolpe, an experience of great value to him intellectually and spiritually, for they were years of intense
study of the great German thinkers, among them
Spinoza, Schelling, Jacobi, and Kant, and they were
years, too, of great burdens of heart.   Through the influence of the Romanticists of Berlin he had been
induced to enter upon literary work, and in 1799, after
two months of close work at Potsdam, he issued to the
world his famous "Discourses on Religion," perhaps
the most important contribution to religion and theology
since the Reformation.   They were a most startling disclosure of a religious, philosophical, and literary genius
hitherto but relatively little known.   This is not the
place for a discussion of the contents of these discourses,
and we are concerned with them at all only as related
to his pulpit work.   It is enough to say here that the influence of the conceptions here embodied were felt and
were manifest in his entire professional career, and that,
although measurably modified subsequently, they were
on the one side the basis of his theology, and reëmerged
in expanded form in his system of Christian doctrine and
have been vastly significant for the evangelical theology
of the last three-quarters of a century, while on the other
side they appeared in his "Practical Theology" and have
significance not only for German preaching but for other
phases of church life and activity.   Answering to the
"Discourses on Religion," there appeared during the following year on the ethical side the "Monologues." These
two works, which are a brilliant defence of the religious
and of the ethical ideal, are the early flower of his liter-

ary and artistic development. That this development should have found its sphere in the realm of religious and ethical thought is proof of the seriousness of his character. In 1804 he is appointed as professor at Halle University, which marks a new period in his career.

4. At Halle, where he remains for three years, begins his ecclesiastical and political as well as professional activity. He lectures on a surprising variety of subjects, Exegesis, Dogmatics, and History, and during a portion of the time he is university preacher. At this time Germany was thrown into confusion by the invasion of the armies of Napoleon. Schleiermacher threw himself, with all the enthusiasm of which he was capable, into this struggle, and proved himself to be a most ardent and uncompromising patriot. In his personal fortunes he suffered much; and when, in 1807, the university was closed and its students were dispersed by order of the invader, he retired to Berlin, where he spent the remainder of his life. All his religious, philosophical, theological, classical, and literary preparation fitted him in a most eminent degree for the position he there held during these last and most fruitful years of his public career. Here he was a popular lecturer and teacher at the university which, in 1810, he aided in establishing. He was an ecclesiastical leader, instrumental in the introduction of notable reforms, and particularly in the union of the Lutheran and Reformed branches of the German church. He, with his family, was an important figure in the social life of Berlin. He was a man of affairs, and as a patriot and statesman his counsels were sought by the Prussian government. To the last he was pastor

of Trinity church, where he preached with ever increasing power to the cultivated people of this university town, and with utmost pastoral fidelity he instructed his catechistical classes and ordered the practical life of his church to the end. It was here that his scientific and practical theology developed themselves into final form, and here they were given to the world. It now remains to consider Schleiermacher's conception of religion and its bearing upon his practical theology, and more particularly upon his work as a preacher.

II

SCHLEIERMACHER'S CONCEPTION OF RELIGION AND THEOLOGY

Schleiermacher's scientific theology is a development of his conception of religion, and his practical theology is closely related to his scientific theology. He valued the science of theology only as related to the life of the church, and the church held a central place in his theology. Theology has no proper source outside religion, and therefore cannot be divorced from the life of the church. It is the product of reflection upon the content of religious experience. It was his aim to do for theology what he declared Kant had done for the human reason, "to bring it from the desert waste of metaphysics into its true appointed sphere," and not from the realm of metaphysics alone, but from every external source. As Lücke, one of his pupils, says: "He brings it back to the facts of the Christian consciousness, as its basis and true object of investigation, and in doing this he in fact secures for it an objective grounding, *i.e.* by showing that it rests on valid facts of Christian faith." A brief statement, therefore, of his conception of religion seems necessary. Religion belongs to the innermost nature of man. Religion therefore is natural. On the other hand, it is supernatural, as involving a sense of the Infinite in the consciousness of the Finite, or a sense of the presence of God in the soul. This conception of religion, as supernatural, of itself disposes of the charge against Schleiermacher, that he was a pantheist. Much of his terminology, influenced by the study of Spinoza and by the rhetorical exuberance of Romanticism, has confessedly a pantheistic basis. But by recognizing the world-ground or world-spirit as both subject and object, he escapes the abyss of pantheism. Since, then, religion is at once natural and supernatural, there can be no contradiction, for both are parts of one complex whole. Thus what was false in the naturalism of his day on the one side and in its orthodox supernaturalism on the other side is undone at a stroke. This consciousness of the presence of God in the soul, which is represented as a sense of the Infinite in the Finite, is not at all dependent for its validity on anything outside of it, whether above it, or below it, or back of it, however closely it may be connected with it. It is not dependent upon the doctrines or beliefs of the church, as the dogmatists would teach ; it is not dependent on any institutional form which religion may take whether of church or of sacrament, as the ecclesiastic would teach ; it is not dependent on state alliance, as the politician holds ; nor upon the nature of thought in its relation to being, as the Hege-

c

lian teaches ; nor upon the moral consciousness, as Kant
teaches; nor is it to be identified with the æsthetic
sense, however closely allied with it, as the cultured
Romanticists would have it; nor with that form of mysticism that consists in union with God through submission of will.   It is deeper still.   Various terms are used
to designate it.   In an explanatory note to the second
discourse, on the " Nature of Religion," he justifies this
variety of designation on the ground of the rhetorical
and descriptive, as distinguished from the scientific, character of the " Discourses."   Religion is a consciousness,
a consciousness of the Infinite or of the Universe, as, with
reference to the audiences to which the " Discourses "
were first addressed, he prefers to call it, presupposing
God as the spirit of the Universe.   It is a sense of or
taste for the Infinite.   It is an intuition of the Universe.
In the later and maturer form of the " Discourses,"
however, the prevailing term is "feeling."   This consciousness, sense, taste, this immediate realization in
consciousness of the Infinite, or of the world-spirit,
within the soul, takes the form of absolute dependence.
The sense of personal freedom belongs to the ethical
consciousness, which, according to Schleiermacher, has
a relative, and it must be confessed, too great, independence of the religious consciousness.   This sense of
absolute dependence, — this only is religion.   It is the
deepmost reality in man.   Relatively independent of all
else in him, it is still the impelling energy of all man's
religious thinking, of all his purest moral convictions,
of all noblest sense of the beautiful, and of all deter-
minations of the will.   Religion, therefore, is the heart
of science, art, and morality.   But these may exist

without religion and in relative independence of it. Only in a secondary and derived sense can they ever be called religion, and never at all save as they are penetrated by the power of the religious sense. Religion has thus a validity of its own, independently of any form our thought may take, even with respect to the being touching whom the sense of dependence is exercised, or with respect to any scheme of doctrine or any institution, or any form of ethics or of art.

Although religion is thus a purely subjective product, as being grounded in the constitution of man and expressing its contents, it nevertheless is evoked and developed under historic conditions. Schleiermacher, therefore, has nothing to do with a merely abstract religion, which is a product of speculation and does not represent the reality of religion. All religions, as historic realities, express, under varying historic conditions, in some degree and in some form, the contents of the religious consciousness. The distinguishing peculiarity of Christianity as religion is that it is evoked and developed by the historic Christ, who brings a new religious spirit into the world, and who in awakening the religious consciousness of the individual Christian imparts the content of his own religious consciousness. If at first Christ appears only as the historic occasion for the development of the individual religious consciousness, he gradually assumes a more positive and creative significance. He becomes the source and norm of the religious life, upon whom the individual Christian is absolutely dependent; and if at first the significance of what we call religious truth for the development of the religious life seems to be minimized,— and he holds the position that religion cannot be evoked by teaching, but must be quickened and nurtured by feeling and imagination, — in the end the value of objective religious truth as found in the Scripture records is more fully recognized. It is this inner reality of religion as an experience of the heart that constitutes its sacredness. It is this that honors the individual soul and life. The rights, the sacred rights, of religious individuality constituted, therefore, one of Schleiermacher's fundamental principles. It is doubtless largely a product of his early religious training and experience, but other influences furthered it. His theory of religion naturally led to an extreme form of individualism, as all forms of mystical subjectivity are likely to do. It has been frequently pointed out that a strict construction of Schleiermacher's theory would leave no place for religion as an associate life. But this was far enough from his conception. It is true that he isolated the element of feeling in religion from the intellectual and ethical factors that border upon it, but it was only in idea, and it was far from his purpose to divorce the emotional from the mental and ethical elements of the practical religious life. These inner religious experiences, as being dependent upon their common quickening source in Christ and as involving a common living relation with him, must express themselves in associate life. These experiences are the basis of all Christian fellowship, and just this is the foundation of the church. Christianity, therefore, as religion is not only an individual Christian life producing religion, but it is a church producing religion. Thus, while he lays great stress upon the sacredness of the individual soul and upon its rights, both in the " Dis-

courses " and in the " Monologues," he lays equal stress
upon the church, and in his hands the church gains
new and vastly increased significance.   No theologian
of the modern world has put such honor upon religious
individuality, and none has put higher honor upon the
religious community.   With him, in fact, the modern
church emerges into new life.   It is the significance of
the church that determines his definition of theology.
It is "the science of the church."   It is more than the
science of Christianity, for we cannot conceive of Christianity as existing practically in complete independence
of the church.   The claims for religion which Schleiermacher set forth in his " Discourses on Religion to those
Cultivated People who are among its Despisers," among
whom were some of his own personal friends, was a
most startling one and made a tremendous impression,
and no wonder, considering the character of the age in
which they appeared.   And it is an influence that is
still felt in the religion and theology of the Christian
church.   In many ways Schleiermacher modified as he
developed.   But, as Pfleiderer suggests in his " Development of Theology in Germany," the " Discourses "
contain his starting-point.   His future theological development was along that line, although constantly toward
a larger measure of harmony with the theology of the
church.   His fundamental positions, however, were
never materially changed.   It is enough to say, just
here, that the work he did has profound significance
for Christian theology, Christian ethics, and for the
practical life of the church, and in many ways especially
for Christian preaching.   It has detached theology
from abstract speculation, and has secured for it an

independent basis.   It has carried out in another direction what Kant initiated, and has laid the foundation
for a new type of Christian apologetics.   It is the
Christian consciousness, reflecting the truth of Christian revelation, that has become normative for Christian
theology, and out of this, as already intimated, Schleiermacher's whole theological system developed.   It has
placed ethics upon a more distinctly Christian foundation, and has resulted in a new development of social
ethics.   It concerns us, however, to consider more specifically the bearing of Schleiermacher's religious and
theological conceptions upon the work of preaching.
In the light of them we may perhaps see more clearly
the influence upon the preaching of our own day.

III

THE PREACHING OF SCHLEIERMACHER

All the wealth of Schleiermacher's genius and varied
acquisitions and culture were made tributary indirectly,
but not the less effectively, to his preaching.   He had the
artistic as well as the religious and scientific equipment.
He displayed rare gifts as a preacher, and attached
supreme importance to the preacher's function.   From
the time of his licensure in 1790 to the close of his life
in 1834 he preached almost continuously, and the preaching interest was, in his apprehension, second to none
other.   While professor at Halle and later at Berlin he
regarded preaching as supplemental to the work of
teaching, and in both teaching and preaching he had
but one aim.   His theological lectures and his sermons

had to a considerable extent the same subject-matter, although presented of course in different form.[1] It has been shown by one of his pupils that the subjects discussed in a scientific manner in his "Glaubenslehre" appear to a very large extent in popular form in his sermons, so that nearly his entire system of Christian theology was interpreted in homiletic form to the people. During his public career he published four large volumes of sermons, the first in 1801, the last in 1834, and with the posthumous sermons they number in all ten volumes. They include a great variety of types of sermons. We have the pastoral and ordinary sermon, the occasional, the festal, the confirmation, the baptismal, the funeral, the burial, the confessional, the parenetic sermon, sermons on family life of great impressiveness and helpfulness, sermons on national subjects like the one entitled "A Nation's Duty in the War for Freedom," and the one entitled "Rejoicing before God" preached on the anniversary of the battle of Leipsic, which greatly stirred the hearts of his patriotic hearers. There are two volumes of expository sermons, or homilies, on the Gospel according to Mark. The series also includes a volume of candidate sermons, which disclose the carefulness of his early homiletic method, the freshness of his thought, and the affluence of his style. There are perhaps no individual sermons that stand out beyond all others as preëminently great. They are of uniform excellence. But the sermon entitled "The Dying Saviour our Example" may be named as a singularly edifying Christian sermon, introduced by a homiletic prayer of great simplicity and beauty, and the one entitled "The Power of

[1] " Reminiscences of Schleiermacher," by Lücke, p. 49.

Prayer in Relation to Outward Circumstances " is a sermon of great elevation and nobility of thought, which
it is almost certain suggested Frederick Robertson's sermon on Prayer.   But let us examine his preaching more
specifically.

1. It is natural that we should consider first his theory
of preaching.   He had his theory; it was a well-defined
theory, and he shaped his preaching by it.   It is fully
discussed in his "Homiletics."[1]   Practical theology occupied a prominent place in Schleiermacher's thinking.
Even as early as his connection with Halle University
he lectured upon it, and in his handling it became a new
branch of theology.   It is that branch which deals with
the life of the church.   The activities of the church with
which it deals are all a testimony, in various lines, of the
inner life of the church.   Now, homiletics is one of the
branches of practical theology, and preaching is one of
those activities that bear witness to the reality of the
inner life of the Christian community.   It is more than
a rhetorical product, more than "sacred rhetoric."   Homiletics is the theory of the utterance of the inner life of
the church in the form of speech.   It is more than the
utterance of certain objectively given truths by the
church official.   It must be assumed to be the expression of what is common to the Christian community,
through its leader, who is identified with them, and
who only leads them in the utterance of their own sacred
religious experiences.   We see in this the influence of
his own early religious education and experience.   But
it is also grounded in his well-defined theory of religion
and of theology, and this theory of preaching has to a

[1] " Die Pract. Theol.," IV Theorie der religiösen Rede, p. 201.

large extent been the theory that has prevailed in the
German churches since Schleiermacher's day.   Let us
therefore try to understand it.   It is the preacher's
function to represent Christianity as religion, not as
science, religion as incorporated and as manifesting itself
in the church, the communion of saints.   It is his work
to represent, to give expression to (*Darstellung*) the
experiences of the common Christian life.   This presupposes a congregation that shares this common experience in adequate measure with the preacher.   Otherwise
it would not be representation, would not be expression
of what is common, would not be testimony, or it would
be fruitless testimony.   The congregation is a Christian
assembly that meets for Christian worship.   Preaching
is a part of the service of common worship, all the elements of which are testimony as to the reality of the
inner Christian life.   This gives preaching a distinctively Christian character, and it must have a certain
liturgical quality.   The congregation cannot be treated
as if wholly without religious life and experience, and as
if practically in pagan condition.   It is true that in the
" Discourses" he represents the congregation as composed not so much of persons who are religious as of
those who are " seeking religion."   He had doubtless
a special purpose in this representation.   But, however
that may be, he does not hold to it in his "Homiletics."
The preaching with which he deals is distinctively
pastoral preaching; evangelistic or mission preaching,
which presupposes a different congregation and has
for its aim the conversion of men to the Christian life,
is a very different product, and the discussion of it does
not properly belong to Christian homiletics.   This con-

ception of preaching, which was regulative for his own ministry, accounts in part for his zeal in catechetical instruction, which he regarded as not less important than preaching itself.   In this way an instructed Christian congregation was prepared for him.   This theory of preaching, defective though it be, has been substantially the prevailing theory in Germany since Schleiermacher's time ; and confessedly it has in part its analogue in the preaching of the apostolic church, whose assemblies were Christian assemblies and whose preaching was of the nature of Christian testimony.   Schleiermacher realized his own theory, and its effect upon his preaching will be evident at once.   We have here the experimental factor with new emphasis, and it has had its influence upon the modern pulpit.   We do not regard that as Christian preaching at all, nor do we tolerate it as such, which con- sists in the retailing of opinions which are purely im- personal, which are based on external authority and have found no appropriation in the innermost experiences of the soul of the preacher.   This, of course, is the old evan- gelical idea, the Reformation idea, the Puritan idea, of preaching.   But it has come in new form and with new emphasis.   Such preaching is likely to assume more for the congregation.   We find here, perhaps, in part an explanation of the large amount of pastoral preaching that characterizes the work of the modern pulpit. Preachers do not divide the congregation as their fathers did.   There is more confidence in the responsiveness of the congregation and in the quickening and edifying power of the truth presented.   And this is in line with the more largely persuasive as contrasted with the dog- matic, argumentative, and one-sidedly intellectual char- acter of preaching.

But its serious defect will be evident at once. It assumes too much for the congregation. This defect in Schleiermacher's own preaching was pointed out by his own followers, notably by Lücke in his " Reminiscences of Schleiermacher." He trusts too much to the religious consciousness. He assumes that all who are in the congregation are the subjects of the same religious experience. He takes too little into account the imperfect operations of grace in men's souls. In a word, he idealizes the congregation and loses sight of facts. He assumes, as Lücke says, " an average measure of grace and leaves the defective stages for other and simpler and more specific forms of instruction." Hence, as Dr. Sack, a Berlin pastor of Schleiermacher's day and a family relative, asserts, the result was a lack of pertinence to the wants of his hearers and to their actual state. Hence especially a lack of the practical quality and an excess of sentiment and feeling, in other words, of the parenetic element in his preaching. Hence a certain lack in popular quality.

The basis of this defect may be due in large measure to a defective conception of religion itself. Pfleiderer, in his " Development of Theology in Germany,"[1] has shown that by isolating the ethical from the emotional in religion, that is by excluding from the conception of religion the consciousness of moral alliance with God, and making it consist wholly in the sense of absolute dependence, Schleiermacher failed to grasp the full content of the conception. Absolute dependence suggests primarily causality — creatorship in God.

[1] "The Development of Theology in Germany since Kant and its Progress in Great Britain since 1825," p. 105.

Pfleiderer finds here the influence of Spinoza. God is causal energy. There can be only one kind of religious experience in such relation with God. There is no chance for qualitative, but only for quantitative, distinctions in religious experience. If the conception of religion is complex, it may involve different kinds of religious experience, and these different kinds of religious experience must be met by the preacher. Schleiermacher did not recognize them and therefore made no effort to meet them. The members of his congregation were all on the same plane. It may be possible that erroneous conceptions of the significance of the baptismal estate may in part account for the perpetuation of this conception of preaching in Germany. A baptized congregation is assumed to be a Christian congregation and should be addressed as such. Perhaps this may in part explain the relative ineffectiveness of German preaching.

2. Let us look secondly at the subject-matter of Schleiermacher's preaching. Religion as an experience, even in its Christian form, must be wholly subjective and personal. It is dependent upon nothing external for its origin. It is neither Scripture truth nor Christ himself that originates the soul's religious experiences. Nothing external originates faith, but what is external may regulate it. That is, it may regulate reflection upon one's religious feelings. Nothing that is external to the soul is creative of religion. It is only regulative. As Robertson said about the sacraments, so Schleiermacher would say about objective religious truth, it cannot produce life, but it may support life. In a letter to Jacobi in 1818, Schleiermacher says: " The

Bible is the original interpretation of the Christian feeling, and for this very reason so firmly established that we ought not to attempt more than further to understand and develop it. This right of development, however, I, as a Protestant theologian, will allow no one to defraud me of." The authority of Scripture, therefore, is in its harmony with faith, not in its creative energy with respect to it. It is regulative only in so far as it is in harmony with the preacher's subjective feeling, and, as Lücke suggests, furnishes a touching-point for his reflection. This position, that Biblical revelation is only the external occasion, the condition or exciting agency, not creative cause of faith, seems to imply that the latter is not dependent upon the former. In this he fails to distinguish between faith and the faith content, between the *fides qua* and the *fidis quae*. This was a position he could not successfully hold. He consequently modified it. We find Christ increasingly regarded as the centre of the soul's spiritual life. The Christian soul is absolutely dependent on Christ for its faith. Without him the inner life of faith is unattainable. Christ therefore is the supreme lord of the soul. He saw that this position was necessary to enable him to distinguish between feeling that is Christian and feeling that may have no Christian character at all. But, after all, while the Christian life is dependent on external agencies, it has an independent reality and validity of its own. As thus relatively independent, it has at hand a test of value for the Christian life of any objectively given truths or facts of Christianity that may be brought to it. It even tests for itself the significance of Christ for it. Consequently historic

Christianity may be treated with a large measure of independence. The Christian life does not feel itself to be absolutely dependent, especially upon the forms of Christian doctrine, and may treat them with freedom. It is not dependent even upon the forms in which Christianity appears in the New Testament. We may therefore discriminate by the test of Christian experience between what is primary and what is secondary in the Christian books, accepting only what faith regards as primary. Large masses of material found in the New Testament may be excluded from acceptance as having no significance for the Christian life. Consequently Schleiermacher dealt very freely with the Christian documents. He did not regard himself as beholden to harmonize his teachings fully with the teachings even of the New Testament. Church doctrine he treated almost cavalierly. The doctrine of the Trinity, as taught by the church, had no significance for him. Thus with the church doctrine of the atonement. He gradually modified in the direction of what is known as the evangelical position, and sought to find basis for a common Christian faith, and his successors and followers carried his modifications still further. But it is evident, as Pfleiderer suggests, that we have here a pretty fully developed scheme of subjective theological individualism, on which, strictly applied, it would be difficult to found a church or to develop a theology. It was necessary to his position that he should find in the Old Testament but little value for the distinctively Christian life. Faith is domesticated only in the New Testament and always returns to it as to its native element, and is competent to test and to reject the Old Testament. He did not find the spirit of

Christianity in Judaism.   No part of the Old Testament
did he greatly value.   He rarely used it in preaching.
In the ten volumes of sermons and homilies there are
less than twenty passages from the Old Testament used
as texts, and those used are in occasional sermons.
They are from the historical books, Solomon's Song,
Ecclesiastes, Job, Psalms, and the major prophets, and
they are the basis, to a considerable extent, of political
and patriotic sermons.   Singularly, there are more from
Solomon's Song than from any other Old Testament
book.   His pastoral preaching is always from the New
Testament, and in the use of the text he plants himself
squarely upon its historic sense.   He holds that such
texts should never be used as mottoes and should never
be twisted by any species of accommodation.   On the
other hand, his Old Testament texts are always accom-
modated, and he justified this on the ground that they
must be adjusted to the spirit of the New Testament
and must be adapted to the needs of the practical
Christian life.   Now it is evident enough that a very
important position has been won for the church and
for the pulpit by Schleiermacher's teachings, despite
their extremely subjective and individualistic tendencies.
We have learned the testing power of Christian experience with respect to the value for the Christian life
of the objectively given content of the Bible, and we
accustom ourselves to apply the test with freedom.
Christianity has been brought back to Christ.   The pulpit has therefore been brought back to Christianity, and
it assigns to the Old Testament its proper place.   The
doctrine of the Christian consciousness as normative for
Christian truth has been lifted into its proper relation

with Biblical revelation and with church tradition.   As
a result the pulpit keeps closer to the centre of Christian
truth.   The preacher is better able to discriminate
between the facts and truths of Christianity that appeal
to and affect Christian experience, and those that are
relatively remote from it.   And all this has had an
important influence upon Christian apologetics.

We have seen that Schleiermacher's conception of
religion involved a modification in the conception of the
supernatural.   Religion as belonging to the constitution
of the human soul is natural.   As having, however, its
inspiring source in God who is revealed in Christ, it is
supernatural, but as having the human soul for the
sphere of its operation, the supernatural itself must have
an element of naturalness.   To the naturalness of the
inner experience answers a corresponding element of
naturalness in the objective agency, revelation.   Revelation as supernatural, therefore, does not involve the
breaking down or suspension of the order of nature.
They are both parts of one whole; even miracles have
an element of naturalness.   It is not my vocation either
to criticise or to defend Schleiermacher's supernaturalism; I have only to say that it has had a very decisive
influence upon the supernaturalism of the entire evangelical church of our age.   It has become a commonplace of the pulpit, and its influence is seen in the
emphasis that is put upon the naturalness of religion.
The close connection between Schleiermacher's theology
and his preaching has already been noted.   It was
Neander's opinion that his sermons were necessary to
an adequate understanding of his theology; and De
Wette, who was an attendant at Schleiermacher's

church, discovered from his preaching his own points of agreement with him in theology. Everywhere and always it is the theology of feeling. But as his theology becomes more clearly defined, we see the effect in his sermons. The difference between his lectures and his sermons is mostly one of form. In a letter to a friend in 1805 he says, " I have a lively hope that by means of the connection between my sermons and my lectures I shall be able to bring clearly home to the minds of the students the true relations between speculation and piety ; and from both places alike, from the pulpit and from the professor's chair, I trust I shall be able to enlighten their minds and to warm their hearts." All the great truths with which Christian theology deals are discussed in his sermons. The centre point of all his pulpit theology, as of his dogmatics, is fellowship with Christ. And it may be said that his theological conceptions are peculiarly well adapted to pulpit discussion. We can see at once why the subject-matter of his preaching is of a theological rather than of a Biblical character. It is his theory of preaching that its subject-matter should consist in reflection upon the content of Christian experience rather than in reflection upon the content of Biblical revelation.

3. The object which Schleiermacher proposed for himself in his preaching, or the use of the material as well as the material to be used, was in harmony with his conception of what Christian preaching should be. As preaching is an expression, not primarily of ideas, opinions, mental judgments, but of the experiences of the heart, its object must be to reproduce, or to develop still further, such experiences in the souls of the hearers.

D

The object is not primarily to develop or direct or shape religious thought.   Preaching is not teaching primarily. It is not the exposition or interpretation of truth, but the utterance of the experience of the heart.   Religion is not developed by teaching.   Teaching, of course, is necessary and is not ignored, but the aim of preaching is not primarily to instruct.   This, in Schleiermacher's opinion, was the fault of the orthodox and rationalistic preaching of his day, against which he strongly reacted. In the introduction to the sermon entitled " The Dying Saviour our Example" he objects to the obtruding of church dogmas relating to the death of Christ into the Good Friday service, and against spending time "in raising questions, in sifting opinions, in instituting discussions, by which minds are not moved for good, — at the very time when we desire to be most cordially united." And this in general was his attitude toward the doctrines of the church.   Nor was the object of preaching to convert man.   Something more than ethical and evangelistic impression is demanded.   The object of his preaching is edification.   His object is so to express the inner realities of the Christian life in forms of Christian thought, by the aid of the imagination and by the impelling energy of Christian feeling, conviction, and affection, that this same Christian life in the souls of his hearers may be furthered and developed.   Preaching is the testimony of the heart in thoughts that are fitted to convey its treasures of experience.   It is not possible to nurture the Christian life by aiming primarily at the understanding, or the conscience, or the will.   It must be evoked by stimulating the imagination and nurturing the feelings.   Hence he denounces the ortho-

dox indoctrination and the rationalistic moralizing of
the preaching of his day, criticising its externality and
unprofitableness.   One must preach from within ; our
words must be the utterance of the heart.   Then they
will be natural and effective.   Schleiermacher doubtless
would not deny that the primary function of the preacher
is that of an interpreter of the truth, or of spiritual
realities ; but he would insist that it must be an interpretation of the truth as transmuted into the content of
spiritual experience, and not of objective truth as such,
and it must be primarily an interpretation to the heart
or to the religious feelings rather than to the understanding.   And the assumption of this position without
doubt involved a relative undervaluation of the objective truth of revelation as such, and of the importance
of increase in Christian knowledge as related to Christian edification.   This would naturally result in a diminution of the didactic and an increase of the emotional
and sentimental element in preaching.   This result we
discover in German preaching in general as contrasted
with English and American preaching, which lays more
stress upon the importance of objective Biblical truth.
In the preaching of Schleiermacher himself it was not
seen nor felt.   The great intellectual resources of the
man and the wealth of his culture demanded and secured
free and full expression in the pulpit as elsewhere,
although his preaching might not be characterized as
prevailingly intellectual.   Schleiermacher's object, however, did exclude conscious effort to secure determinate
and immediate results, and there is a lack of definite
ethical and evangelistic purpose.

How far the direct influence of Schleiermacher with

respect to the problem of the proper object of preaching is being felt in the modern pulpit may be uncertain. But it is perfectly evident that edification, not by the direct inculcation of objective truth, but by the interpretation of truth as vitalized by ethical and spiritual experience, is the prevailing object of the modern preacher. Not to regulate the doctrinal opinions nor the ethical behavior of the congregation, but to meet its spiritual needs, is the aim. The processes and agencies of spiritual nurture are honored, and imagination and the emotions, as distinguished from the dialectical faculties, are brought into fuller exercise. Consequently the intellectual character of our preaching has been modified but not lost.

4. As might be expected the tone of Schleiermacher's preaching was emotionally and religiously elevated in a very high degree. It was wealthy in its subject-matter, the product of a capacious, well-stored, well-trained, and highly suggestive mind, holding as in solution for pulpit use all the vast treasures of his learning and disclosing at times, although in wholly simple form harmonious with the work of preaching, the immense dialectical abilities of the man. But it was always exceedingly earnest and affectionate, yet always dignified, and so most nobly persuasive in its character. It bore the mark of the cheerful, hopeful, optimistic, even supremely idealistic, character of the man, and thus disclosed itself in the earnestness of his manner and in the sympathetic tones of his voice. It was always his conscious effort to elevate and ennoble the hearer, and to leave him a little further advanced in the Christian life as the result of his effort. He would never have the sermon end with any-

thing but a tone of cheerfulness, hopefulness, and encouragement. The sermon must always be tributary to the worship of the congregation. It is an organic part of worship itself. Preaching, prayer, and song are parts of one whole. He would enlist the service of song in the interest of preaching, at one period selecting his own hymns from the liturgical treasures of the church, and having them printed for the use of his congregation. He compiled a new hymn-book, and sought to influence the worship of other churches. The Moravian service he exalts as a model for all the churches. It was this liturgical influence, the elevated, idealistic character of the man, and his theory of what preaching ought to be, that fostered this elevated tone in his work as a preacher. His theology also fostered it. Fellowship with Christ received supreme emphasis in all his theological thinking and in his entire religious life, and this imparted a nobility and dignity and tenderness as well to all his preaching. His message came warm and fresh from the fountain of life. It was this elevated, penetrating quality that Humboldt had in mind in writing thus of him: " Of Schleiermacher it may be said, as of the greater number of very distinguished persons, but in an incomparably higher degree, that their speaking exceeded their writings in power. Those, therefore, who may have read his numerous writings ever so diligently, but who never heard him speak, must nevertheless remain unacquainted with the most rare power and the most remarkable qualities of the man. His strength lay in the deeply penetrating character of his words. It would be wrong to call it rhetoric, for it was so entirely free from art. It was the persuasive, penetrative, kindling effusion of a feeling, which seemed not so much to be enlightened by one of the rarest of intellects, as to move side by side with it in perfect unison." Religious thought that is caught up and penetrated by religious feeling and affection, and that undertakes to interpret the significance of the experience of the inner life and to impress its power, will of necessity be an earnest, sympathetic, dignified, emotionally elevated, and ennobling utterance. It was his conviction that the content of preaching should never go outside of Christianity as a subjective religious experience, and to interpret in terms of rational thought the inner significance of religious life was his conscious supreme vocation. Hence his objection against making any additions to the content of pulpit thought from outside sources. Doubtless he wrought into his own discourses material that came from the wealth of his own humanistic culture, but it was contrary to his theory and contrary to his conscious purpose. To present Christian thought unmixed with human speculation and to interpret only what is real to Christian experience was his aim. Doubtless his preaching was deficient in many respects in what calls itself the evangelical note, and notably so in the evangelistic note. It may have obscured or even neglected Christian truths that are necessary to further Christian piety, for in maintaining the position that piety is normative for truth, he forgot that truth also may be normative for piety. But it was always a most deeply spiritual and devout utterance, as from the consciousness of fellowship with the Redeemer. It is this "pectoral theology" that has given an earnest, sympathetic, devout, and elevated spiritual tone to the best type of modern preaching.

Because his own preaching was an outpouring of the
heart Schleiermacher found great joy in it.   His letters
indicate the satisfaction it gave him.   He has a "constant hankering after the pulpit," even when at work
upon the beloved Plato, and his discourses to the
students of the university formed, as he says, "no
slight addition to my happiness."   Elevated in tone and
adapted to an educated and cultivated audience as was
his preaching, he still sought to reach the common
people, and at Berlin he adapted the afternoon service
to their needs.   It was his opinion that "all sermons
and mine more especially are only intended to be
heard."   Hence he was opposed to the publication of
his sermons and only yielded after the earnest solicita-
tion of his friends.   He was also opposed to written
sermons.   At first he carefully wrote, but in the interest
of greater impressiveness and effectiveness he abandoned
the practice, because he found that it hampered him.
He introduced the change by dropping one part of the
written product after another, beginning with the conclusion and ending with the introduction, till nothing
was left, and he at last spoke wholly without writing;
and this became tributary, not only to the freedom and
the cogency, but to the elevation of his preaching.   The
sermon that is the free outpouring of the life from
within must be elevated and spiritually impressive.

5. Looking at the formal aspects of Schleiermacher's
preaching, or at the ordering and expression of the
thought, we are at once impressed with its organic
quality.   There is no external manipulation of material,
no mechanistic combination of parts.   The sermon is
not built.   It is a simple, free outflow and onflow.   It

is an instrument for the expression of Christian feeling in the form of Christian reflection for the purpose of Christian edification. The chief interest is the subject-matter. The form is subordinate to it, and is so shaped as to bring out the material to the best advantage. The fulness, the wealth, the affluence, the apparent spontaneity, is apparent at once. The form is simply the natural and easy unfolding, as by organic process of the subject-matter. To secure this, he abandoned the manuscript, as already suggested. This freedom which he sought does not imply that he was at all careless with respect to his work. In his early ministry he labored to perfect his instrument. At that time he gave his father an account of his sermon preparation. "I cannot," he says, in a letter from Schlobitten, in 1793,[1] "commence writing down a sermon, until I have thoroughly arranged it in my thoughts, even to the smallest details; for otherwise I run the risk of anticipating some things or of putting them in the wrong place." And he says that the unwritten sermons gave him "much more trouble than any I have ever composed." Then follows a description of his method which is interesting: "I first made a very careful disposition of my subject, and then sought various modes of expression for each thought. Next, I took first one part of the discussion, then another and another, and preached it in thought: and then returned again to the first, probably changing the terms in some measure, and then I delivered my sermon bit by bit, several times over, and also committed to memory the entire plan." This habit of careful preparation in the early period stood by him all

"Life and Letters," Vol. I, p. 106 ff.

through his ministry. It resulted in great clearness of
method. The structural form is more manifest in the
early period, and gradually becomes more flexible and
free, but it is always the unfolding process. He does
not anchor closely to his text, but uses it freely, not,
however, in the way of accommodation, save in his use
of the Old Testament. He takes the exact thought of
the text, or some thought that is easily and naturally
suggested by it, and not by some remote process, as the
basis of his discussion; but in the formal sense the
thought of the sermon is not closely bound to the text.
The introduction is of a general character, and is rarely
explanatory. It is not his purpose to unfold the subject
in a strictly expository manner. He will rather draw
freely from his own resources. Even in his expository
discourses, although merging himself fully within the
sphere of the writer's thought, and making it his own,
as the first and necessary step in his work, he nevertheless draws abundantly from the wealth of his own inner
life, and the thought unfolds itself very freely in line
with his own mental processes. The thought, once appropriated, expands and takes new form under the
vitalizing touch of his own personality. He is thus a
most quickening and suggestive expository preacher.
The theme of the sermon always comes naturally from
the text and is not forced upon it. He discusses but
two or three topics, which are a natural partition of the
subject, and the topics are generally textual. The theme
is definite and frequently stated in propositional form,
which calls for definite, and yet admits of free, treatment.
"That we should not be the servants, but friends of
God!"   "Only he can free who is above all the

prophets." "The Redeemer is born as the Son of God." "That the joy of the advent of Christ is enhanced by the consideration that he came to bring a sword." Themes like these suggest at once the largeness of the thought discussed and the definiteness with which it is conceived. The topics are frequently stated at the outset, and restated in the discussion. In the development of the sermon we rarely find Scriptural citation. This is in harmony with his conception of the relation of Scripture to the religious life. The sermon material should never come directly, but indirectly, out of the Scriptures as they are spiritually appropriated. He uses his material in a large, free way, but bridges the path from topic to topic by skilful transition, so that, while the sermon has a large, free movement, the continuity of thought is observed and made clear and the whole discourse is held in unity. There is therefore great variety of method and there is nothing stereotyped. The rapidity with which the final preparation was made and the influence of the audience upon him in his extemporaneous movement of thought, especially in the later period of life, furthered this freedom of development. The thought of the sermon was with him for several days. But not till Saturday evening did he outline his material. As to the development, he leaves much to the inspiration of the audience, believing that the material should never be wholly reproduced, but that a good deal should be left to the productive energies in the stimulating process of discussion. In this we are reminded of Henry Ward Beecher. His enthusiasm for preaching was a stimulus to his productiveness. His reserve in private intercourse, especially

in the presence of strangers, was in striking contrast to
the spontaneity and joyfulness with which he poured
out the fulness of his soul in the pulpit, and in this he
reminds us of Phillips Brooks.

The diction of the sermon is always characterized
by his reflective habit of mind, but bears the mark of
his earnest, sympathetic feeling, and is always dignified
and measurably concrete. The style is descriptive, but
it is descriptive of the inner world of consciousness,
hence it is not abstruse, but reflective in its quality.
The "Discourses on Religion" are more exuberant in
their diction than his sermons. The earlier sermons are
the more stimulating, the later more contemplative and
more edifying. They bear the mark of pastoral experience with the sorrows and sufferings of life. There is
nothing obtrusive in his diction; the sentences are
German-like, long and complex, but they are clear and
accurate. They demand careful attention, but from the
German point of view the style is adapted to its work.
The absence of Biblical diction and of Biblical material
in general, as already suggested, is notable. Moreover
there is but little material from secular life, and but
little coloring from his humanistic culture; but the sermon always rings true to the Christian life, and is lifted
into a great height by a noble Christian feeling. For
his success as a preacher he was to no considerable extent dependent upon his physical personality. He was
short of stature, and as to his shoulders slightly de-
formed; but he had a broad forehead, firm-set lips,
strong Roman nose, a keen eye, and an altogether serious and vigorous countenance and a penetrating voice,
and this was doubtless tributary to his impressiveness.

During his whole public career, he was infirm of body, and, like Robert Hall, often preached in great pain. In preaching he began slowly and deliberately and with complete self-possession and composure, but warmed with his discourse, and then, though always under control, his speech became a torrent. Altogether his preaching illustrates the triumph of the spirit of the preacher. The method was well adapted to the substance, tone, and aim of the sermon, and all were tributary to the spiritual ennobling and enrichment of the hearer.

6. As to the type of Schleiermacher's preaching, it is not altogether easy to classify. In the general sense of the term, he was an intellectual preacher. His discourses met the needs of educated and cultured people. But they are not obtrusively intellectual. We are not at first impressed with their intellectual wealth. There is a basis of rich mental culture, but it makes no exhibition of itself. He was a highly emotional preacher, but it was not evangelistic emotion. He was a reflective and not an obtrusively rhetorical preacher. He never permitted the exuberant rhetoric of the " Discourses on Religion " to disclose itself in his sermons. In general he should be characterized as a pastoral preacher. He took personal direction of his parish affairs, notwithstanding his arduous duties as university professor, and his more public duties as a patriotic citizen, continuing to care for his catechetical classes, even up to the close of life. This pastoral spirit he carried into the pulpit. All this is in line with his conception of Christian preaching as the utterance of the content of Christian experience with reference to the edification

of the congregation.   An examination of his sermons
will show how largely the great truths of Christianity
as related to Christian experience appear in his preaching.   He is eminently a didactic preacher, in a modified
sense, even a doctrinal preacher, for, as already suggested, the content of his system of Christian doctrine
appears in homiletic form to a large extent in his
sermons.   But he made no distinction between the
doctrinal and ethical aspects of Christian truth.   The
only distinction is of form.   All doctrine is practical
and the end of doctrine is life.   In this we are reminded
of Bushnell and Brooks and Robertson, and of other
preachers with the modern spirit.   Schleiermacher
therefore may be called a pastoral preacher of the
higher ethical type.   In order to secure a proper analysis of the nature of religion, he would isolate it.   But
of course he never allowed his religion to evaporate in
emotion.   Emotion was but the inner impulse that inspired all his varied activities.   He says, indeed, that
religion is to act with morality, rather than to produce
morality.   But practically religion is with him the very
life of morality.   Despite his extremely subjective and
individualistic conception of religion and its tendency to
isolate the religious feeling from other contents of experience, he nevertheless in his scientific work developed Christianity on its ethical side, and especially on
the side of social ethics, more fully than it had ever been
developed before and made to it the most important
contribution of the last century.   And with equal fidelity in his pulpit teaching he carried out this development on its practical side, thus realizing his conception
of Christianity as the religion of life and not primarily

of thought. His sermons consist very largely in the application of Christianity to the practical interests of life, individual or social. He devoted himself largely to the interests of domestic life, and his sermons upon these subjects are of permanent value. As we have seen, he was an enthusiastic patriot, and his patriotic sermons are among his noblest utterances. He exalted Christ as the realization of the ideal of true human life. The sinless completeness of Jesus is central in his Christian apologetics. Christ is presented, not only as the one in whose spiritual fellowship we nourish our own spiritual life and so find fellowship with God, but as our ethical ideal in accordance with which our life is to be shaped as well as inspired. This practical quality is the more striking when we consider the profoundly reflective, introverted, speculative, as well as poetic, quality of his mind. It is still more striking when we recall the mystical basis of his religion. He was not a practical mystic as Tauler was. Religion does not find its centre in the will, but in feeling. He might easily have been a sentimental and contemplative mystic, and but for his humanistic culture and his serious sense of the ethical significance of human life, he would have been such. It was therefore quite the necessity of his rich, full inner life of feeling to push vigorously over into the domain of thought and then to take the product of his thought, penetrated by the life of his emotion, out still farther into the world of practical reality. And he demonstrates that true religious feeling cannot be isolated from mental and moral life. The " Monologues" interpret the " Discourses." They disclose his own sense of the might of his moral man-

hood, which he carefully cultivated and defended as a
most sacred possession, and the like of which he would
encourage in every human being.   These ringing words
reveal the strength and the enthusiasm of that manhood.
"Yes, my mind shall preserve its vigor in advancing
years, never shall spirit and courage forsake me; what
I rejoice in now, I will rejoice in forevermore; firm
shall my will remain, and strong my imagination.
Nothing shall deprive me of the magic key which un-
locks for me the mysterious portals of the world above;
never shall the fervor of my love be extinguished.   I
will not behold the dreaded weakness of age; I vow to
despise every calamity which does not affect the objects
of my existence, and I swear to preserve myself in
eternal young."   These are the words of a man whose
wealth of religious feeling found its noblest expression
in mental and moral life, and it found vent in the pulpit,
not only in noble thought, but in the inculcation of a
noble moral life.   The man who in old age could stand
at the grave of his only son, and, while shaken to the
foundations by a stroke from which he never wholly
recovered, could with calmness commit him to mother
earth, and speak strong words of hope to those who
mourned with him, proved his own fidelity to a noble
ideal of a manly moral life.

How far and in what ways the development of the
religious life of the modern church has influenced its
practical or its ethical or philanthropic life would be a
profoundly interesting inquiry.   It is doubtless true that
modern philanthropy has its distinctively secular aspect,
and that it has developed to a considerable extent as a
distinctively ethical interest, and independently of the

church. There is a moral life that has had a very vigorous growth apart from religion, and it may almost be called a characteristic of our time ; but it is questionable, at least, whether it may not ultimately be the product of the Christian conception of man that has been so fully domesticated in modern life. It is at any rate certain that the revival of religion in the latter part of the eighteenth century and the early part of the nineteenth, in Germany and in Great Britain, has resulted in a mighty quickening of the moral and philanthropic life of the church and has had wide-reaching results in what is called secular society. The immense vitality of Christianity and its demonstrated power in practical life was one of the most striking phenomena of the last century. It is also certain that all the great leaders in modern German evangelicalism who were influenced by Schleiermacher have been profoundly interested in the problems of practical theology and of Christian ethics, and in the development at once of the piety and of the practical morality and philanthropy of the churches. The great modern missionary movement is the direct product of the revival of evangelical piety, and all this illustrates the great truth, enunciated and exemplified by Schleiermacher, that religion is the soul of morality.

CHAPTER II

FREDERICK WILLIAM ROBERTSON

In passing from Friedrich Schleiermacher to Frederick Robertson we are at first strongly impressed with their points of contrast. But after all between the two men there are notable points of likeness. In much they are kindred spirits, and they hold the same general point of view in their estimate of religion, of theology, and of the practical significance of the Christian church. They are alike in their spiritual insight, their delicacy of religious susceptibility, their ardent affectionateness, their fervid emotion, their sturdy independence, their manly courage, their tolerance, their patriotism, their devotion to the practical interests of men, their humanistic culture, and they are both intrenched in the position that "in all matters of eternal truth the soul is before the intellect." It will always be an honor to the Anglican church that it was the spiritual home of Frederick Robertson. But it cannot be claimed that he is a distinctive product of the Anglican church. He was the product of a broader world than that in which his church moves. He had nothing of the churchliness that characterizes the typical Anglican preacher, nothing of his conservatism, conventionalism, and devotion to institutional religion. He was subjective, independent, revolutionary, open-hearted, and fiery. He was immensely human, and no ecclesiastical establishment could bind his free, imperial spirit.

E
49

I

INFLUENCES DETERMINATIVE OF ROBERTSON'S DEVELOPMENT

In point of time, Robertson belongs to the first half of the nineteenth century; in point of influence, to the last half. He was born in 1816 and died in 1853, at the age of thirty-seven years and six months. His public life covers a period of only thirteen years, during which he was not very widely known, even in his own country. It is since his death that his place as a preacher has been established, and it is hardly too much to say that among the educated classes, throughout the English-speaking world and throughout Germany as well, his name has become more widely cherished, and his work more widely influential, than that of any other English preacher of his century.

1. In looking at the career of this singularly gifted and impressive preacher, we note at the outset his distinctive English qualities. Although in remote lineage he may have been Scotch, he had become thoroughly Anglicized, and he disclosed English rather than Scottish traits. He was, in fact, every inch an Englishman, and he bore the marks of the English culture of the first half of the century. He was, indeed, a man of much finer fibre than the average Englishman, even than the English preacher. His mind was much more speculative, it had a subtler insight, a richer æsthetic sensibility, a much more delicate emotional susceptibility, than most Englishmen possess. But in his basal qualities, those qualities that gave solidity and balance to his

intellectual and moral character, and in which lay in large measure the secret of his strength, he was a thorough Englishman. He was an idealist of high degree, but to his singularly delicate poetic insight and to his artistic taste there was added the broad, Saxon common sense that reaches its best development in the typical Englishman. He was trained in the realm of abstract thought, and was at home in the high altitudes of speculation, at once intuitive and dialectical in his mental operations, but he had the objective realism of the English mind. It was this mental bias that led him away from the transcendentalism of his early years, "the rock on which I split." It was this that led him to the study of the physical sciences, — chemistry, natural philosophy, geology, and botany, — for "the effect of certainty which they produce on the mind is always a healthy feeling." It was this perhaps that inclined him toward the Biblical type of preaching, in which he could deal with religion in its objective, historic form, in which he, shunning the artifice of allegory, always grasped the historic sense, and in which, despite his brilliant imagination and skill in detaching the inner suggestiveness of Biblical truth, he always proved himself to be a sane and reliable critic. He had a very keen and delicate sense of the idealistic or poetic aspects of nature, but he also had a sharp eye for its external and local aspects. It was, in part, this English realism that led him from Shelley's "atmosphere of profligacy" to the wholesome tranquillity of Wordsworth and to Shakespeare's "spirit of sunny endeavor," and to his "acquiescence in things as they are — not incompatible with a cheerful resolve to make them better," which he testifies is "good for

the mind." It was this English common sense that
led him to take a balanced view of all things and
secured him against the one-sidedness of his impulses.
No modern preacher has entered more deeply than he
into the life of Christ, and his spirit of self-sacrificing
devotion became almost a passion with him. It might
have become a superstition and a supererogatory sort
of passion. But he held himself in moral poise, and
could say, "I believe the spirit of exceeding self-devo-
tion, as a mere romantic instinct, is but folly." He was
almost feminine in his emotional susceptibilities and in
the tenderness of his sympathy, but all this was matched
by a masculine strenuousness of will that increased in
force with the passing years, and held him steadfast to
his goal. To a shrinking sensibility that was intensified
by the contradictions of life and made morbid by physical disease, was added a virile individuality and Saxon
independence of character. He was humble, yet in
high measure self-asserting. He respected the opinions of others, yet in his own opinions he refused to be
a partisan. "Save yourself from sectarianism; pledge
yourself to no school," is his counsel to the working-
men of Brighton ; "cut your life adrift from all party;
be a slave to no maxims: stand fast, unfettered and
free, servants only of the truth." He kept his own
precept, and in the spirit of this independence he spoke
with a courage that is an honor to the manliest race of
the modern world. What he declares to be true of the
poet is true of himself, who also had the poet's mind
and heart. "Every great poet," he says, "is a double-
natured man, with the feminine and manly powers in
harmonious union, having the tact and the sympathy

and the intuition and the tenderness of woman, with the breadth and massiveness of the manly intellect, besides the calm justice which is almost exclusively masculine." It was this manly independence of character that gave a martial heroism to his too short earthly career. He had the English ethical mind. Gentle toward the weak and suffering, he was fierce in his moral indignation and terrible in his denunciation of cowardly wrong. He had no weak, sentimental notions about punishment, human or divine. "Once in my life," he says, "I felt a terrible might. I knew and rejoiced to know, as I spoke, that I was inflicting the sentence of a coward and a liar's hell." He hated and denounced all sham and hypocrisy with the intensity of Carlyle. But he had the reserve of a gentleman, and the patience of a Christian in all his denunciation.

By the patrons of tradition and convention he was regarded as an iconoclast, and it must be acknowledged that in effect, although not in spirit or method, he was revolutionary in his teaching; but still he had the Englishman's caution and his conservative habit of mind. He taught freely and boldly, but positively and constructively. "Let them draw the conclusions, I state truths," he says, and for this reason he was left "unmolested in spite of great grumbling, dissatisfaction, and almost personal hatred." He was democratic in principle while he was aristocratic in sentiment. "My tastes," he says, "are with the aristocrat, my principles with the mob." And in all this he is conscious of fellowship with John Milton. He was the recognized friend of the working-men of Brighton, but he never allied himself even with the Christian socialists. He thought that

he could not preach to the privileged classes, and at one
time he was ready on this account to resign his charge
at Cheltenham; but he felt himself in sympathy with
their traditions and strenuously advocated their rights.
He was an advocate of revolution with reference to the
advancement of the rights of the common people, but
he hears with a pang " of the extinction of great names,
gray with the hoar of innumerable ages " and laments
"the passing of great ancestral estates under the hammer of the auctioneer."   He was catholic in spirit
beyond the measure of the ordinary Englishman, elevating the church above the sect, and humanity above the
nation; but he had the heart of a true English patriot.
His sense of justice and of philanthropy led him to
distinguish with respect to the objects for which a nation
might fight; but his chivalrous martial spirit would have
led him to die for England for almost any cause, and
there were times when he even seemed to covet the
honor.   He followed the English campaigns of the
past with an almost boyish enthusiasm, and described
them with singular skill and exactness.   The English
sense of patriotic duty and patriotic devotion fired him,
and he could glory in a nation whose sons "can die at
their posts silently, without thinking that forty centuries
were looking down upon them."

2. In Robertson's career we are also impressed with
the influence of his early English home.   The first five
years of his life were spent in a military fortification,
the next four amid the Yorkshire hills.   Till he was
seven years of age his parents were his only teachers.
During the following seven years, a portion of which
he spent in France, where he mastered the French

language, his father seems to have had a general direction of his studies, till, at the age of sixteen, he was sent to Edinburgh. During all these years, parental influence, nature, books, solitude, were laying the foundations for thoroughly trained and cultivated character. It was then that his habits of study were fixed, and here we trace that accuracy and conscientious devotion to his intellectual tasks that marked all his later years. Here, amid these influences, was developed that purity of heart and life that enabled him in later years to say, " I know from personal experience — and I do know — that feelings such as these, call them romantic if you will, can keep a man all his youth through, before a higher faith has been called into being, from every species of vicious and low indulgence." Here, in solitude, at his intellectual tasks, or in the companionship of nature, he developed that tendency to self-isolation that always characterized him, and which is connected with that sense of loneliness that he often felt in later years. In a thoughtful and reflective habit of mind, he developed a maturity beyond his years. He is a student of Shakespeare, and even as a boy he wonders at his knowledge of the human heart. In his early companionships he exhibits that chivalrous tenderness of affection that made him an intense and steadfast friend. In subsequent life he recalls his love for one of his schoolmates, and his reference indicates the almost womanly delicacy, and at the same time manly chivalry, of his affection. He familiarized himself with nature and with all forms of animal life, and this developed his poetic tendencies. He knew the " power of English scenery and life to calm, if not to purify, the hearts of those whose lives are habitually subjected to such influences;" and he could testify from experience that "a man's character and mind are moulded for good or evil, far more by the forms of imagination which surround his childhood, than by any subsequent scientific training." It was in early life that he nurtured that "delicacy and depth of feeling" which he regarded as a necessary prerequisite for the apprehension of poetry, and it was thus that he learned to associate poetry with religion. It is his judgment that no man can understand poetry "who has led a slothful life, or who has not at one time or other loved to rise early — no man who in his early walks has not mingled with a love of poetry a deep religious sense; who has not felt the consecrating effects of early dawn; or who has not at one time or another in his early days, in a moment of deep enthusiasm, knelt down amid the glories of nature, as the ancient patriarchs knelt, and feeling that none were awake but the Creator and himself, bowed down to consecrate and to offer up the whole of his life, experiencing also a strange and awful and mysterious feeling, as if a hand invisible were laid upon his brow, accepting the consecration and sacrifice." It is utterances like these that disclose the power of the associations of his youth. Then also was developed that soldierly spirit that was so notable a characteristic of the man and of the preacher. He "breathed the atmosphere in which the English soldier lives," and he never lost the impressions of those days upon his susceptible and fiery spirit. As is well known, he was inclined to the military service, and was turned aside from it only by a combination of circumstances to which, in after years, he attached a sort of fatality, and to him it illustrated the divine predestination. One is strongly reminded of the critical and sometimes seemingly fortuitous character of our earthly life by recalling how slight a thing might have committed Robertson to a life in which some at least, if not all, of his choicest gifts might have been buried, or at least greatly obscured, and the modern English pulpit have been robbed of its brightest ornament. No one can fail to see that all the influences above specified were tributary to his power as a preacher, nor can, nor should, one forget that the piety of that early home, a piety that can flourish even in a soldier's life and perhaps nowhere else so well as in the homes of many of the officers of the English army, wrought powerfully upon his fine religious susceptibility. We should not forget that Robertson was nurtured in the atmosphere of an Evangelical piety. In subsequent years he was accustomed to speak with severity of the unreality of much of the piety that he found in Evangelical circles. It is not unlikely that he was correct in this estimate, although some allowance must be made, perhaps, for the overwrought feeling of a theological antagonist, and especially of a man who felt the sting of personal wrong. But whatever the truth of the matter may be, he could not and would not deny, nor could he ever forget, the reality of the piety of his early home, nor could, nor did, he escape the influence throughout his life.

3. Robertson's relation to the Anglican church is an interesting and an important feature in the history of his development. In the broader estimate, as already suggested, he was a product of modern life, rather than of the modern church. His culture was characteristically

humanistic rather than ecclesiastical, yet in a restricted but important sense he was a product of his church. Each of the schools, the high, low, and broad, into which, fortunately or unfortunately, as one may be inclined to consider it, the church is divided, and which represent tendencies of thought at work in various forms and degrees in almost all sections of the modern church, exerted an influence upon him, and he was at one or another time affiliated with them. On the æsthetic, as well as on the devotional, and, perhaps the philanthropic side, and to a considerable extent on the theoretic side (for he held that some of the fundamental tenets of this party were true), he had a bias toward the high church, or what was later called the Ritualistic party. The lofty, although unhistoric, conceptions of the dignity of the church held by its chief representative men, their elevated conceptions of the sanctities of worship, their reverence for the past, their devoutness and earnestness of character, their devotion to a life of beneficence, and the fact that this party numbered in its ranks many of the most gifted and cultivated minds in the church, like Keble and Newman, had strong attractions for him; and he seemed at one time, as by his own tastes and poetic inclinations, destined to be numbered with them. Indeed, so near to superficial observation did he seem to come to them, that at one time they were almost tempted to claim him. In fact, not more than five months before his death, he confesses that "with a thoughtful and large-minded high churchman I believe I could sympathize more than with any other section of the church." It was his belief "that in all the tenets and practices of the high church body there is an underlying truth."

While at Oxford University he had come into connection with its most prominent representatives. He must have heard Newman at St. Mary's, and could not have failed to be impressed with his intellectual brilliancy and religious intensity, although he could not accept the " forms of statement " in which they all sought to express their fundamental truths. But when he came to apply his critical methods and to state the truths they had formulated, in his own terms, they found that he was far removed from them. In the last period of his career his conceptions of God were modified and enlarged, and he found himself putting the ubiquitous presence of God over against the high churchman's localized deity, and balancing a pantheistic pervasiveness against an anthropomorphic personality. The conceptions of the church and of the sacraments also which prevailed in this party were too narrow for him, and he refused to ally himself with them. Moreover, his sense of reality revolted against their effort " to represent the piety of the past through the forms of the past, instead of striving, like true prophets, to interpret the aspirations of the present in forms that truly represent and foster them."

On the emotional and affectional and measurably on the practical side of his nature, as well as by early education and association, he was allied with the so-called Evangelical branch of the church. Like Newman, he, as we have seen, was nurtured in an Evangelical atmosphere. During his university course, from 1837 to 1840, although to a certain extent influenced by the Anglican movement, he was still regarded as a low churchman, and there is no evidence that his religious or theological views underwent any material change. In his first ministry of two years at Winchester, from 1840 to 1842, and during his ministry of the five following years at Cheltenham, he was also regarded as a low churchman. His preaching was for the most part of the pronounced Evangelical type, using the term Evangelical in its ecclesiastical sense, although it may be questionable whether it was more Evangelical in the proper theological sense than that of his Brighton ministry. His aim was "the saving of souls," as the term was understood among the Evangelicals, *i.e.* the bringing of men to a decision for Christ, the winning of them to a conscious religious life, and to the fellowship of the church. In its austerity, his piety was of a pronounced Evangelical type. It was mystical, and in a way transcendental and distinctively ascetic; but before he left Cheltenham a change in his views had taken place, and he began to recognize himself as moving in a larger world of thought. The unreality, as he regarded it, of the Evangelical type of piety was apparently one of the influences involved in this change. He detected a certain pietistic cant behind the Evangelical phraseology, and he was convinced that it represented a great amount of religious pretentiousness and of unsound ethical character, and his sensitive moral, not to say æsthetic and religious, nature vigorously reacted against it. This, however, was only one, and perhaps the most trifling, of the causes or occasions of his break with the Evangelical school and of his subsequent religious and theological revolution. The criticism to which he was subjected on account of his free utterances in the pulpit, and a certain tone of worldliness and frivolity which he detected, or thought he detected, under the pietistic cant of the

Evangelicals, may have still further intensified his revulsion of feeling. And it is not altogether unlikely that, had their piety been more genuine and their type of religious character broader and manlier, he might have continued to be more closely allied with them to the end.

On the intellectual, as well as ethical, side of his nature, he was allied with the broad church school. It is noteworthy that, seemingly, so far as the records of his life testify, he did not know very much about this school and was not in close relation with its leaders.

So far as I recall no special mention is made of it as a movement in his biography, but it was already in existence, and was a distinct and most significant movement in the church against which Tractarians and Evangelicals alike reacted. In fact, it was one of the chief incentives to the Tractarian reaction. It was a relic in modified form of the earlier Oriel school, of which Whately was the leader and with which Arnold, and at one time Newman, was in a sort connected. It was the school of Coleridge and the Hares, of Maurice and Stanley and Kingsley. It is significant of Robertson's independence that he says almost nothing about this movement. He probably did not wholly agree with any one of them in their conceptions of Christianity and of the church. But in their general humanistic tendencies, in their intellectual freedom, their catholicity of spirit, and their ecclesiastical comprehensiveness he was in sympathy with them. In the partisan sense he belonged to no particular section of the church. In a way, they all contributed to him. In accounting for his development, we cannot fail to detect their influence; for with all his manly independence, he was responsive to influences from all quarters, not the less from individual friends than from books, that represented a new spirit and suggested a new and better method in theology. He gathered from all, yet he stood alone. He could not be a party man. He formed no alliances in furthering the schemes of this broad school. He was too sensitively individualistic and independent for such alliances. This solitary position, result partly of inward and partly of outward conditions, while it was the necessity and the glory, was yet the sorrow, of his life.

But it was singularly tributary to the persuasiveness and power of his preaching. It contributed to that intensity, that reality, that peculiar penetrating, experimental quality that can come only from independent personal conviction. It was experimental preaching of the most pronounced type, the testimony of the soul and message bearing, intensely subjective, yet anchored to a historic basis in the life of Christ. There is no note of conventionality about it. It was a new prophetic voice in the Anglican church, a voice as in a wilderness of party confusion. It was the utterance of a man who had fought his way through and out and beyond party lines, who was willing to stand alone and was able to do it, and who spake what he felt in the deepmost soul of him. He spake the things he had seen and heard and felt, and there was consequently a tremendous power in what he said.

4. We have seen that the agencies which wrought in Robertson's general change of religious and ethical experience, and in his change of theological position, are somewhat occult and difficult to trace. Perhaps they were not fully known even to himself, and therefore

could not be known to those about him. This seems to
be particularly true of those influences, whatever they
may have been, that wrought a change in the philosophical basis of his beliefs. All such changes are
likely to come gradually, and the process is likely to
be obscure. Without doubt, in his case, the transfor-
mation was more gradual and inward and silent than
appears at the surface of his life, although the culmina-
tion was rapid and seems to have been limited to the
course of a few months, after which he emerged into a
new and singularly sudden consciousness of power, and
his growth, thence onward, is marvellous. It is evident
also that a basis for the change cannot be traced back
to his university days. At Oxford he was a careful
and accurate student, and became somewhat familiar
with Plato and Aristotle. But his student life was
somewhat miscellaneous, and, according to his own ac-
knowledgment, lacked concentration. He left the university, apparently, without any thorough grounding in
modern philosophic thought; and his theology, as regards its philosophic basis, seems to have been of the
traditional sort. It is altogether likely that we might
trace the beginnings of his ultimate change to the
literature with which he became familiar, and which
became the medium for interpreting to him new philosophic conceptions. A modification in the ethical character of his religious experiences was also doubtless a
conditioning factor in the intellectual revolution; but,
whatever may have been the genesis of the change, ultimate modified philosophical conceptions of Christianity
become manifest, and it is altogether unlikely that a
man of Robertson's penetration should never have rec-

ognized this change of philosophic basis and never have given an account of it to himself.   It is a well-known fact that a new idealistic and spiritualistic philosophy was becoming current, and thinking men, in a great variety of ways, were becoming subject to it and largely through the new literary spirit of the time.   It is interesting to note how silently fundamental changes in thought are effected.   It was some time after Kant's death that his works were translated into English. It was almost a half-century after Schleiermacher's death before his " Discourses on Religion " were given to the English public, but the results of Kant's philosophic criticism and of Schleiermacher's " Discourses " were already manifest in English thought, and Robertson in England and Bushnell in this country disclosed the traces of this influence.   Coleridge's " Aids to Reflection," published in 1825, embodied the results of his investigation of German philosophy and became a fruitful source of influence.   His philosophical idealism, which may be called a combination of the ethical idealism of Kant and the religious idealism of Schleiermacher, directly or indirectly influenced Robertson. From Robertson's published works it becomes evident that he was familiar with some of Coleridge's philosophical positions, especially with his theory of religious knowledge.   In his ever recurring declaration that religious truth "is felt, not reasoned out," we note the influence of the idealistic philosophy.   We find also a changed conception of the immanence of God in the universe, and especially in humanity and in the individual soul.   And here it is not unlikely that we may trace an influence from Carlyle.   For it was

Carlyle's message to the world that religion is the intuition of the divine in the universe. Robertson, in one of his letters, criticises Carlyle's tendency to pantheism, or the tendency to find "the divine everywhere and to make little distinction between the amount of divinity which is contained in different forces, provided only that they be Force." But he is at one with Carlyle in his general conception of religion, and in Robertson we detect the ethical idealism, the hatred of sham, and the respect for hard, honest work that characterized Carlyle. It is not unlikely that the influence of Carlyle's literary Romanticism was even more potent with him than the philosophical idealism of Coleridge. But whatever we may conclude as to this matter, it is perfectly clear that Robertson's change of theological views was connected with changed philosophical conceptions. The fundamental change was in his conception of God's relation to the universe. With this was connected a modification in his conception of the way in which the soul comes to a knowledge of God and of divine realities, thus securing to him a more spiritual theory of religious knowledge. With this was included a broadening of his conception of Biblical inspiration, as involving that action of God within the soul by which it becomes able to recognize religious principles of universal validity. With new recognition of the soul in the totality of its powers as the organ of religious knowledge, and with new recognition of the self-evidencing power of Christianity in the experiences of the soul, came a modification in his conception of the validating force of miracles. "I hold," he says, "that the attempt to rest Christianity upon miracles, and the

F

fulfilments of prophecy, is essentially the vilest rationalism." With his changed conceptions of God's relation
to the world, it is natural that the incarnation should
become central in his Christology and soteriology, and
that his conception of the atonement should have been
modified. And his conception of the church and of the
sacraments is in line with his fundamental conception
of the character of God, of the mission and work of
Christ, and of man as the child of God.

5. The influence upon Robertson of modern literature has already been referred to. Especially to be
recognized is the influence of the great modern poets,
Wordsworth and Tennyson. He possessed the artistic
temperament in a high degree, and from an early age
was strongly impressed by all the artistic forms in which
truth is expressed. Science, and especially physical
science, met the needs of his intellectual life. In it he
found relief "from the dim religious light of theology,
in which one seems to make out the outline of a truth,
and the next moment lose it in hopeless mystery and
shadows." But truth in artistic forms was his great joy,
for these forms "feed the heart." He regards poetry
and religion as in close alliance because "the laws of
both are the same, and the organ of both intuition, and
both satisfy the needs of the heart." Therefore, in his
maturer years, he studied theology almost wholly in the
forms of literary expression, rather than in its scientific
forms. It was Wordsworth, especially, who realized his
highest ideal of a poet, and of the man who, as poet, is
also the prophet of the soul. As regards his knowledge
of Wordsworth, he thinks himself competent to say of
him what "should be heard by his fellow-men," because

he "has for years studied Wordsworth, and loved him,
and year by year felt his appreciation and comprehension of Wordsworth grow, and has during all those
years endeavored to make Wordsworth's principles the
guiding principles of his own inner life." He finds
much theology in his poetry. He especially finds in
him the harmonizing of the seeming contradiction
between the quasi-pantheistic conception of the divine
immanence and the theistic conception of the divine
personality. As poet, Wordsworth was pantheistic; as
a Christian, he was theistic. He found the divine everywhere; he also found the divine in specific and determinate localities; hence he can be a high churchman,
and at the same time can maintain the essential
sacredness of all forms of existence. And Robertson,
with his genius for comprehension, defends the seeming
contradiction as embracing a higher truth. The subjective and idealistic quality of modern literature found
response in his own subjective and idealistic tendencies.
He recognizes the truth of Schlegel's distinction between
ancient and modern poetry, viz. that "the characteristic
of the former is satisfaction, that of the latter aspiration."
Therefore, he could even tolerate Byron and Shelley.
It is this note of self-consciousness, of struggle, of
aspiration for the unattained ideal that found him, and
the influence of this poetic expression of human aspiration is seen in all his culture, in all his preaching, in all
forms of his literary activity, and in his whole life. It
expressed what was most real to himself. But in
Wordsworth, especially, he found tranquillity as well as
quickening of aspiration. Wordsworth's peacefulness
calmed his turbulent soul, and he found relief from the

storm and stress of life in this refreshing realm. And
for something the same reason he turned to the fresh
objective, descriptive mind of Sir Walter, for there " was
no morbid spot in that strong, manly heart and nature,"
and he is "the most healthful restorative of any."

In this realm of tranquillity he trained his imagination to work and calmed his turbulent emotions, and all
this commerce with poetic forms, whether as stimulus
or sedative, heightened the prophetic quality of his
preaching. He lived a lonely life. One suspects, and
indeed hears, of an unrealized domestic ideal, and he
was the victim of such distempers as a highly sensitive,
intense, overwrought organization is exposed to. Hence
the tremendous earnestness, the almost preternatural
intensity, the sometimes depressingly sad and solemn
impressiveness of his utterance. He threw all the
great emotions that were stirred within him by the political and social agitations of his time, by the conflicts
of the church, by the opposition to which he was subject, by his lonely life, by the kindlings of the imagination and the quickenings of aspiration, in his high
poetic world, by sympathy with the " man of sorrows,"
whose pains had penetrated his soul, into his preaching ;
and with all the comforts of literary fellowship, all the
solace of friendship, all the grace of his Master, it was
more than the mortal frame could bear. He saved his
life for other generations, but he lost it in saving it. He
did not know how well he wrought. He did not know
the full import, reach, or measure of his prophetic utterance. He did not know how deeply he spoke into the
lives of men. Never was man more unconscious of
what he was doing for others, for the church, for the

world, ultimately for himself. It was in much a sad history, but most precious for the multitudes of needy men whom he has helped. More fully than any other English preacher of his century has he spoken the true prophetic word for hungry and disquieted human hearts. In our effort to interpret him, we may not forget his identification of poetry and religion, nor his poetic and religious interpretation of human life.

II

THE DISTINCTIVE QUALITIES IN ROBERTSON'S PREACHING

What is distinctive in his preaching may perhaps be made apparent in an attempt to point out what is most helpful and impressive in it.

1. Perhaps the first thing that arrests our attention is the distinctively Biblical quality of his preaching. He illustrates most suggestively the value of Biblical preaching, demonstrates the fruitfulness of Biblical study for homiletic use, furnishes the most attractive model of an effective Biblical method, and has exerted an important influence upon the best Biblical preaching of our day. The foundation was early laid, and it became his chosen and only method. At the university " he took special delight in Scriptural and Greek Testament readings." " He literally learned by heart the whole of the New Testament, not only in English, but in Greek." " His love for the Holy Bible was exceedingly remarkable, and especially for those parts that are full of Christ." His inclination and his training,

therefore, both drew him from the first to this type of
preaching. At Winchester his preaching was, in the
substance of its thought, doctrinal after the Calvinistic
type of the Evangelicals, but it was Biblical in form.
He was a careful student, devoting the morning hour to
study, " getting up early and eating almost no breakfast
in order to apply himself to his work. He chiefly at
that time devoted himself to the study of Hebrew and
Biblical criticism, though he read all sorts of books."
" He was no contemptible scholar," and " of general
information he had a large store." All this became
available in his Biblical expositions. At Cheltenham,
his doctrinal beliefs, as we have seen, began to modify,
and this somewhat affected the substance, but not the
form, of his preaching. The best type of his preaching,
however, both as to substance and form, is seen in his
Brighton ministry. Here his unique skill as an interpreter of Biblical truth, and of human life in the light
of that truth, reaches its supremacy. In his sermon on
the " Illusiveness of Life " he suggests his own conception of the preacher's work. " The very essence of it is
to justify the ways of God to man — to interpret God."
His letters also, profoundly interesting in their simplicity,
perspicuity, freshness, and grace of diction, indicate how
thoroughly familiar his mind was with Biblical truth.
We detect his habits of Biblical study, not only in his
expository discourses upon the books of the Bible, in
which he alternated between the Old and New Testa-
ments, but in his discourses from isolated texts. He
wrought the results of this study into his Sunday-
school work, especially into the instruction given his
teachers. His catechetical work had a Biblical rather

than a dogmatical or ecclesiastical quality, and his large confirmation classes attest, not only his pastoral zeal, but his attractiveness as a teacher. He availed himself of the expository method, as a wise homiletic and pastoral device, in getting difficult and offensive themes before his congregation. A result of this Biblical habit of mind was that his ordinary preaching always took the textual form. It was very likely the method in which he, in his associations with the Evangelical preachers of the church, had become familiar, but he greatly improved upon the method. No textual preaching of his day, and none since, is comparable with Robertson's in freshness, suggestiveness, and forcefulness. His preaching shows how thoroughly he had grasped the homiletic significance and value of the Bible, and it demonstrates how fully he understood the importance of historic religion as interpreted through experience, for the practical lives of men, notwithstanding his brilliant speculative and dialectical abilities, and his possibilities thereby, for the most effective type of topical preaching.

Let us now note some of the prominent features of this Biblical quality in his preaching.

(1) And first, his grasp of the historic sense. He must know first of all, and so must his hearers know, the explicit thought as it lay in the mind of the Biblical writer. This historic sense is always present as groundwork. Hence his Scripture passage is always held in its contextual relations. His expository discourses especially, as for example those on the Corinthian letters, the exposition of the last chapter of which closed his earthly ministry, show how well he had mastered the whole situation, how well he understood the historic

conditions, and how wide-reaching was his grasp of the whole course of thought and how clear his conception of the experiences in Paul's life that furnish a background for these letters.

(2) His penetration into the inner suggestiveness of his texts. He gets down under them, sinks himself into them, and throws up into the light what lies hidden there. He combined these two requisites in all successful Biblical preaching, viz. definite comprehension of the historic sense, and skill in detaching its inner ethical and spiritual suggestiveness. Defective preaching of the Biblical type has always disclosed a failure in one or the other of these conditions. Robertson's preaching combines duly the historic and the suggestive, the literal and the poetic, truth for the understanding and truth for the imagination, fact for our sense of reality, and principle for our practical guidance. The historic, however, appears only as the background and base of his procedure. He had what Rothe, speaking of Augustine, calls " exegetical divination," by which he means power of insight into the ethical and spiritual suggestiveness of the Scriptures, and which may be called as well, indeed more appropriately, homiletic divination. He seizes the inner suggestiveness of his passage as by a kind of inspiration. " He did not," says his biographer, " choose his text in order to bring a doctrine out of it, but he penetrated to its centre and seized the principle it contains. It was the kernel, not the shell, for which he cared." This penetrating and suggestive quality is seen in the light he throws upon his texts in the broad processes of his discussion. He cultivated his imagination and his sympathies, and these

two qualities were greatly conducive to his suggestiveness as a Biblical preacher. His mind acted spontaneously and intuitively. He was, indeed, as already suggested, strong in dialectic, he was a master in subtle reasoning ; but imaginative insight was his most marked intellectual gift. It was preëminently the gift of the interpreter.

The best interpreter in any field of knowledge is the man who combines patient investigation and ratiocinative skill with that sharpness of insight which is often only a happy guess of the imagination. The best interpreter of religious truth, and so far forth the best preacher, is the man who combines exegetical analysis with that sharpness of insight which is the gift of a trained imagination. Facts or truths are of but little significance or value without ability to detect their inner meaning. With a trained imagination, Robertson combined trained sympathies. He had a most delicate sense of ethical and spiritual realities, because he approached them through his sympathies. It is his conviction, very frequently expressed, that without the capacity of sympathy, spiritual truth cannot be interpreted, as it cannot be apprehended. It is especially true that without it the character and life of Christ cannot be understood nor successfully presented. His vivid apprehension of Christ, his delicate sympathy with him, and his skill and persuasiveness in interpreting Christ's character and life illustrate this. " He had," says his biographer, " spent a world of study, of reverent meditation, of adoring contemplation, on the gospel history." To a friend, two years before his death, he gave this counsel, and it suggests the habit of his life. " Receive, imbibe, and then your mind will create. Poets are creators because recipients. They open their hearts to Nature, instead of going to her with views of her already made and second-hand; so with Scripture, — patient, quiet, long, revering listening to it; then suggestiveness."

It is this quality of insight that enables him to grasp the underrunning principles of Biblical revelation. He has great skill in applying these principles. In his hands particular truths acquire new significance by reason of their vital relation to general truths. We discover the inner meaning of the specific truth in the light of the larger truth that is brought to bear upon it. He was confident that in his preaching he had got at what was fundamental. He speaks with confidence in one of his letters of having mastered Paul's "root thoughts." He sought what was fundamental in the character and life of Christ. No modern preacher has been more successful in finding the centre of this character and life or in making the discovery of it the key-note of his preaching. He felt that he had struck bottom. And it can hardly be doubted that his new, clear vision, and his quickened and expanded sense of the significance of Christ for his own and for all human life, was one of the influences that wrought in the change of his theological views. He found that the doctrinal standards of his church did not harmonize with his broadened conceptions of Christianity, and that they did not stand the test of broader Biblical criticism. He was driven back the more centrally and fundamentally to historic Christianity, as he found himself relaxing his hold upon the doctrines of his church. He found himself forced to look for fundamental principles, and when he had found them his pulpit power was doubled. The contrast, not so much in form as in substance, between his earlier and later preaching, is notable, and has been a matter of frequent comment. He felt at last that his feet were upon the rock, and it is because of this experience that Robertson became the most comprehensive, forceful, and persuasive interpreter of Christ and of all human life in the light of his person, character, and work in his century. Other preachers have brought human life to the interpretation of Christianity. He would bring Christianity to the interpretation of life. Other men have been students of humanity, and have found its best experiences, even its common experiences, even its experiences of sin and suffering, vindications and verifications of Christian truth. Robertson was indeed a student of life and of men, but he was first of all a student of Christian revelation, a student of ideal humanity as it exists in Christ, and he finds here the realization and the interpretation of all that is truly human. The message of Phillips Brooks to the world is this: Religion is human, religion is truly natural. Know yourself in your deepest needs; know the deepmost significance of your own experiences; know the world in its deepest principles; get at its deepest meaning; interpret yourself and interpret the world aright, — and then you will know Christ, you will find an echo and a vindication of His revelation to your soul. On the other hand, Robertson's message was, Know the deepest inner meaning of the life of Christ; know it as containing the root principles of all human life, then you will have the key to your own human experiences, the key to all truly human life.

(3) We are thus brought to consider briefly Robertson's skill in applying to ethical and spiritual needs the content of Biblical truth. He had far more than the ordinary mental and moral impulse, which every genuine preacher must have, to reach out into the lives of his fellow-men and to apply the truth to their practical necessities. He was a diligent student of his age, and he sought to apply the principles of Christianity to its special wants. He was strongly moved by the political, ecclesiastical, scientific, economic, social, and philanthropic questions that were in agitation at the time of his appearance in public life. The democratic spirit that has since made such head in England and has exerted so powerful an influence in public life was making itself felt in many ways. The conflict in the church, that resulted in Newman's break with it, was at its height when he took orders. Scientific theories were challenging the truth of the doctrines of the church. Carlyle was prodding the sluggish English public and rallying them to action with respect to the problems of poverty. Maurice and Kingsley were engaged in pushing their schemes of Christian socialism. Robertson was profoundly impressed and influenced by all this. He gained a powerful ascendency over the working-men of Brighton, and he interpreted Christianity to men of wealth with rare skill and balance of judgment. He was a student of social and economic conditions and problems, and applied the truths of Christianity and the spirit of Christian morality to them with great discretion and effectiveness. He was a student of physical science and of Biblical revelation

as related to scientific problems, and he brought the results of his studies to his people in expository discourses upon the Book of Genesis. He was a student of his church, and he brought his regulative conceptions of Christianity to bear upon the church problems of his time. He studied the political questions of his day, sharing in large measure the democratic spirit that was gaining ascendency, and applying the principles of Biblical revelation to those problems of government that were stirring the minds of men, the concrete results of which appeared in his expository lectures upon the Books of Samuel. He grasped the fundamental principles of all these problems, bringing them into relation with the fundamental principles of Christianity, and became the most skilful interpreter of Christian morality, as applied to the problems of associate human life, of any preacher of his day.

(4) In the formal as well as material aspects of his preaching, that is, in the organizing of the material of the sermon, we find the prevailing Biblical quality. In a word, it is always the textual method. In his choice of a text, he prefers more than a single isolated passage. The topical preacher who abandons the text in his discussion of the theme needs but a single passage. But the textual preacher will not isolate his passage. He will relate its elements in his discussion. Contrast, in this regard, Robertson with Brooks. The Biblical quality of Robertson's introductory approach to his discussion is seen in its explanatory character.

The object is so to deal with the Biblical material of the text as to clear the way for the discussion. At one time it is a contextual explanation, disclosing the inner connection of thought and holding it in continuity. At another time it is verbal explanation, interpreting the meaning of stress words. Now it is the principle of contrast that is introduced for the purpose of heightening the significance of the truth in hand. Again the approach is through some hedge of difficulty that must be cleared away before a path can be opened to the discussion. Sometimes our attention is directed to the importance of the truth suggested, and the proper method of treatment is pointed out. But whatever be the method of approach, the text is the point of departure, and the substance of his introductory thought is in some way explanatory. That the sermon has no formulated theme simply indicates that the content of the discussion attaches itself directly to the text, and is not drawn out of or through a theme that is assumed to represent the substance of the text. The topics, drawn in some way, in general directly from the text, but applied liberally in the way of accommodating application, are stated at the outset, and restated in the process of discussion. They summarize the most important truths of the text. This textual habit prevailed in all periods of his preaching. The entire development is but an unfolding of the content of the textually suggested topics. It is his chosen process, "from within outward." This was a fundamental homiletic principle, from which he never varied. Thus he unfolded Biblical truths as an interpreter, and was on principle, therefore, a textual preacher. First, interpret the inner significance of the truth that is given, then apply it. This is the gist of his homiletic science. The conclusion consists of a vigorous use of the truth discussed with reference to practical results, either the truth as a whole or some deduction from it, or the application of some of the most prominent points of the discussion, generally the last. Thus from text to conclusion we have the Biblical quality. And this illustrates his theory of the preacher's function, namely, that he is an interpreter of the truth of revelation. And so his preaching has a prevailingly objective quality, and, considering his subjective tendencies, it is the more significant that it should be so objectively real. It shows the dominating power of Biblical religion; and that his preaching should be so suggestive to the imagination and so impressive to the feelings demonstrates at once the fruitfulness of the truths of Biblical revelation, and the genius of the preacher for making these truths supremely attractive, however unattractive they may have become through commonplace handling.

2. Robertson's helpfulness as a thoughtful and edifying preacher is a natural suggestion from what has already been said. He recognized Christianity as a religion that may and must be taught. It is something objectively given, not merely subjectively felt. It is not only an inner experience, but a historic fact. It is to be interpreted, therefore, not merely as an expression of pious feeling, but as a content of historic truth. Christianity is life, but it is also light. It is the heart that appropriates it, but it is the mind that mediates it. Hence he would be known first of all as an interpreter. To nourish life he would furnish light. Truth is the

pabulum of growing manhood.   No preacher of his day
in the Anglican church was comparable with him in
wealth and range of material.   There were more distinctively intellectual preachers, perhaps, but they were
so much the less real preachers.   He was not an
intellectual preacher, either as to type or measure,
such as Mozley was.   He was, indeed, a preacher
for the more thoughtful and intellectual class of hearers,
but he was not deficient in those qualities that characterize the popular preacher in the truest and best
sense.   His preaching took hold of the heart and conscience, as well as the mind, of his hearers.   All of
his published sermons disclose the depth and scope of
his intellectual life and the wealth of his spiritual life;
but there was probably an emotional and ethical intensity about his preaching of which these sermons,
impressive as they are, hardly give us an adequate
conception.   He was not a whit the less practically
effective as a preacher, that he was also an exceptionally thoughtful preacher.   He threw all of his fiery
intensity into his work, and he profoundly moved his
audience.   But there was always a solid basis of strong
and dignified thought, and his mental poise always mastered his emotions and made them the more impressive
and effective.   He was a man of thorough mental training.   From the beginning of his student life he had grappled valiantly with his intellectual tasks, and he was
not satisfied with vague conceptions of any subject.
He had a poetic conception of religion and was something of a mystic, but he knew that when the mind is
brought into intelligent commerce with religious truth,
it should yield definite and apprehensible results.   He

was a clear, keen thinker. His power of intellectual discrimination and analysis is most notable. He not only
mastered the individual sermon, being exceedingly jeal-
ous of all intrusions during the sacred hours of preparation, but he mastered the theory of preaching. He
had gradually formed a comprehensive conception of
the preacher's work and worked in the light of it, but it
emerged into a more definite form in the crisis of his
life. He put the stamp of his own genius upon it, and
carried it into effect most brilliantly in the Brighton
ministry. It is evident that he saw from the first that
the effectiveness of preaching, for incentive as well as
for instruction, will depend upon orderly method. Even
in the early years of his ministry, before his intellectual
life had reached its full development, he was exceptionally methodical in the ordering of his thought, and
so extraordinarily clear. He was willing even that his
method should be stereotyped, so only it proved to be
definite and clear. " All public speakers," he says,
" know the value of method. Persons not accustomed
to it imagine that a speech is learned by heart. Knowing a little about the matter, I will venture to say if any
one attempted that plan either he must have a marvellous memory, or else he would break down three times
out of five. It simply depends upon correct arrange-
ment. The words and sentences are left to the moment,
the thoughts methodized beforehand, and the words, if
rightly arranged, will place themselves." This utterance is biographical. It indicates not only his intellectual conscientiousness in the work of preparation, but
it suggests the secret, in large measure, of his remarkable success as an extemporaneous preacher. It is the

discriminating quality of thought that characterizes the sermon from beginning to end. The process of analysis and discrimination is one of his most characteristic didactic methods. By the process of exclusion and inclusion he opens the way to the definitely conceived principles that he will discuss, and the entire movement of thought has a corresponding discriminatingness, distinctness, and clearness, speaking at once to the mind and with scarcely less effectiveness to the emotions.

As already suggested, he states his topics distinctly and clearly at the outset, and, for the purpose of aiding the mental processes of the hearer, he restates them in the course of the discussion. He handles his subjects with an easy mastery, for the truth comes out of the broad fields of his study and reflection, and has been excogitated along the line of a careful, logical method. The whole discussion has an admirable unity, although no comprehensive theme covering the entire content of thought may be suggested, and although these sermons as we have them are confessedly fragmentary, they still have such completeness and symmetry as best serve their practical purpose, and the discussion is always intellectually and spiritually suggestive rather than exhaustive. He trained the man, and the individual sermon, although carefully wrought out, was the product of such training. He had acute analytical power, as well as most extraordinary facility of statement, and his imagination and emotions never ran away with him. He was a student of the dialectical Aristotle, of the philosophical and metaphysical Edwards, as well as of the idealistic Plato, and of the world's great poets, and "their writings," he says, "passed like the iron atoms of the blood into my mental constitution." This early and continuous intellectual discipline was of immense value to him, especially in his later years. When once emancipated from what he regarded as the early limitations of his theological thinking, this habit of mind stood by him and helped him through the great intellectual and religious crisis of his life. He insisted upon the formation of such conceptions of Christianity as could be preached, because they would be free from all incomprehensible vagueness.

It is surprising that any man who carried such physical infirmities as he did should be able to present in extemporaneous form and with such freedom and facility, truth so thoroughly discriminated and so precisely stated. No man could have done it who was not a thoroughly trained man. Robertson demonstrates, therefore, that one may be a thoughtful preacher in the best sense, and yet a popular preacher. Common people, so called, the working-men of Brighton, heard him gladly. He shows how strong an influence it is possible for a Christian preacher to exert upon the people of his time. A preacher of less firm mental fibre, no matter how fervid, could not have done it. He dealt with living questions. He had a comprehensive grasp of the main facts and features of his subject, and they were presented most effectively in definite, dignified, impressive, often intense, and yet graceful form. He had a high conception of the dignity and sacredness of the pulpit, and he never made use of it for the purpose of political, social, or ecclesiastical propagandism. He interested himself in living social and political subjects, and he made both pulpit and platform a throne of power in the discussion of them from the Biblical, or ethical and religious point of view.   No class mourned for him when he died more sincerely than the hard-handed working-men of Brighton.   But he bears witness that the pulpit must keep in line with the intelligence of the age, or it will be shorn of its power.   It is the work of the thoughtful, studious preacher that endures.

3. Robertson's career is helpful as suggesting the value for the preacher of deep and varied religious experiences.   It is true that he had a special gift for religion.   His ethical and spiritual susceptibility reached the measure of genius.   But this gift had been cultivated from early years, and his religious life deepened, enlarged, and enriched itself in all varieties of experience.   We do not ordinarily think or speak of Robertson as a saint, although the writer has frequently heard young Englishmen thus designate him.   But if we do not regard him as a saint, it is because we have learned to attach an inadequate significance to the term.   He was not a faultless man.   No saint is ever faultless.   But with all his defects, which were temperamental and superficial, he was a modern saint, and this saintship was a moral and religious achievement.   It was the conquest of his manly conscience and will.   One of the notable things in his religious experience was its vitalizing power in his intellectual life.   He laid great stress upon the experience of the power of the truth in the heart, in order that it may become a more real and vital mental possession.   And this was a recognized fundamental principle in his preaching.   A religious truth was of no special importance as a mere intellectual possession.   He must feel its moral and spiritual power.   It was not enough

to think it out clearly; he must feel it profoundly and, holding it as a possession of the heart, it had new significance for the mind.   He found a good deal of religious experience, especially in the Evangelical communion, that did not seem to touch the intelligence of men.   It lingered in the realm of feeling or sentiment or practical zeal.   Such religious experience could not produce preachers of Robertson's type.   He knew the importance of an experience that dominates the intellectual life, and it was the depth and compass of his own experience that stood by him in the tempests of that life.

His religious life was varied as well as profound. The story of his mental and moral struggle, and the revolution it wrought in his life, is known to the world, and it may almost be called one of the treasures of the modern church.   It is the story of a great triumph.   Its lesson is the power of a pure heart, of a good conscience, of a great piety, to steady the soul in the storms of doubt, of the vitalizing power of religion in the mental life, and it is most precious.   He seemed to waver between the different schools that touched him, passing from the austere piety of the Evangelicals through the high churchliness of the Tractarians to the liberalism of the broad churchmen, but at bottom he was stable as a rock.   During the Evangelical experiences of his early ministry, he led an unworldly, even an ascetic life, yet he was as saintly in the later breadth, as in the earlier limitations of his piety.   He fasted often.   He prayed long and strivingly.   He read religious biography.   He labored for the conversion of souls.   He " was in the regular habit of reading daily, with scrupulous adherence to a plan, the works of eminently holy persons, whose tone was not merely uprightness of character and high-mindedness, but communion — a strong sense of personal and even living communion — with God besides." In later years he recalls "how far more peaceful" his mind used to be at that time in connection with this habit of life, and he resumes the habit, but under changed conditions. The experience, however, was too narrow for him. In his delicate ethical sensitiveness, he suspected that his moral life did not correspond with nor justify his emotional life. His intellectual struggles brought him into a large place, where his larger mental, ethical, and spiritual wants were more fully met, and where his free nature had broader range. These experiences illustrate, not only the staying power of piety, as we have seen also in the case of Schleiermacher, and its vitalizing energy in the mind's commerce with truth, but the anchorage ground that is furnished by the moral factor in religious experience. And in all these aspects the experiences of Robertson and Bushnell were similar. It was this variety of his experience also that fitted Robertson to understand and appreciate the truth in conflicting parties and in diverse statements thereof, and thus he became a mediator. No modern preacher has seen more clearly the truth that lingers beneath the forms of error, the good that is hidden under the forms of evil, and the higher unity that embraces all the seeming contradictions of truth.

It was this breadth of experience that gave him touching-points with men of different schools, liberated and liberalized his mind and heart, made it possible for him to receive truth from men as diverse in theological opinion as Channing and Newman, and that gave him, in the catholicity of his spirit, a most commanding place in the modern pulpit. It may not be appointed to every minister, nor may it be possible or necessary, to pass through such experiences as those of Robertson. But no man who is called to it and is as true to his own intelligence and conscience and heart as he was, will fail to be greatly enriched by it.

4. Robertson illustrates the power, for the preacher, of a refined and forceful personality. He was a man of most extraordinarily quick and delicate sensibilities, and he was so much the more a preacher because of it. For the true preacher is the man who not only sees clearly, but feels strongly. No man can preach with effectiveness who is not emotionally responsive to those to whom he ministers. Few men have ever given themselves as he did, body and soul, with such utter self-forgetfulness, to the work in hand. A delicate organization, rendered more painfully acute in its sensibilities by disease, made him, in later years, subject to violent revulsions of feeling. He had strong antipathies, was not a man of easy good nature, although of a most generous and noble disposition, not a wide liker, and was probably not an altogether easy man to get on with. He was incapable of smallness or of malignity, but there were people whom he intensely disliked, and men who were base he detested with all the intensity of his high-strung and highly trained moral nature. And there was something immensely attractive about this ethical fierceness of the man. But he was a man of broad and tender sympathies. He declares, and with utmost truthfulness, that no class of human beings, except possibly the epicureans,

nor indeed would he exclude them, was ever beyond the reach of his fellow-feeling. He conscientiously cultivated this. It was the realization of his Christian principles as well as manifestation of his Christian affection. He cultivated his poetic susceptibilities and his heart was softened and tranquillized by it. It made him more intensely human. We have seen his love for the great poets. He was capable of great reverence, and Wordsworth especially filled the longing of his heart for a realized ideal of human greatness and goodness. Tennyson's "In Memoriam" expressed and interpreted for him, as it has for many another of his fellows in the modern ministry, his own deepest experiences and wrought productively in his feeling and imagination. He loved this pleasant world, and, although a sadly burdened man, who often sighed that the end might soon come, rejoiced in it as his transient home. He had a poet's eye for its beauties, and he described them with singular felicity. All this was greatly tributary to his power as a preacher. It quickened his insight, cultivated his perception of analogies, gave him increasing skill in illustration, and enriched his literary style, which is notable for its simplicity, clearness, dignity, and intensity. It enriched and intensified his sympathies, nurturing a broader and more delicate love for men. It fitted him to receive impressions from them when he stood before them. He was able to see them in their ideal manhood. With all his manly British sense, he had great facility in idealization, and his poetic studies furthered it. He fled from the world into fellowship with his poets and tarried in this high realm as in a sanctuary and a refuge. He forgot men in their individual weaknesses and meannesses and sins. By reason of this delicate susceptibility of feeling he was a man of notable weaknesses. He was too sensitive for this rude world and became morbidly so. It brought him sometimes to the verge of unmanliness. He longed for a sympathy which he did not get, or thought he did not get, or did not know that he did get, and it was not always easy for him to believe in its reality, even when the demonstration was before him. He was frank to a fault and poured out his complaints into the ears of his friends. He could not conceal what was going on within him, and if he had forced himself to do it, his preaching would have been shorn of half its power. But on the whole it is surprising that we detect no more specifically in his public utterances the struggle of his life. His strong manhood saved him. He never lost himself in his dreams nor in his emotions. His strong mind and valiant heart and sturdy will dominated all tendency to excess of sentiment or of emotion, and all his studies but added fuel to the flame of his devotion to men. His tastes, as we have seen, were aristocratic, but his sympathies democratic, and no one can fail to see and feel that he is in contact with a man of superb manliness. Intellectual independence and moral courage are the two strong traits of his manhood, and the intensity of his emotional nature but made them the more impressive. He was a born intellectual leader. The Brighton ministry was one of transcendent power. He was a free man, at last emancipated from an intellectual thraldom that had crippled his pulpit power. The power of the Christian pulpit is conditioned by its freedom. No man can speak force-

fully who cannot speak freely. This intellectual courage of Robertson's was an immense power. It had
a martial quality. He was rash at times, but what
soldier in the thick of the fight will not sometimes
adventure rash things? Practical wisdom is a pastoral
virtue. A preacher must know his resources and the
conditions of his message. But if any man on earth
needs a soldierly courage, it is he. This combination
of delicacy and forcefulness, of fine feeling, strong
intelligence, and strenuous will, made him the preacher
for many classes of people. The so-called common
people felt the power of his sympathy and respected
his manly intelligence and sincerity. They saw his
large- and tender-heartedness, but felt too that he was a
man. Imaginative people were attracted by the semi-
poetic glow of his speech. The young were attracted
by his earnestness and grace, and the sceptical by their
confidence in his ability to sympathize with them, or at
least to understand them, in their intellectual perplexi-
ties. He illustrates most strikingly the tremendous
power in pulpit oratory of a sympathetic heart and a
forceful will. Without them one may be a pulpit
teacher of a sort, but not a preacher.

All this is connected with what in our day calls itself
the magnetic quality in the personality. He was a man
of Grecian beauty of face and grace of form, and altogether of a singularly attractive physical personality.
He was charged with physical nerve force, and he spake
with a musical sweetness of voice, with grace and force
combined of physical movement, that sent his words like
flying arrows, swift and straight, into the quick. He
never wrote his sermons. They were carefully studied,

and came out of the broad fields of his culture and training. They bear the mark of thorough, earnest thought and comprehensive study. They are a testimony as to the importance of training the man in habits of clear, broad thinking. He has a strong and comprehensive grasp upon the main facts and truths of Christianity. He develops his subject in its broad outlines in an altogether quickening, suggestive, and attractive manner. It was one of his homiletical principles to preach suggestively rather than dogmatically. He would not present the truth in abstract or dialectical form for the indoctrination of the understanding, but in such way as to secure an emotional interest in it, and it was the more sure to reach the heart of the hearer. His preaching is clearly discriminated thought, conveyed by the language of feeling and imagination, and it suggests more than is said. His biographical sermons, which are masterpieces of this type of preaching, are eminently of this suggestive order. The sermon on Balaam and on John the Baptist illustrate the quality above mentioned. " The Parable of the Sower," " God's Revelation of Heaven," " Jacob's Wrestling," " The Good Shepherd," " The Irreparable Past," " The Illusiveness of Life," which are among his most impressive sermons, all bear the same mark of breadth, insight, and suggestiveness. The singularly impressive character of his preaching is largely conditioned by its penetrating suggestiveness. This is also connected with its fragmentary character and its not infrequent suggestion of inadequacy to the full demands of the subject. But it was his purpose never to treat the subject exhaustively. The truth comes to us in glimpses, but they are glimpses

of great and fruitful truths, and the mind follows the subject discussed because the feelings are enlisted and the
imagination stimulated, and thus impel the mind to action.   He carefully prepared the outline, jotting it down
on slips of paper, sometimes fully and sometimes mea-
grely, not infrequently leaving only salient stress words.
But the sermon was always well in hand. He permitted
nothing to turn him aside from careful preparation, and
he always gave his mind free movement along the line
of an orderly logical plan.   Thus he went into the pulpit.   He begins with the deliberation of self-mastery,
but soon warms with his theme, and launches out uncon-
strained upon the broad stream of his thought.   His
frame would sometimes quiver with the intensity of his
emotion, his keen eye seemed to shoot his congregation
through, and with most graceful movement, in absolute
unconsciousness of himself, he would pour out his
treasures upon them ; and in all this there was no loss of
self-possession.   His delicate instincts, his refined tastes,
his firm mental poise, always rescued him from going to
pieces.   In this combination of intensity and self-possession he proved himself to be an orator.   He speaks
deprecatingly, indeed, of oratory as an art.   But it is
evident that he had carefully cultivated his rare gift of
speech, that he had mastered an impressive literary
style, and he knew its real worth.

5. The rhetorical qualities of Robertson's preaching
are a helpful study, and our discussion would be incom-
plete without some reference to them.   It is true that
the sermons in their present form are not the original
product.   It was probably fuller and more complete
than what is left to us.   And yet the product as we

have it may be assumed to represent adequately his literary style, for the sermons were either written out by him after they were preached, before the tide of the preaching impulse had ebbed, or were revised by his own hand from the notes of friends, or were taken down stenographically. Moreover, the sermons in their present form bear a common mark, and when compared with his lectures and letters, we discover the same general literary characteristics, although confessedly the letters are sometimes more accurate in expression than the sermons or lectures. We catch at once the note of reality in all his utterances. He detested all artifice in speech. " I believe I could have become an orator," he says in one of his letters, " had I chosen to take pains. I see what rhetoric does and what it seems to do, and I thoroughly despise it, . . . and yet perhaps I do it injustice ; with an unworldly, noble love to give it reality, what might it not do ! " He certainly did no injustice in this utterance to the stilted, artificial rhetoric that has sometimes been introduced into the Christian pulpit, but he did scant justice to the best type of modern pulpit rhetoric, and least of all did he do justice to his own rhetoric. He not only might have become, he did become, an orator of great effectiveness, although confessedly the orator is lost in the preacher ; and it is perfectly evident that he did "take the pains " with his rhetoric at least, if not with his oratory, such as all effective public speakers have taken, and without which no man can expect to be effective. And it was precisely that " unworldly noble love " of his that rescued him from all artifice and gave to his speech the ring of reality. His words always express what is true to his thought, feeling, and conviction.   Form as such he did not cultivate. He was careful and conscientious in his rhetorical culture, and it is perfectly evident that he had trained himself to use his mother tongue with effectiveness. We hear of skilful debate and of careful literary culture during his university days.   But his diction was alive with the energy of his thought and feeling. Hence there is but little in his style as such that arrests attention to itself, and nothing that is odd or obtrusive because self-conscious, as in the style of Carlyle, with which Robertson was familiar, but which he never allowed to influence him in his own method of expression.   The notable thing is that there is so little that is noticeable.   We are impressed with the thought and feeling, and not with the form that is their instrument. Form is wholly subordinate to substance, and the result is that the style is impressive in its general fitness to do its work, rather than in any salient peculiarities. Hence, simplicity and naturalness are its fundamental qualities.   It is the moral sincerity and reality of the man that explain this unobtrusiveness of diction.   It is in harmony with the best rhetorical and literary culture of our time and is the most appropriate instrument for the work of the pulpit.   For this reason Robertson's rhetorical and literary form is worthy of the preacher's study.

The note of reflection is also recognizable in his style. It suggests the serious, solid, discriminating thinker, the man who is a searcher for the truth and who lives in fellowship with it.   We find here the diction of a man who never obtrudes the result of his philosophic reflection, but who has been trained to deal with what is fundamental. By entering the fibre of his thought "like iron atoms into his blood," the products of his study penetrated his diction. It is a type of speech, level to the apprehension of the average man, but it is the speech of a thinker. Hence the quality of perspicuity, of solidity, and of intellectual dignity. Because of this intellectual dignity and strength, it is a balanced style, without an excess of intensity or an overexuberance of fancy. The teaching quality is fundamental, according to his conception of what the preacher's work should be. It speaks to the mind. It is the speech of a man who has taught his mind to deal with principles, and his tongue to utter them in clear, definite, forceful, and often graceful speech. The quality of intellectual comprehensiveness is manifest in his style, and discloses his skill in crowding large thoughts into small compass of form. But the quality of intellectual discrimination, definiteness, and accuracy is not the less manifest, and the discriminating quality of his statement is often associated with cogency and felicity of statement.

The idealistic quality of his mind is also manifest in his style. Thought is represented in the diction of the imagination. It is therefore the suggestive style. He illustrates from nature, art, literature, and from the higher ranges of human experience, and his language is attractive in its semi-poetic glow. He draws largely from the tragic aspects of human life, and his sympathy with suffering and sorrowing men, and especially with the Great Sufferer, imparts a tone of seriousness, often of sadness, and not infrequently a tone of most impressive solemnity to his speech. The diction that expresses his moods, whether of the higher inspirations or of the sadder

sympathies, are most felicitous in their grace of movement, as well as most forceful in their intensity, moving
at once the conscience and the heart as with great
prophetic voice.

Perhaps the emotional and ethical intensity of his
nature, what may be called the martial quality of the
man, is most readily recognized in his style. It is the
language of a soul keyed to the highest pitch of intensity.
The opening sentences of his discourses are deliberate,
reflective, and discriminating, speaking tranquilly to the
mind, and awakening mental interest in the truth in
hand. The close of the sermon is sometimes shot
through as with a flame of moral and emotional passion
that is almost overwhelming. The words are short, the
sentences are compact, great thoughts are crowded into
small compass, and great emotions explode in short,
sharp, abrupt vocal utterances. It is like the short,
sharp, double-quick of a soldier. It is no leisurely
movement, for passion sways the soul. The architecture
of the sentence is twisted, words involuted, stress words
repeated, ictus thrown where impression is sought, order
of the sentence wrecked, and fragments regathered in
new form. It is the vocabulary and the syntax of concentrated energy. It is the voice of a prophet who is
straitened within himself till his message be given, and
his mission be accomplished.

We have lingered wholly with the beneficent lessons
of Robertson's short and remarkable life, for one finds
almost nothing that was not beneficent. But if we were
looking for admonition, we might find it in his too
subjective life. He lived too much in his emotions, and
could not emancipate himself from their tyranny. He

had his own inner world, where he did not always find a comfortable home. He brooded too much upon his own subjective states. It was in much an unhealthy life. It lacked a certain steadiness which is the gift of the healthier mind. He was restless and the victim of extreme revulsions. Physical disease, temperament, an overwrought brain, the conditions of life, explain it. If he had not anchored at historic Christianity, he might have been wrecked. Even as it was, he sometimes laid disproportionate stress upon the subjective experiences of the individual in validating the claims of Christianity, and as the measure of all objective religious truth. Hence he wavered : and yet, when we recall the singular impressiveness of his solemn earnestness; when we remember that those penetrating utterances, those outcries of his restless spirit, were wrung out of the agonies of that wondrous inner life; when we remember that his great message came out of the struggles of his soul and that these struggles are part of its very substance and form, — we come back to the conviction that just here was the hiding of his power, and we say with ourselves that we would not have this disquieted, passionate soul other than it was. We echo the words that stand upon the marble at Brighton : " He awakened the holiest feelings in poor and in rich, in ignorant and learned. Therefore is he lamented as their guide and comforter."

H

CHAPTER III

HENRY WARD BEECHER

FROM the most gifted English preacher of his century we readily pass to the most brilliant of American preachers. Robertson and Beecher belong to the same period, came into prominence at the same time, and may be classed as representatives of the same broad school. Beecher was the elder born by nearly three years, but the same year in which Robertson entered upon his short but brilliant career at Brighton Beecher began his longer, more varied and eventful, and not less brilliant, career in Brooklyn. Strikingly divergent in type of genius and of culture, in delicacy of intellectual and æsthetic fibre, and in the processes of their development, they still share much in common. They were born preachers and intellectual leaders of men. They were men of like independence of spirit, breadth, and intensity of sympathy, and of the same quenchless Anglo-Saxon courage. They belong to the same general school of religious thought, and they look out upon God's kingdom from the same general point of view. They were both subject to influences that wrought strong intellectual and spiritual revulsions, and they both modified and enlarged their views in the process of their development. They exhibit like humanistic and philanthropic tendencies, are path-breakers in the work of the Christian pulpit, and may be classed as epoch-making men in modern preaching.

THE REPRESENTATIVE AMERICAN PREACHER

Mr. Beecher was a typical American. He came from a Puritan ancestry, and his youth was spent in Puritan communities. It is no small honor to Litchfield County, Connecticut, that it produced and nurtured two such representatives of Puritan Americanism as Henry Ward Beecher and Horace Bushnell. In his prophetic intuition, his high aspiration, his vivid imagination, his intense love of freedom and detestation of all forms of tyranny, Beecher was a Puritan idealist. In his practical common sense, his knowledge of human nature as distinguished from his knowledge of individual men, his grasp and free handling of facts, and in his skill in adjusting the high ideals of religion to common life, he was a Puritan realist.   He had the nervous intensity of the typical New Englander.   He was an enthusiastic democrat. He inherited in a most extraordinary measure that independence of spirit that gave birth to our popular institutions, and no man of his day did more in all ways to foster that spirit.   In him American patriotism found an almost ideal embodiment. In birth, training, culture, as in genius and spirit, he belonged to us wholly, and it has been well said of him that he was "the pride of America." No man in the nation could more appropriately, and none more effectively, have spoken for us in England during the War of the Rebellion. By the power of his personality and the skill and cogency of his speech he turned the tide of opposition against the Union cause. The hostility of the ruling classes evoked all his patriotic and belligerent instincts, and it is fortunate for us that those courageous utterances of his found so ready a response among the manly middle classes of the mother country. From a small spark, the consciousness of vocation to speak for his people burst into a flame that scorched the arrogant, hostile government, and kindled the democratic enthusiasm of the common people. And this awakened consciousness of vocation was an index of his supreme fitness for his task, for which his countrymen will be forever grateful. It was as if all the forces of the loyal nation, with its political idealism, its patriotic devotion, its broad philanthropy, its love of freedom and hatred of tyranny, its prophetic outlook into the future, and its firm grasp of the case in hand, were stirring within him, as the forces of the German people were stirring in the soul of Luther. In that brilliant campaign he stood as the embodiment of the spirit of American freedom and loyalty and nationality, as Luther, at Worms, as the embodiment of the German Reformation. It was one of the most signal triumphs of oratory in the history of human speech. It was also one of the most significant exhibitions of the power of a great personality as the unofficial representative of a nation. But we have chiefly to do with Mr. Beecher as a representative American preacher. In larger measure than in any other modern American preacher, there appeared in him always, in his own unique and inimitable manner, many of those qualities that distinguish the preaching of this country. That he has exerted so effective an influence in modifying our preaching is due to the fact that he was so distinctively American in his qualities. It is for this reason that he has contributed more, perhaps, than any other American preacher to the production of a

67258

modern type of American preaching. He gave expression to the half-consciousness of the need, and the half-blind groping after, a better homiletic spirit and method. Of Mr. Beecher's place in American citizenship, of his influence in the cause of reform, of his significance in various lines of secular activity, it is not our purpose to speak; nor is it possible, within permissible limits, to attempt an exhaustive analysis of his singular gifts as a preacher. It remains for us to direct attention to a few of those salient qualities which are in a degree representative, but which appeared in him in his own peculiar manner and measure.

1. The strongly individualistic quality of Mr. Beecher's preaching at once arrests attention. In his article on the "History of Preaching," in the second edition of the "Real Encyklopädie,"[1] Professor Christlieb of Bonn presents the following estimate of Mr. Beecher as a preacher: "He was without question the most highly gifted and versatile of modern American preachers, the Shakespeare of the pulpit of our day. The earlier period of his preaching, however, as of his work for social reform (note especially his self-sacrificing coöperation for the abolition of slavery), as disclosing his full greatness, is to be distinguished from the later period. A sound understanding, lively imagination, an altogether inexhaustible wealth of genius and wit, religious earnestness, dauntless courage, fiery patriotism, good will toward all men, ardent self-sacrificing love, responsiveness to all that is human, to politics and ethics, education and religion, art and philosophy, mechanics, agriculture and horticulture (so that he once said, 'I study everything except

[1] Vol. XVIII, 1888, p. 644.

theology '), profound knowledge of human nature, and of all classes in human society, great facility of expression, were blended in this preacher in an altogether phenomenal manner, and contributed to him a many-sidedness so kaleidoscopic and a freshness of treatment so original that he was for a long time the pride of America. Other preachers before and contemporaneous with him were greater theologians, and had profounder knowledge of the Scriptures, but no one gathered material for pulpit discourse from so wide a realm.   He spoke upon no subject that he had not studied.   But he was wholly averse to systematic theology and could often make it a subject of ridicule.   The din of conflict between Old and New School Presbyterianism, that raged about him in his youth, had made theology distasteful to him, and in general all abstract methods of preaching.   If he had to touch upon moot questions in theology, he preferred to leave the exact point at issue indeterminate.   Christ and love were the centre of all his theology, and in laying stress upon the love of God, His righteousness failed of due recognition.   In his exposition he never dealt with dry abstractions, but always penetrated to the full, fresh life.   Few could electrify and sway an audience as he could.   He moved them to tears, often very copiously, as well as to laughter.   He could change his voice and delivery from the quiet, gentle, and confidential tone to the most penetrating severity, and then suddenly he became fiery and his eye flashed and cheek glowed.   But when he depicted with moving pathos, for example, the miseries of mankind, so that all were melted to tears, just then would come those jests and witticisms that are almost never lacking in his preaching, by means of which not only is the assembly provoked to loud laughter, but even the force of his piercing thrust is at once broken.   Under the influence of these witticisms impressions of sin and wrong are soon forgotten.   Edification gives place to entertainment; and, alas, it is precisely this irresistible humor, this lack of reverence in the treatment of sacred things, that draws many to Plymouth church, while at the same time it must be acknowledged that the more serious-minded Americans openly condemn it.   Add to this his great dramatic gift, whereby for example he would imitate with singular exactness the movements and speech of a drunkard, or of a blacksmith, or a fisherman, or a backwoodsman, in their various callings.   But even in addition to such transgressions of the bounds of ecclesiastical dignity, there was the frequent introduction of social, political, educational, and such like subjects, which, according to our taste, have too little direct reference to edification, while at the same time he theoretically and practically exalted good will above conscience.   On the other hand, it was to have been wished that the element of spiritual experience had been represented less fragmentarily and more richly and edifyingly in his preaching. • He did but little pastoral work in his church. • For the last fifteen years of his life, the theology of this anti-Calvinist and theistic evolutionist, probably through the influence of the writings of Herbert Spencer, showed itself to be in essential features unscriptural, as for example in his doctrine of creation and of reconciliation, his Christology, his views of the specific authority of the Scriptures; and his reputation and influence decidedly declined. He always preached extemporaneously.   Even when he brought written notes into the pulpit (as I myself saw him make use of them), his best thoughts seemed to come to him in the course of his address under the inspiring influence of the thousands that gathered about him.

" By reason of the introduction of new thoughts, there was often no very close coherence in his discourses. But practical application, as exactly fitted to the American character, was never lacking. In wealth of genius doubtless the superior of Spurgeon, moving often, by reason of the peculiarities of his theological culture, his versatility and wide reading, in realms that were foreign to Spurgeon, and by reason of his use of the language of scientific culture more attractive to and more effective with the cultivated classes, Beecher is nevertheless, by reason of those questionable defects and idiosyncrasies, and at last by reason of the confusion of his theological point of view, greatly inferior to Spurgeon with respect to concentrated and fruitful efforts among his hearers and readers, despite his great services to his country as philanthropist and social reformer."

The value of this estimate is not materially diminished by our failure to agree with it at all points. From some of its criticisms Mr. Beecher's countrymen, who knew most of his preaching, would dissent. It may be questioned whether the critic has formed an adequate judgment of the weight and permanence of Mr. Beecher's influence as a preacher, patriot, or reformer. Doubtless his personal influence diminished during the last years of his life, but his work is a permanent possession. He was not a close thinker upon theological subjects, but it may be questioned whether the critic's theological point of view furnishes an adequate test of Beecher's theological soundness. Those who know Mr. Beecher's work, and can justly estimate its permanent value, will dissent from the critic's judgment of the sensational, dramatic character of his preaching, and will regard it as exaggerated and as conveying an erroneous conception of its edifying character. It is a mistake to estimate him as a trivial, sensational preacher. But Professor Christlieb's estimate as a whole is of value. It comes from an independent, outside source. It is the judgment of an exceptionally intelligent historical student and critic of Christian preaching, and of one who was trained in a very different homiletic school from that in which Mr. Beecher was trained. Particularly valuable is the estimate of Mr. Beecher's greatness and uniqueness as a preacher, and of his striking individualistic qualities. He has been universally regarded as unique among the preachers of his day ; by most he has been estimated as superior in popular effectiveness to all other American preachers of whatever period, and by not a few as the greatest pulpit orator of the Christian church. In the quality and measure of his pulpit power he was unquestionably altogether exceptional. It has been said of him, and perhaps no more pertinent word was ever said of him, that he was a great original personality, rather than a great original mind.[1] He certainly was not a path-breaker into new realms of truth or into new methods of conceiving truth, as Bushnell was. In the ordinary sense of the term, he was not a student, not a patient investigator or discoverer. The speculative understanding was for him to no con-

[1] Rev. II. R. Haweis, *Cont. Review*, Vol. XIV, 1873.

siderable extent the organ of religious knowledge. He had neither the deep intellectual penetration nor the delicate speculative subtlety of Bushnell. He used his imagination, his feeling, his sympathy, as the organ of religious knowledge. His scientific equipment was meagre. He knew but little of the philosophical, historical, or critical method in modern theological investigation. His prevailing intellectual interests were not so largely theological as were those of Bushnell, notwithstanding Bushnell's affiliation with Beecher in the habit of decrying theological science. He had not the subtle intellectual penetration of Robertson, nor his close mental training, nor his skill as an interpreter. Hence Beecher's influence upon the more thoughtful, cultivated, and better-trained portion of the community has not been equal to that of Bushnell or Robertson. But upon the masses of the American people, upon the laity of the churches in all denominations, it has perhaps been much greater than that of any other American, or possibly any other English-speaking, preacher within the last century. And it is precisely the originality and the size of his personality, its freshness, its vitality, its sympathy, its irresistible energy, that accounts for this influence. It was a battery charged with psychical and physical impulse and energy that, breaking through all barriers, found copious discharge according to its own free method. It was his vocation to deal with the old truths of evangelical Christianity, modified in conception and statement in accordance with the native energy of his large, rich imagination, emotion, and sympathy, in which he disclosed no strikingly original insight and no scientific grasp. These modifica-

tions were in line with a broader and more humanistic
view of human life, of the nature of man and of God,
of Christ and of the kingdom of redemption, than was
prevalent in his early years. But, after all, the truths
with which he dealt were at bottom the old truths of
evangelical theology. It was largely his unique method
of stating the truth, it was his impulsive, extravagant
utterance, that often obscured the substantial evangelical
quality of his preaching. It was one-sided and fragmentary rather than unevangelical, at least during the
greater portion of his public career. At the close of
life his point of view doubtless materially changed, and
the earlier thinking was not adjusted to the later. But,
taking his career as a whole, it was his conscious vocation to give new accent to the old truths of the redemptive love of God in Christ, to clothe the old truths in
new, fresh, concrete forms, and to quicken and impress
his hearers rather than to indoctrinate them. Not that
he failed to be an edifying preacher, not that he was
deficient in clearness and cogency as an interpreter of
truth, but the energies of his emotion and imagination
dominated him, and he was more persuasive than he
was convincing. He gave new emphasis, if not significance, to the old truth of the presence of God in the
soul of man, and to the love of God as the unifying
principle of the moral character of both God and man.
His Christology and soteriology had from an early
period the modern note, not as the result of a clear
apprehension of the historical and critical method of
approach to the study of the person and work of Christ,
but as product of his own intense personal religious
experiences and of the reaction of his own capacious

human sympathies against the traditional Christology and soteriology of the church. And while in all this there was but little contribution in the formal or material sense to the stock of our pulpit theology, in the wondrously blended elements of his complex personality he was a distinct and original product.

Freedom from conventionalities, large indulgence for personal peculiarities, unrestricted vent to personal impulses, bold assertions of the inalienable rights of the homiletic personality, are the dominant characteristics of his preaching, and he more fully than any other man has been influential in furthering this tendency in the preaching of the country. In him it reached nearly its extreme limit. His freedom is sometimes almost homiletic lawlessness, approximating the grotesque. There is a lack of delicacy of sentiment, as of a personality too vigorous and virile to be mindful of æsthetic requirements, in some of his noblest and most helpful discourses. They are marred by expressions that may be tolerated, but barely so, in the heat of extemporaneous speech, and may be carried by the uplifting power of the sermon as a whole, without those violent revulsions of feeling that are fatal to salutary impression; but which, in fact, check its movement toward the highest altitudes and which in the printed form are inexcusable, and especially so in the treatment of themes that have become exceptionally sacred in Christian experience. Foreigners, whose homiletic training had been more formal and conventional than that of this country, and who could not readily enter into the spirit of American license, naturally reproached Mr. Beecher with an almost irreligious irreverence. But those who are able to measure him by a larger homiletic standard, and who know the preponderance of his influence, understand that, after all, these are but surface imperfections. At bottom, there is a strong genuine moral and religious earnestness, and those who listened to him continuously learned to pass such demonstrations of individuality, as surface incidents that were not chargeable to fundamental defects. These free manifestations of personal impulse were, in fact, largely inseparable from the sources of his singular power as a preacher, and we easily forget its grotesque features, for it is part of a great beneficent force. This individualism was an inheritance. He belonged to a family, each one of which made a distinctive mark upon his or her generation. Each was notable for striking idiosyncrasies. Mr. Beecher was not unaware of the defects that were involved in the idiosyncrasies of his genius, and did not regard himself as wholly responsible for them personally. He recognized their source in a temperament which was an inheritance. In an address of singular interest and power, to the New York and Brooklyn Association of Ministers,[1] near the close of his career, he refers to his personal peculiarities and to the misapprehensions to which they exposed him as a preacher, in the following language: "I am what I am by the grace of God through my father and mother. I have my own peculiar temperament, I have my own method of preaching, and my method and temperament necessitate errors. I am not worthy to be related in the hundred thousandth degree to those more happy men who never made a mistake in the pulpit. I make a great many. I am impetuous, I

"Life of Beecher," by Abbott and Halliday, p. 485.

am intense at times on subjects that deeply move me.
I feel as though all the oceans were not strong enough
to be the power behind my words, nor all the thunders
that were in the heavens, and it is the necessity that
such a nature as that should give such intensity at times
to parts of doctrine as exaggerates them, when you
come to bring them into connection with a more rounded
out and balanced view. I know it. I know it as well as
you do. I would not do it if I could help it, but there
are times when it is not I that is talking, when I am
caught up and carried away, so that I know not whether
I am in the body or out of the body, when I think things
in the pulpit that I never could think of in the study,
and when I have feelings that are so far different from
any that belong to the lower or normal condition, that I
can neither regulate nor understand them. I see things
and I hear sounds, and seem, if not in the seventh
heaven, yet in such a condition that leads me to understand what Paul said, that he heard things that it was
not possible for man to utter. I am acting under such
a temperament as that. I have got to use it, or not
preach at all." It is this emotional exuberance, this
passionate intensity, this irrepressible energy of physical
and psychical personality, this irresistible impulse of
nature, which is the demon of genius, that must be our
starting-point in estimating these peculiarities in the
conception, exposition, representation, and enforcement
of the truth. Now, I venture to affirm that it is precisely this sort of personality, individualistic, unique,
transcendent in power though it be, that becomes representative of the national temperament, of its intensity,
force, self-assertion, independence, emancipation from

bondage to tradition and convention and custom.   All the forces that have been at work in the development of national character seemed to play through him.   It was this impressibility, this quick responsiveness to all that is human, that rendered it impossible for him to keep any question of human interest out of the pulpit, or to discuss it with tranquil deliberation.

The conditions of his life also contributed largely to his individualistic qualities.   His early home life, employments, free access to the outer world, his own self-preoccupations, all contributed to the awakening of the sense of freedom within him, and all became tributary to his independence of character.   He always looked back upon those early years with peculiar interest and knew what they had done for him.   In all important matters of family training he was held with a firm hand, but in the minor matters of the household there was a good deal of freedom, and this freedom furnished scope for his individual impulses.   He was left to shift for himself largely, and this "gave him early habits of vigor and reliance."   Like Bushnell, he knew the early " salutary limitations."   He worked upon the parsonage farm, had but few luxuries, and these occupations and limitations, in his, as in Bushnell's case, fostered that healthy, manly independence that stood by him through life.   In constant contact with nature, he entered into sympathy with its wild freedom.   He "had a world of things to do," and " he did not come much in contact with the family government."   He did not come early to the consciousness of his power.   It was wild impulse, rather than intelligent sense of power, that incited him to revolt against the restraints that would check the free expression of his personal forces. Later on, as is the case with every man of genius, he became conscious of his gift, and then he freely chose such courses as would secure fullest and freest play to his individuality. His early habit — or lack of habit — of study was conducive to the same result. In college he would not be limited by the curriculum, and became a sort of free lance in every sort of intellectual combat. Whatever may have been the ill result as regards closeness of mental training, one fancies that his free range in the college libraries may have furnished, as in the case of Phillips Brooks, an important stimulus to his slumbering mental, æsthetic, and emotional energies. His training in debate in the college societies, his free expression of religious feeling in the college prayer-meetings, his addresses in neighboring towns on religious and other subjects, were all promotive of the same result. Even the defect in his speech, which he was obliged to master by the most painstaking effort, became ultimately tributary to the same end. Those oratorical efforts under difficulties and the thorough training in elocution, then begun and continued through many years, served to awaken the free preaching impulse, which soon developed itself strongly on the didactic, the ethical, the æsthetic, and emotional sides. Such training gave him vent. Self-expression evoked the slumbering orator. The great English preachers of the seventeenth century, particularly Barrow and South, at first in a formal manner which involved unfruitful imitation, but ultimately in the larger material sense, were early tributary to him, awakening his own preaching gifts. A close study also of apostolic preaching

was a source of awakening and guidance. That he was
not long shut within the limits of city life in Boston,
where in his boyhood his father had moved, but was
sent for study into the country he loved so well, was at
once a security against his roving impulses and a
positive educative influence. That in his college days
he came into a new experience of the grace of God and
won a new conception of His character, which carried
him beyond the limitations of a traditional faith, secured
for his religious life a more intensely personal character.
That in his freedom and native catholicity of spirit he
reacted against the polemical theology of his day and
against the violence of theological controversy is an
index that points the way to his future life. That in the
divinity school he pursued an independent course, collecting what his free spirit could readily assimilate and
rejecting the rest, that he came to the knowledge of his
own expository powers in the work of teaching the
Bible in Sunday-school, — all this had its part in the
culture of those qualities that were most distinctive and
individual. Moreover, it was quite a necessity that the
freedom of the relatively unorganized life of the great
West, to which he went while yet a young man, and
where the first two years of his ministry were spent,
should still further and more rapidly have developed
his native gifts. In this early ministry he found himself. The influences of those pioneer experiences upon
his future career can hardly be overestimated. What
might have been the result upon his development as a
preacher if he had begun his career in staid and conservative New England one may seriously question.
Doubtless the genius of the man, as in Bushnell's case,

I

would have triumphed measurably over whatever barriers. But he certainly would not have found so
congenial a sphere for the expression of his irrepressi-
bly free impulses. It is no wonder that men who feel
stirring within them the preaching impulse have turned
their faces towards the great, free West. Nor are we
to forget the troublous times into which he was thrown.
Not only did the violence and injustice of theological
controversy awaken the love of fair play and zeal for
the non-partisan and non-polemical presentation of the
gospel, in his catholic mind, but the social and political
agitations of the day stirred an intense hatred of all
public wrongs in his patriotic heart. Before he left the
West he had already entered the lists as an agitator and
reformer, and when, in 1847, he came to Brooklyn he
soon found himself plunged into the midst of the controversy that was to ultimate in the Civil War and in
emancipation. This great national struggle furnished a
sphere where he felt himself at home in the exercise of
all his powers, and where they were developed to the
utmost. It was the great inspiration of his life. Apart
from the pulpit, he never could have exerted the power
upon the platform he did exert. But on the other hand,
the political conflict doubled his pulpit power. Then
came the War of the Rebellion, and no one man outside
political life stands out more prominently than he in those
days of struggle. That great conflict was for him, as
for many another Christian minister, a mighty inspiration,
and it was a unique foster-school and training-school for
powers that else had been half known. All the elements
of his life and all its conditions from the first tended to
the awakening of a great, free, forceful personality. And

of the influence he has exerted upon the country at large
by the breadth and wealth and strength and impetuosity
of this colossal personality, there can be no doubt.

2. In the popular estimate, scant justice has been
done Mr. Beecher's distinctive and varied intellectual
qualities as a preacher. He was transcendently a persuasive preacher, and in his power to sway the emotions of men the intellectual fibre of his preaching has
been measurably lost sight of. But his preaching was
the more effectively persuasive that it had a firm didactic basis. In Christlieb's article above referred to, he
directs attention to the prevailingly didactic character
of American preaching in general and refers to three
aspects of it, the logical, the philosophical, and the
doctrinal. As a student of homiletic literature he has
in mind the preaching of a past period. From the
early period and on into the first quarter of the nineteenth century, American preaching was largely doctrinal
in its subject-matter, logical in form, and philosophical in
spirit. It has ceased to be doctrinal and logical in the
formal sense. Church doctrine no longer constitutes its
subject-matter and dialectic is no longer the instrument
of defence. But in the broad sense of the term it has
never ceased to be philosophical when at its best, and the
demand for a reasonable interpretation of religious truth
has not ceased, nor has it greatly diminished ; it has
only been modified. To this modification in the didactic
type of American preaching Mr. Beecher, equally with
Dr. Bushnell, has been powerfully tributary. His personal religious experiences, not less than the type of his
genius, were determinative of his didactic method. A
man of intense intellectual activity, he was also nurtured

in a most stimulating intellectual atmosphere. His father was a man of robust character and of stimulating mind, the most effective preacher, perhaps, of his day, and could not fail to make a strong impression upon so responsive a mind. The entire intellectual life of the household was most stimulating. One can hardly conceive of conditions more favorable to independent, sturdy, varied intellectual development than were found in that home. The life of New England and measurably of the new West, settled largely by New England people, was charged with intellectual vitality. It was a time of theological controversy. The conflict between the old and new schools of so-called orthodoxy was at its height, and the Unitarian and Universalist controversies had not yet subsided. This polemic temper, with all its bad results, developed strong mental fibre in the preaching of the day. Mr. Beecher inherited and perpetuated much of this intellectual virility. Against the form in which the thought of the sermon was put he strongly reacted. His exuberant emotions and his vivid imagination were intolerant of its dogmatic, polemical, and dialectical quality. His catholicity of spirit and love of brotherly concord reacted against its bad tone and temper. His practical sense reacted against its excessive indoctrination as the supreme homiletic aim. His habits of study, his neglect of doctrinal theology, his devotion to general literature and to rhetoric and oratory, his own intense personal religious experiences, which resulted in a new conception of God and of his Christ, his familiarity with revivals of religion, belief and interest in which, with their emotional intensity and practical aims, he never lost, as well as his own habits of extemporaneous preaching from college days, — all this and much more of a practical sort, together with the more direct intellectual influences, which are somewhat obscure, had for their result a modification in the character of his preaching and yet a perpetuation of its mental vitality. From the beginning of his ministry, therefore, he ignored the doctrinal type of preaching and became an evangelistic preacher. In an address to the Congregational ministers of London in September, 1886,[1] in which he gives a sketch of his ministerial life, he refers to the reaction against the preaching of his earlier days, and the result in turning him to pulpit evangelism. The address is of value as giving us an insight into his early ministerial development. " Seeing this fight," he says, " degenerating oftentimes into the most scandalous enmities, I turned away in absolute disgust from all these things and said, My business shall be to save men and to bring to bear upon them those views that are my comfort, that are the bread of life to me ; and I went out among them, almost entirely cut loose from the ordinary church institutions and agencies, knowing nothing but Christ and him crucified, the Saviour of mankind. Did not the men around me need such a saviour ? Was there ever such a field as I found ? Every sympathy of my being was continually solicited for the ignorance, for the rudeness, for the aberrations, for the avarice, for the quarrelsomeness of the men among whom I was, and I was trying every form and presenting Christ as a medicine to men ; and as I went on and more and more tried to preach Christ, the clouds broke away, and I began to have a distinct system in my own mind." Here is a knowledge

[1] " Life of Beecher," by Abbott and Halliday, p. 608.

that is the product of religious experience, and that does not come through the processes of the understanding alone. And yet all his previous training in theology and all the activities of his quick, capacious understanding conditioned the value of this experience, and they all bore fruit in his preaching. In all this reaction he did not lose mental fibre. In fact, his preaching constantly increased in intellectual power. The exuberance of his rhetoric tends to obscure the strength and range of his thought. The early period was the evangelistic period. The mid period, covering the years of the antislavery controversy and of the Civil War, was the ethical period, in which he dealt largely with the moral aspects of religion, particularly as related to the duties of associate life, although always from the Christian and even evangelical point of view. He handled ethical subjects in a masterful manner. This country has produced no preacher who was his equal in the cogent presentation of political ethics. His study of human nature and of human institutions gave him exceptional power in the handling of such subjects. The later period may be called the didactic period, in which he sought to be the teacher as well as inspirer of the people, and to give them the results of his investigation and thinking upon the problems of religion as related to new world-views. But in all these periods there was never a lack of energetic thinking. His appeal to men always had a rational basis. And in all these periods he was influential in leading American preaching away from a dogmatic basis and a semi-scholastic form into a more popular and practically effective method, at the same time conserving its substantial intellectual basis.

But let us look a little more fully into his intellectual outfit.

(1) The quality that makes the most immediate and perhaps the strongest impression is his immense intellectual productiveness. It is said that Mr. Lincoln once characterized him as "the most productive mind of ancient or modern times." This may be an over-estimate, but certainly few in this country, if any, have been his equal in this regard. There have been those who struck into deeper depths and whose product was more weighty, those who produced more elaborately and more gracefully and more in accord with the classical standards of rhetoric and oratory. There have been American orators who were in many respects his superiors. Webster was more massive in his mental product, more stately in his mental movement, and more elevated and dignified in his rhetoric. Calhoun was more subtle and acute and plausible; Everett, more scholarly and finished; Clay, more graceful and fascinating in elocution; Prentiss, more habitually impassioned in his eloquence; Phillips, more incisive and pungent in the oratory of invective, and much more concise and classical in his style. But no one of these men had his vast intellectual productiveness. None produced with such rapidity and intensity and affluence of mental movement, in so many fields of intellectual activity, and with such wealth of imagination and emotion. A ministry of forty years in one parish with ever increasing power, nearly to the end, and with surprisingly little diminution of popularity in the face of a scandal that would have put most men beyond recovery, attests, not only his amazing intellectual pro-

ductiveness, but his power to hold the affections, the confidence, and the allegiance of men ; and the way in which he bore himself during those years of trial, the undiminished freedom of his mental and moral energy, the poise and balance of all his powers, and the continuous unembarrassed devotion of all his productive forces to the welfare of men were evidential of his own consciousness of innocence, and it effected much in disarming his enemies and in holding the confidence of those who would be his friends.   His success in other fields, and those widely different from the one in which lay his life vocation, which he loved supremely and to which all his best powers were devoted, also attests his productiveness.   On the platform, as a lecturer and especially as a political orator, he was unrivalled.   His success in England in quelling the tumults of audiences that had become mobs, and in forcing a hearing by the might of his personality and the skill of his oratory, was one of the great historic triumphs of human speech, worthy of record for future generations.   He lectured successfully on a great variety of subjects.   As magazine writer and editor, he handled a free and facile and vigorous pen.   He made a respectable figure in fiction. He was an authority on many and widely different subjects of human interest.   In all these lines of activity and in every specific effort he made, there was always the impression of unlimited and unfailing resources. The ease of his mental movement, the affluence of his style, the quiet colloquial manner of his address, no less than its passionate explosiveness, the torrent rush, the variety of his themes, the diversity of his methods, the tropical luxuriance of his rhetoric, all attest the wealth of his resources. No one could hear him talk, now with subdued tranquillity, and again with the bubbling vivacity as of a brook, without being impressed by it. In his early ministerial life, while doing the work of an editor as well as of a preacher and pastor, he preached daily, "and once through eighteen consecutive months, without the exception of a single day." A striking illustration of his productiveness, and of the ready command of his resources, may be seen in two different consecutive speeches made by him in New York, in connection with the meeting of the Evangelical Alliance. He had made a very effective address to one of the assemblies, and passing immediately into the presence of another assembly, he, within a few moments, made a second address, as different in substance as if made by another man. The man who can, within so short a period of time, develop two lines of thought so thoroughly divergent, has met the supreme test of intellectual productiveness. This fertility was, of course, the gift of genius. He was a man of singularly quick intuitions. He saw straight and quick into the inner meanings of things. All forms of external reality found ready response, and awakened myriads of echoes within him. He had the "imagination penetrative." His organization was keenly susceptible to impressions from without, — from nature, upon which he looked with a poet's eye; from art, for which he had a delicate native and trained aptitude; from science, whose materials and principles he made available for religious use; from literature, whose treasures he had stored, and by which he had enriched himself; from his fellow-men, who nurtured his feelings and affections and sympathies; from the invisible and eternal world, with which, through his faith talent, he was always in easy contact, and the vision of which always stirred all that was best within him.   With all this responsiveness was associated that power of reaction from within which is the gift of genius ; that creative activity, the activity of the poet or maker, that takes the results of all impressions, and organizes them into all varieties of fresh forms ; that plastic inventive power that manipulates all material from without, and converts it from within, into new, fresh, living forms.   With all this was associated that impulse to objectify, to communicate, to relate with other living souls the thoughts that burdened the mind, and that ethical impulse to turn all truth and all thought of it into personal, moral property in the interest of character and conduct which is the gift of the true preacher.

(2) This productiveness was not superficial and showy. Thoroughness was equally a characteristic of his mental movement.   His product was in its main outlines fundamental.   It was his habit to examine the foundations of things, to get at their inner reality and to set forth their relations.   He dealt with principles.   One who allows his attention to be preoccupied with his intellectual brilliancy is likely to lose sight of his intellectual thoroughness.   The very brilliancy of his diction, by which he expresses weighty thought in attractive form, obscures its fundamental character to the superficial hearer or reader.   But below the rush of his diction, below the concrete illustrative forms of his thought, there was generally solid substance.   He had not only intellectual irritability to a surprising degree, and the impulse to utter what was stirred within him, but he had great expository skill.   It was a close and harmonious blend-

ing of the interpreter and the advocate. He studied his
subject in its elements. He grasped it in its relations
and made it clear and reasonable. He never forgot
the object of the sermon and he lived with his audience
in the hours of preparation. But he never forgot his
subject, knowing that justice to the audience is in part
justice to the discussion. This expository tendency was
increasingly developed. In the early period he indulged
in the descriptive style more fully than in the later
period. It was pictorial and dramatic. But it was the
use of the descriptive method, to set forth the inner
realities of human experience and the occult realities of
human life. His lectures to young men were perhaps
as effective a series of discourses as he ever preached,
and have exerted a wide-reaching influence. They
portray, with master hand, the passions and the struggles of the human soul. They belong to the first decade
of his ministry. His style became less exuberant and
his discourses took broader range. He grappled more
fundamentally with his subjects. His methods of getting his thought before the mind are always prevailingly
concrete and illustrative, but the thought itself is fundamental. His method is analogical rather than logical.
He appeals to experience. His thought moves in the
realm of life. He illustrates, does not argue; but the
truth that lies under his concrete form of exposition is
substantial. His skill in analysis is great, particularly
his skill in portraying the workings of the human soul; and
few preachers have ever reached his mark or measure
in expounding the principles that are at work in social
and political life. He handles these questions with the
consummate art of the orator, but he handles them fun-

damentally. Estimated superficially, as by their first and surface impressions, nothing will seem less carefully deliberate and less elaborate than the speeches he delivered to the howling mobs of Englishmen during the Civil War. They were uttered with extreme difficulty, amid continuous interruptions, that taxed to the utmost all the powers of the orator, and these difficulties would have vanquished most men. As to their form, they were struck out with great rapidity, but they were the ripe fruit of long years of study of the Constitution, of the political institutions of the country, of the slave system in its economic, political, domestic, and moral aspects; and they everywhere show a firm grasp of the special subjects discussed and of the general principles that underlie them. They are all interrelated, have unity of plan and progressive movement, reach the climax sought, are all tributary to one great definite object, and are not the less evidential of the grasp of the political and ethical philosopher, than of the skill of the orator. The first speech deals with the growth and development of the slave power that led as by "irrepressible conflict" to the clash of arms. The second, with these historic facts before the minds of his hearers and readers, takes up the effects of the slave system in degrading labor, and has for its immediate object to convince the working-men of Great Britain, to whom it was addressed, that their interests were with the cause of free labor. The third, with these data in hand, takes up the political aspects of the conflict, and deals with the struggle between the North and the South, for supremacy and for control of all departments of the government, executive, legislative, and judicial. The fourth deals with the commercial, as the second with the industrial, aspects of the subject, *i.e.* with the relation of the slave system to the commercial classes, and has for its object to show that a nation of capitalists engaged in manufacturing and commerce is preëminently interested, or should be, in the support of free institutions. The fifth is a lucid and skilful exposition of our representative system of government, in which there is a blending of autonomous state with national government: it shows the impossibility that the national government should deal successfully with the slave system as a national question, and that, under existing political conditions, in which it was impossible for the national government to legislate state institutions out of existence, civil war was inevitable. These speeches, popular in form and artistic in oratorical method, are full of sound economic and political science and moral philosophy, and show, on the part of the man whose chief pride and joy it is to be a minister of the gospel, a thorough comprehension of the problems at issue in that great historic struggle. Beecher had trained himself to think, vigorously and independently. He was not a close nor accurate thinker according to the standards of logic, but he was a strong and aggressive thinker. He was trained even in theology. His expressions of contempt for theology, his rejection of the theology of his day, and his abandonment of all attempts at a systematic presentation of his own theology, are misleading if they lead us to infer that he was ignorant of theology. He had examined the chief systems of theology in his day. He heard these matters discussed at home and in the seminary class-room and was familiar with them. He early cultivated the method of the inter-

preter, and it became the basis of his persuasive method.
His habits of study and of expression, and even his dab-
bling in phrenology during his college days, were all in
a way tributary to this didactic habit. His interest in
Biblical studies during his seminary course and his
experience as a Bible-class teacher intensified his didactic impulse, and these were the decisive influences that
led him to the final choice of the ministry. It was his
life habit to deal with substantial truth, interpreted and
vindicated in terms of human experience rather than of
human speculation, and translated into vivid concrete
forms. In the early part of his ministry he was, as has
already been suggested, a diligent and enthusiastic student of the Old English preachers, Howe, Sherlock,
Butler, and of our own Edwards, and especially of
Barrow and South. He absorbed South and made his
method of handling texts and his style his model. The
influence of Barrow is also evident. Their diction and
structural method were thoroughly impressed upon him.
His own homiletic method, although always natural and
sufficiently individualistic, always varied, suited to the
subject and object of the sermon, and never stereotyped,
shows at once the influence of these old homiletic masters and the prevailing habit of his own mind. His own
injunction to students, never to preach two sermons alike
in treatment on two successive occasions, he obeyed.
But if there is one method more characteristic than
another, it is the twofold process of exposition and
application. His first object is to set forth the truth
in hand to the intelligence of his hearers, to set it in its
true light, to secure a clear understanding of its elements and relations, and thus to secure an intellectual

interest in it ; and then he will impress upon the heart
and conscience the practical implications of the truths as
thus set forth.   Despite the popular impression to the
contrary, he is therefore a Biblical preacher.   Not
infrequently the entire discourse is at once expository
and applicatory and is in the homily form.   But more frequently it is in topical form, with an expository basis
and an inferential application, and reminds us of the
English Barrow and of the French Saurin.   Thus he
gets at the main teaching elements of the truths discussed and at the subordinate truths bound to them and
deduced from them.   All this is done in a singularly
vivid, illustrative, and popular manner, yet bearing evidence of a mind that deals with broad principles which
in a modified, but true, sense of the term, may be called
the philosophic habit of mind.

(3) Intellectual range is another notable quality in
Beecher's preaching.   His mind was capacious and
wide-reaching in its movement.   He took large views
of all subjects, and always wanted a wide field for his
discussion.   His thoughts ran along broad avenues.
Facts, truths, and suggestive impressions poured through
the wide gateways of his capacious mind ; and under the
touch of his discriminating, analyzing, and constructive
intelligence, and the quickening power of his vivid
imagination and intense emotion, they arranged themselves under broad principles.   He grasped the broad,
generic features of his subject and did not linger with
small details of elaboration.   By native tendency and
by training he was an extemporaneous preacher.   In
his way he was an enterprising and diligent student.
From all sources of knowledge he appropriated omniv-

orously.   Nothing that was human was foreign to him.
He exploited every field of human interest and was no
mean authority in various and diverse departments of
knowledge.   He was rapid in his movement and undertook nothing he could not handle with ease.   It was the
habit of his life to look at all things from the humanistic,
rather than from the ecclesiastical, point of view, and in
this his influence has been very great.   He trained the
man, and the preacher was simply the man disclosing
himself in all his fulness.   To dip into horticulture and
agriculture, while preaching daily, was only recreation.
By drill in oratory, by practice in addressing public
assemblies, and by literary culture, he fitted himself for
platform speaking.   While discharging the most exacting duties of a large parish, he wrote editorials that
were felt all over the country, and he was regarded as
one of the great journalists of his time.   So great was
his versatility and fertility and range of thought, and so
exacting was he, that his lectures were never quite the
same on two successive occasions, but were always re-
shaped and made new.   He was a slow reader, but a
rapid assimilator and producer.   Everything was tributary to him.   All he saw, heard, felt, read, became
pabulum for his preaching.   He had the high sense of
his calling, the love of man, the ethical purpose to use
the truths for the bettering of men or to bring some
determinate moral result to pass, the teaching impulse,
the eager observation, the comprehensive grasp, the
assimilative vitality, the imaginative suggestiveness, the
emotional earnestness, the sympathetic responsiveness,
and the professional enthusiasm that mark the homiletic
mind in its highest range.

No modern preacher has ever foraged so widely and so eagerly for the material of his preaching. He stored during the week, holding his mind in a condition of constant responsiveness and of intense aggressive activity, his imagination always at work, his sympathies kept fresh by contact with human life in all varieties of experience, always mindful and wisely careful of his physical health ; and on Sunday morning he had only to organize the accumulated mass of material that was seething in his capacious mind, and to let it expand under the vitalizing action of his creative energy. In the method of his pulpit preparation he reminds us of Schleiermacher, with the difference that Schleiermacher's sources of material were found in the realm of theology and of inward experience, while Beecher's were more largely the realm of life. This method of preparation accounts for many of the peculiarities of his preaching, its wealth of subject-matter, its freedom and largeness of movement, its vivacity, its carelessness with respect to close structural method, and its homely colloquial diction. All his stores were poured out freely from within, the form was always subordinate to the substance, and structure and style were never very important considerations. He was not a supreme master in the artistic handling of his material. His artistic sense was disclosed in his diction, particularly his vocabulary, and in his illustrative material, rather than in the organization of the material of the sermon. The rhetorical dominated the logical interest. He did not value the highest cumulative effects, and in so far as the highest rhetorical impression is dependent on cumulative force, he often failed to realize it. He apparently sought a

K

continuous, rather than a cumulative impression, or rather a series of striking and not altogether closely related impressions. It was a vast accumulation of varied homiletic supplies that was tributary to this quality of range that we are considering. Everything is on a large scale. He will not tie himself down to fine points. There is plenty of delicate shading of thought, but he indulges in no unpopular subtleties. His statement is large, often complex and diffuse. It is sometimes in the form of a proposition, but more frequently in broad rhetorical form. Sometimes there are two statements of his subject, reminding us of Phillips Brooks in this regard, whose mind had something the same large, rapid, free-running movement. The second statement is more specific than the first, but both are likely to be discursive and diffuse and sometimes embrace a whole paragraph. He is not careful to trace the connection between his text and theme, or to justify the use of the text. He has his material, at least in its germinal form, and he wants a text to fit it. He takes what he can get most readily, and is not over nice about it. As he starts out from his text he approaches his subject in a large, free way, always, indeed, in a way that is pertinent, but not artistically skilful. Here at the start, as elsewhere, there is the suggestion of extemporaneousness about it, not in the substance of thought, but in the methods of relating and expressing thought. If the introduction is explanatory, as it generally is, it does not deal with minute points of exegesis, but in large general statements. It is much less concise than Bushnell's introductory work, but always concrete, and, as with Bushnell, not infrequently put in a paraphrastic manner. The outline always has wide range, not so much in the number of main topics as in subordinate thoughts. In his discussion he runs into side issues a good deal. He darts suddenly into side tracks, and returns to the main line only to dart off again. He turns up in the most unexpected quarters. He brings out the most novel conceits. His lines of mental association are manifold and wide-ranging. He has the poet's eye for likenesses. His mind is analogical. He sees things, not under the relation of cause and effect, or of logical contiguity, but of resemblance. He therefore indulges in such expository methods as are peculiar to a man of genius. The result of all this is, as regards method, not most helpful for permanent educative results. But it is always vividly and often dramatically impressive. It is a series of impressions, vigorous and stimulating, while at bottom there is substantial and helpful thought. He is not flashy and superficial, but his mind works with such amazing rapidity and fertility that he must let it run on in its own free way unshackled. He violates approved homiletic principles, and in the matter of homiletic method he is not so helpful as many an inferior preacher. This will do for a man of genius. There is a certain Shakespearean freedom about it all; it has the merit of directing attention to itself as a unique homiletic type, and there is always enough in the sermon to overmaster whatever defect. But it is a type that cannot be perpetuated even by a man of great genius, and it would be imbecility itself in the hands of a man of only ordinary power. He had transient aspirations and made sporadic efforts after a better method, for the artistic sense was strong within him, and he knew the worth of homiletic as of literary form, but in the rush of life they never came to much. He wrecked everything in the stormy activity of his powerful mind, in the turbulence of his intractable emotions, and in the strenuousness of his militant life.

The extemporaneous method, to which for years he had accustomed himself, of course contributed to wide range in his handling of subjects, and he illustrates signally the demand for freedom of range in this method of presenting the truth.

(4) Another quality in Mr. Beecher's mental equipment was his intellectual catholicity. That he was tolerant in his feelings was the necessity of his broad humanity, of his Christian estimate of men, of his large and delicate sympathy with all classes of men, of his supreme valuation of the religious significance of truth, of the peculiarities of his own religious experience, and particularly of his religious conflicts. It was impossible that a man of his breadth of sympathy, who especially had learned the difficulty of winning firm footing for his own faith, who knew the assaults of doubt, who had learned to undervalue the formulated doctrinal statements of truth and was intensely hostile to polemical theology, should not hate all intolerance of feeling. But he was tolerant in his intellectual judgments as well as in his sympathies, and this was a necessity of his general mental attitude toward the truth. It was his habit to recognize what is true in different types of theology and in the tenets of different sects, and he could not be a partisan. He was a very sympathetic and generous interpreter of other men's opinions. He was inclined to find truth under all forms of error, and for the man

whom he regarded as in error he had only sympathy
pity, and good will.   This intellectual tolerance was
due also in part to the experimental quality of his own
theology, and not to indifference with respect to the truth,
nor to undervaluation of correct religious thinking.   His
theology came from within, out of his own religious life, not
as the product of speculative thought; and he approached
all theological questions with a religious spirit and valued
all theological truth chiefly with reference to its significance for the religious life.   As a mere matter of
thought no truth had for him much value.   Hence he
was the more ready to value what others thought, in
so far as it related to their own religious interests, even
though he had no intellectual agreement with it.   For
this reason his own theology was somewhat ill-defined.
He held stoutly to what he regarded as the truth and he
had a clear conception of it as truth, but he knew that
the field of truth is broader than the field of doctrine,
that there is more in any truth than can be crowded
into a definition; and he held the truth in the large, held
it in solution, and never subjected it to the closest and
most critical analysis or particularity of statement.   For
this reason he found but few theological boundary marks
across which it was difficult for him to pass into fellowship with men of other sects.   He had a good word for
all theological and ecclesiastical parties, and found warm
friends and admirers among them all.   In days of detraction and ill repute he found no more ardent defenders
and supporters and admirers than in communions with
which he had no ecclesiastical affiliation.   His influence
in breaking down the spirit of intolerance and of denomi-
national exclusiveness has been very great.   His own

theology was a gradual development, and it became more
definite in the latter part of his ministry. He valued
sound and positive belief, but insisted upon the distinction
between belief and faith, and laid chief stress upon those
truths that faith appropriates in the interest of character and conduct. In his theology, using the term in its
primary significance, he was a sort of Christian pantheist. He accepted the theory of evolution, adjusted it to
his theological thinking, and became an intelligent defender of it. This theory fell into line with those conceptions of God and of His relation to the world which
he had held with measurable definiteness for many years.

It was because he conceived of God as a living presence and power in the world, carrying on to triumphant
issues His purpose of mercy for sinful, suffering men, that
he laid such emphasis upon the element of compassion
in the divine love. In his doctrine of the Trinity, he
was, as was Bushnell, substantially a Sabellian, following
Sabellius even in his illustration of the Trinity, from the
symbol of the sun, as the source of light and heat, the
two elements being manifestations of the one fontal
source, as Christ and the Spirit are moral manifestations of the one God. His preaching had a Christological centre. What he knew of God, he knew chiefly
through the heart of Christ, and in his soteriology he was
a Patripassianist, holding that God was incarnate in a
human body as the historic Christ and that God suffered
in the sufferings of Christ. In his doctrine of the
atonement he held the position of a modified Socinian,
agreeing substantially with what calls itself the "moral
influence theory," as held by Bushnell in this country, by
Robertson and by the broad churchmen of England, and

by the Ritchlians of Germany. In his anthropology he reacted vigorously against the doctrine of total depravity as it was held and expounded by the traditional Calvinism of his early days. In his doctrine of regeneration he was nearer the Arminian than the Calvinistic position. Miracles he accepted as genuine supernatural events, and his adherence to the doctrine of evolution never compromised his faith in and allegiance to Christianity as a supernatural revelation. In his eschatology he was agnostic, but became increasingly hopeful and indeed confident of the complete final elimination of evil from the moral universe and of the ultimate triumph of the good, and at the close of life seemed to be in substantial accord with those who accept as a positive tenet the final restoration of all men. He abandoned Calvinism in early life, and his influence in this country as well as in England, in the modification and subsequent substantial abandonment of Calvinism by the Congregational churches, has been very strong. This freedom from school theology, and this readiness to accept as truth teachings that were allied with those that have been regarded as heterodox and over which the churches have quarrelled, were the product of his catholicity of mind and spirit, and this is one of the sources of his wide influence in all denominations. But with all this freedom, which has generally been regarded as loose theological thinking, it must be acknowledged that, as contrasted with the theological latitudinarianism of our day, he held a substantially evangelical position. And no one can read his sermons without being convinced of it, or at least one cannot fail to be strongly convinced of their evangelical spirit. From the first his preaching, which was practical rather than doctrinal, ethically applicatory rather than dogmatically didactic, dealt with what he regarded as Catholic Evangelicalism. The present generation of preachers, that has come into a pretty well established order of evangelical freedom, can hardly understand the change which the preaching of this country has undergone within the last three-quarters of a century. The average preacher takes his homiletic inheritance as a matter of course, and it is well-nigh impossible for him to estimate adequately the influence of Henry Ward Beecher in the change that has brought the new order. Of course he was not a model for the theological thinker, nor even for the preacher. He was not a well-balanced man. His powers were not coördinated as were those of Phillips Brooks. He was so many-sided, so kaleidoscopic, in the combination of his faculties, so subject to inward revulsions and changes of mood, so impulsive and emotional, that a disturbance of balance was inevitable, and his instincts were more trustworthy than his judgments. But in his breadth and catholicity of mind and heart, he has had wide-reaching influence in all the Protestant churches of this country, and is widely known in all the churches of Christendom. With a less catholic mind and spirit he never could have exerted such an influence. In many ways, but especially in the quality of breadth and catholicity, — the present generation of American preachers is the more influential and effective and the next may be still more so, because of the work he has left behind.

3. No adequate estimate of Beecher's power as a preacher will fail to recognize his transcendent gifts of expression. It is his diction that has won for him

the title, " The Shakespeare of the Modern Pulpit.'
His nimbleness and fertility of mind, vividness of
imagination, and passionate intensity of feeling were
all tributary to this linguistic facility. These are the
gifts of the artist. But in his case they all found their
most natural and characteristic manifestation in speech,
rather than in other forms of artistic expression. He
was an artist in speech. His diction is a distinct gift,
and he cultivated it with ceaseless assiduity. It is notable for its ease and affluence, its wealth and variety. It
combines all the qualities of an effective pulpit style.
It is at bottom an expository style. There is often,
especially in the early period, an Oriental gorgeousness,
a tropical luxuriousness, of diction that is likely to draw
attention to itself, and in these more salient and obtrusive characteristics the ordinary hearer or reader is likely
to lose sight of its intellectual qualities. But his conceptions are mentally discriminating, and the perspicuity of the expression matches the perspicacity of the
thought. He is an analyst in thought, and deals with
the important and practical considerations suggested by
his subject. In his discussion of states of soul, and
especially of the moral elements in character, he is
sometimes singularly definite and discriminating. It
is not a style that has the precision of scientific accuracy, but of vivid representation. It flashes light into
the mind by the vividness of its suggestion. Perspicuity is, after all, the notable mental quality of his style.
Thought is expressed in colloquial, often homely, diction
and in simple, unartistic sentences, so that with all its
brilliancy of imagery it is at bottom a plain prose style.
The expansiveness of the style discloses the expository

quality.   There is a multiplication of the elements of
thought for the purpose of clear interpretation, and a
consequent expansiveness, sometimes even to diffuseness, that becomes an increasing tendency with him.
The style of early years was much more compact than
that of later years, therefore more vigorous, although it
was never lacking in freedom and facility of movement.

The ethical quality of naturalness is another and
equally noteworthy quality.   Out of the abundance of
his inner life his speech flows copiously, easily, rapidly.
There are no artificial twistings of sentences, no pedantic straining for effect, no strange, remote, barbarous,
unidiomatic vocabulary.   It is fundamentally the simple
colloquial style.   It utters itself with perfect freedom, as
of one who knows himself as talking with his hearers.
But its most salient quality is its concreteness.   The
American pulpit has in general been distinguished for its
power to grapple with abstract thought and at the same
time, which is especially true in our own day, to translate
it into the language of practical life.   The illustrative
style of preaching has displaced the argumentative.   Of
this type of preaching Mr. Beecher was the most striking representative, and in it he was a pioneer.   His
theology is anthropomorphic.   His conceptions of God
are derived from human analogies.   Of the Absolute of
philosophic thought he knew nothing.   Apart from His
disclosure in humanity, and especially apart from the
fact that He is historically revealed in Christ, he does not
know God.   It was therefore necessary for him, with
his vivid imagination and intense emotion, to represent
God concretely, under human images.   All his discussions of the remote and difficult problems of the Invis-

ible are crowded with human analogies. All subjects
are discussed illustratively, all brought out into the
sphere of life and experience. But few abstract terms
are found in his diction. It is the descriptive vocabulary. He deals not with things as they are supposed
to be in themselves, not in our abstract notions of them,
but as they seem or may be represented in concrete
images. His rhetorical figures are largely those of
resemblance. Few preachers have ever equalled him
in the sense of poetic likeness. It was Shakespearean.
He thought in images, and his gift for illustration has
perhaps never been surpassed by any preacher of the
Christian church. It was as natural and as easy as his
breath. Whether in public address or in private conversation, he would hardly open his lips without an outflow of most exuberant and felicitous imagery. It was
a highly poetic gift. It appears in his preaching, not
only in formal illustrations, but in his ordinary vocabulary. Formal comparisons are found on almost every
page of his sermons, and quite as frequently the more
compact and sententious metaphor. Nature, with whose
scientific as well as æsthetic aspects, he showed himself
familiar, in large measure furnished his images and illustrations; but human life also, business life, industrial
life, artistic life, and particularly domestic life, furnished
abundant material. His vocabulary was large and rich
and varied, and came from many sources. In its range
and in its suggestiveness, few preachers if any, have ever
surpassed him. The most occult realities of the inner
life are described in most graphic style, in terms that
represent them to the senses. If he spoke of motives
that readily disclose themselves, they were described

as "jutting motives." If he would represent God as a being of power, He becomes the "Arch-thunderer of the Universe." He likes descriptive Latin words and their resonant rhythm, and uses them as freely as the more compact and vigorous Anglo-Saxon words. If he would speak of the foulness of sin, it shall be represented as "feculent vice." If he would describe the selfish greed of man, he must use the worm as his symbol, and we are introduced to the "vermicular human race." Christ, in his sympathy with men, "carries the core of their hearts." Men who are in unsuspecting peril "stand at the edge of unspeaking precipices." Everywhere his thought appears in symbols. The all-devouring activity of his mind leads him into widely different fields, and his creative imagination forages everywhere for the treasures of his vocabulary and for his more formal illustrations. Hence his discourses are always pictorial and often dramatic in high degree. His style has vivacity, intensity, rush. He compacts his thought and speech by turning nouns into verbs. Eager boys "enterprise after" all things that lie before them. His lectures to young men are notable for condescension of style, and at the same time there is a rush and a sparkling vivacity in the sentences which we do not find in equal measure in his maturer style, and we are reminded somewhat of Newman's intensity in the marshalling of compact, descriptive clauses. The conclusions of some of these lectures carry a passionate intensity that must have sent shivers through his audiences. He knew the value of literary form, knew that the literary product will not live without it; but in the rush of his life, he sacrificed some qualities that he admired, and in which he might have become complete master ; and while his tendency to expansiveness and diffuseness enhanced his expository power, it diminished the artistic impressiveness of his preaching. And yet it must be said that the style of the latter period, while less intense and more reflective, less artistic and more free and colloquial, never lost its descriptive clearness, and was always rich in figurative suggestiveness. It is precisely this concrete quality that measurably accounts for the colloquial homeliness of his diction. His use of homely, often rough, colloquialisms was perhaps more common in his lectures and addresses ; but they were not lacking in his sermons. It is a sensational feature in his preaching that grew upon him, and while it gave a certain pungency and dramatic forcefulness to his preaching, it also became offensive. But the point to be noted is that it all originated in this energetically descriptive quality of his style. If he wishes to characterize the trashy quality of a large amount of the religious literature that is current, he calls it " wishy-washy," the "swill of the house of God," and says it is like the "locusts, the lice, and the frogs of Egypt." Of two descriptive terms, he will always use the stronger. It is not enough to say that criticism is trenchant — it is "sneering." A pronounced infidel is an "acute infidel." The Bible is not severely criticised, it is "riddled." Mission schools are "chickens under the wings of the church." The rich give to the poor their "scraps and mouldy rinds." Impracticable effort is "running the thing into the ground." Any excess is a "gorging of ourselves." This is the emotional intensity and the colloquial familiarity and rudeness of his descriptive style.

In conclusion and in brief summation of what has

been said, Mr. Beecher, perhaps more fully than any
other modern preacher in this country, and if so, surely
more than the preacher of any other country, illustrates
the preacher's assertion of the rights of personality.
Intellectual productiveness, emotional intensity, and
æsthetic sensibility are combined in him in an altogether
phenomenal manner, and he illustrates the value of
training the man in a comprehensive way. Because of
this combination, his preaching was of the most animat-
ing sort.   It stirs all the activities of the soul.   It will
not fail, even in the printed form, to quicken the aspiration to preach effectively, the ambition to reach and
influence men.   It suggests the value of the study of
the human soul and of human life, in order to realize the
highest pulpit effectiveness. And beyond the measure of
any other modern preacher does he illustrate the power
of the illustrative type of preaching.   As to many things
that are important for the highest and most permanent
usefulness in preaching, his value is relatively little.   He
has doubtless influenced the lay mind more strongly than
it was possible for him to influence the clerical mind as
regards the substance of his preaching.   His influence
upon the platform and through the press has perhaps
been nearly as great proportionately as from the pulpit,
and everywhere and always it has been tributary to personal rights, to the higher moral and religious ideals of
human life, and to the permanent welfare of human
society.   Taking his brilliant career as a whole, notwithstanding the shadow that rests unjustly, we may believe,
upon his declining years, and which will at last, we may
surely hope, wholly pass away and no longer darken his
name, his influence, it must be acknowledged by all who
know the record, has been a most beneficent influence.

CHAPTER IV

HORACE BUSHNELL

I

BUSHNELL'S HOMILETIC GENIUS

HORACE BUSHNELL was preëminently a preacher. His genius for religion, the struggles of his intellectual life, his supreme interest in religious truth, his way of apprehending it, his impulse to impart it, and his method of presenting it, all fitted him in a notable degree for the work of the pulpit. By this it is not implied, of course, that he was nothing but a preacher. He was a man of varied gifts, aptitudes, and interests, and it is very likely that he might have been highly successful in any one of many departments of intellectual or practical activity. He certainly had in him the making of a philosopher. Using the term in the popular rather than in the technical sense, it may be said of him that he had a certain philosophic habit of mind, without which no man can ever be a preacher of the highest type. He had the intellectual impulse to grapple with what is fundamental in any subject; had an easy grasp of principles and an orderly method of expounding them. It is said of him that "he had no unrelated facts." His facts must be related in order to be interpreted. For simply as unin-

terpreted facts they had no significance or value for
him.   All that came under his observation, whether in
nature or in art or in the ordinary events and experiences of life, took connection with fundamental and
regulative ideas.   This tendency to get at the inner
relations and the inner significance of things, which was
so marked a trait in him, is substantially the philosophic
habit of mind, however remote it may be from any
special, formal philosophic method.   The world to him
had meanings that lie far below the surface aspects of
things, and their superficial and commonly interpreted
significance had but little interest for him.   He was not
content to linger even with the higher artistic aspects of
life.   He was gifted with the artistic temperament, but
the tendency to get at the rationale of artistic expression led him below the surface of artistic forms.   He
had, for example, a great love for music.   But he was
not satisfied to cultivate the mere art.   He sought to
interpret its inner meaning in terms of thought.   He
had an eye for the forms of art, notably of architecture, of which he was a competent critic.   He had, in
fact, a rare susceptibility to all artistic forms.   But it
was the necessity of his mind to get at the sources of
artistic impression and to interpret the artistic in terms
of the rational.   He had a trained sense of the beauty
of natural scenery, but the philosophic explanation of
its impressiveness had seemingly quite as much interest
for him as the æsthetic impression itself.   In a word,
Bushnell's interest in the world and life was preëminently intellectual and philosophical.   This habit of
mind he took into his investigation and discussion of
theological questions, and he always sought to penetrate

to the core of the question in hand and to get at what is fundamental. He had indeed no philosophy of his own in the formal sense of the term, and he never adopted another man's philosophy, but this habit of searching for the rationale of things came from the philosophic impulse, and it was a source of the greater power for him as an interpreter of truth. Yet he ignored and despised, or affected to despise, philosophy in all its formal aspects. He even went so far as to deny the possibility of any mental or metaphysical or moral science. A philosophy of nature is possible, because "nature is a system," but in mind and in morals such system is impossible. His highest estimate of metaphysics was that its first and chief use is to "show that metaphysics are impossible." He seemed never to understand the significance of philosophy for religion, and spent the greater part of his life in battling against all attempts to apply a philosophic method to the interpretation of the facts of Christian experience and to the objectively given truths of Christianity. For a mind so enterprising and penetrating and logical, all this seems highly absurd, as it doubtless is. But it should be borne in mind that, after all, what Bushnell was fighting was primarily not philosophic thought or philosophic method as such, but the philosophic system current in his day, which he characterized as "a soulless matter-born philosophy of mind." He was cast into the breaking-up period of religious thought. He was too late for the old and too early for the new. Because he had outthought the old philosophy and had not yet discovered the new, he fought the whole thing. He saw that in its materialistic basis and tendency the old philosophy "reduces the

L

spiritual and material creation to the same dead level,"
and " regarding all his actions as the successive products
of a systematic mechanism, it sees in man no heaven-
ward tendency, no yearning of his nature after God and
goodness." It is doubtless true that he did good service
in his contribution to the disintegration of the existing
scheme of philosophic thought as applied to the interpretation of religion ; but he went too far, accepting a
somewhat fanciful theory of language that rendered
impossible any philosophy of religion, and this unfitted
him for any adequate apprehension of religion in its
philosophic aspects.

But the practical, and for Bushnell himself one might
almost say the beneficent, result of all this was that it
led him the more determinately to the cultivation of the
preacher's habit of mind, and the aggregate result for
the world was doubtless more and better than it would
have been had he been a more consistent philosophical
thinker.

Dr. Bushnell was a theologian and has left behind a
theology sufficiently distinctive to bear his name. It is
a curious turn in the course of events that our theological
institutions, as in a sort of defence of the Christian faith,
should to-day be expounding the theology of a man who
spent his life in antagonizing theology, and who denied
that anything like a system of theology is possible.
But the fact is that Bushnell had the full outfit of a
notable theological interpreter, and might have made a
competent theological investigator. He had a robust
intelligence, a keen insight into the realities of religion,
such as stimulated him to bring that intelligence to bear
upon the problems of religion, a great hunger of heart

for the invisible, the eternal, the spiritual, a strong grasp
of the truths and facts of religion, and a logical faculty
that fitted him to relate those truths and facts, and to
bring them into a fairly well-ordered whole. He was
not a theologian of the type of his teacher, Dr. Na-
thaniel W. Taylor, whose method and results he stoutly
antagonized; and his own method, or as some might say
defect of method, perhaps incapacitated him for recognizing the significance of his teacher in the development of New England theology, and for assigning to his
work its true value. He refused to employ the dialectical
faculties with which he was equipped, and rejected a
method in which he could easily have become a master.
As he denied the possibility of a philosophy of mind and
of morals, so he denied that the experiences of religion
could ever be brought within the limits of scientific
statement. In this he is for this country a pioneer in
movements that developed after he left the stage, and
that have become domesticated in the religious thinking
of wide-reaching circles in our own day. But it would
be idle to deny that, after his own kind, he was a theologian of high degree. His theology was "pectoral,"
but it was a theology. It was more than a subjective
experience incapable of rational interpretation. He
was not at all content that his own or any other man's
religious life should remain a vague, undefined emotional
and ethical experience. It was the necessity of his
keen, sturdy New England mind, trained in intellectual
gymnastics, to grapple with religion as an intellectual
problem. He stoutly maintains that Christianity is not
a gift to the intellect, but to the imagination and the
heart, and that language is wholly incompetent to formu-

late the content of religious experience into an intellectual system. But it is as impossible for him to detach his sturdy mind from the problems of religion as it is his impressible heart from its experiences. In his own way he was a rationalist, and there is a certain *naïveté* in his vigorous onslaught upon theology, since in the very process of his criticism he is bringing out a theology of his own. The real object of his assault is not theology as such, but the kind of theology that is current in his day, and particularly its methods and results. He believed in theology, as every man who does any thinking upon the problems of religion must, and he was not without an orderly and consistent method of developing his own theological thought. But the point is that it was his own, and not other men's, theology that commanded his interest and respect. In the sense of the term that was accepted in his day, he was not a theologian. His method was that of the preacher, and no American preacher within the last century has succeeded in introducing more theology into the pulpit or in discussing theological problems in a more interesting and effective manner than he. The significance and value of Dr. Bushnell for the Christian church is not in the fact that he antagonized theology and denied the rational possibility of it, but in his battling a theology that had a false philosophical basis and a wrong method, and perhaps especially in the fact that he brought to the investigation of theology the spirit and method of the preacher, and therefore brought theology out into the practical lives of men. He had no theology that he could not preach, and he believed in none that could not and should not be translated from the realm

of thought into the realm of life. It is here that we see
the genius of the preacher. It was the spirit and the
method of the Christian prophet, rather than of the
Christian dialectician. The mystical has somewhat
obscured the dialectical element in Dr. Bushnell. But
Dr. Henry van Dyke's characterization of him as " the
most logical of mystics and the most mystical of
logicians " is strictly correct. He understood thoroughly
well the laws of thought, and he was the better preacher
on that account. It is true that he could not or would
not hold the truth he discussed under the limitations of
close formal definition, nor use in its presentation the
categories of dialectic, and he was the more a preacher
for that very reason. But he had a strongly logical
mind ; he presented the truth in an orderly, logical
manner and carried his hearers by the cogency and
cumulative energy of his presentation. In early youth
he showed those judicial qualities of mind that won the
confidence and respect of his elders. It is said of him
that when a youth of sixteen years he showed unusual
ability in sifting evidence and in forming correct judgments upon important questions, and it was very likely
this quality of mind that gave him a bias or inclination
to the study of law. It can hardly be doubted that he
would have had a distinguished career in the legal profession. He was skilful in debate and early developed
the debating habit. His mind was quick, keen, and
eager, seizing as by logical instinct upon the strong
points of a subject, and the impulse for discussion is a
marked characteristic in all his work. His method from
the first was eminently logical and always continued to
be. Yet it was the mystical and poetical rather than

the dialectical quality in him that won the ascendency, and which disclosed itself in various ways in his development.   And here again we see the preacher.   He was profoundly interested in political questions, and had a sound working knowledge of their theoretic aspects, but always discussed them from the ethical and religious point of view, and he made himself strongly felt as a Christian citizen.   He undoubtedly would have made a notable figure in civic life and might have become a statesman of wide-reaching and most beneficent influence.   But all his patriotism and all his knowledge of public affairs were made subordinate and tributary to the work of the pulpit.   It was the impulse of the preacher that dominated the impulse of the patriot and the citizen.

He had ready insight into the spiritual significance of Biblical truth, seemed less dependent than most men by reason of this insight upon the science of exegesis for his apprehension of the truth of Biblical revelation, and he had a great deal of skill in a species of compact, sententious, expository, often periphrastic, statement of it. His explanations of Scripture are always in rhetorical and popular literary form.   But he knew little or nothing about the modern science of exegesis and Biblical theology.   His interpretations are highly interesting, suggestive, and helpful, but often fanciful, and lack the support of recognized exegetical canons.   He was master of " exegetical divination," not of exegetical science.   In this too, as in the case of Augustine, he was the preacher.

In the modern acceptation of the word, he cannot be called a student or scholar.   He did not even read very widely, and his attainments in profound and connected knowledge of any subject that demands scholarly investigation were meagre. By patient, protracted, toilful research he never mastered any subject. He had a great many ideas upon a great variety of subjects, and even upon subjects he had not investigated he could talk interestingly and instructively. By independent reflection he was able to penetrate the depths of a subject, but what others had thought and said upon it he did not know, nor did he much care. In fact, he was less dependent than most men upon research for the formation of his intellectual judgments. His keen mental penetration measurably served him instead, and he was generally worth listening to on almost any subject on which he might choose to speak. His neglect of what others had done and thought and said, however, was the serious fault of his life. His mind was singularly quick and keen and penetrating, but from early years he lacked the concentration of the student and scholar. Even when he undertook to examine and state the results of others' investigations, he proved to be somewhat untrustworthy, for he was likely to read his own vigorous, creative thoughts into the process. Scholars like Professor Shedd could easily bring him to book and put him to confusion by showing the misapprehensions and mistakes of his subjective prepossessions in attempting to interpret a theological work like Anselm's "Cur Deus Homo?" When brought to the test of scholarly judgment much of his thinking was unreliable. And yet it is true that his eager mind sought commerce with the sources of intellectual training and culture, and in various ways he showed the results of it in a scholarly habit of mind. His scholarship, such as it was, showed itself in a trained capacity for vigorous intellectual grasp of the weighty problems of life, rather than in stored intellectual acquisitions or in a scientific method of investigation. He bore the result of years of varied mental activity in the fibre of his thinking, and he was one of the most interesting, helpful, and intellectually stimulating thinkers of his time. In this intellectual independence, this creative activity, this lack of scientific method and limitation of scientific acquisitions, we see once more the preacher.

Dr. Bushnell was a realist as well as an idealist. He had a strong, manly grasp of things as they are. To a poetic insight and the prophetic vision of a higher invisible world, which was a gift from his Puritan ancestry, and which seems, as is so often the case, to have come through his mother, or his maternal ancestors, was added that sturdy common sense and that firm grasp of reality that is not less the Puritan gift. It was this, very likely, as in the case of Robertson, that gave him a taste for the natural sciences. Considering his habit of intellectual thoroughness, his tendency to go to the bottom of things, his respect for nature as the realm of causation, and his general respect for the causal relation of things, together with that tenacity of will that led him to the mastery of whatever he undertook, he might have made, one fancies, a respectable figure as a scientific student, had he been early turned in that direction. He had a trained eye for topography, and a habit of throwing out imaginary highways and railroad lines and bridges and of throwing up military defences with mathematical accuracy of measurement, and it is not unlikely that he might have had a successful career as

a civil engineer. There was nothing human seemingly
that was foreign to him. He was far-seeing and sagacious in practical affairs. He was intelligently interested
in the pursuits of men's daily lives. He knew something about the markets and the laws of trade, was at
home with men in their ordinary business life, could
sometimes give them " points " worth considering in
their business management, and might himself apparently have been a successful man of affairs. But these
multifarious gifts were after all subordinate. They
heightened his value as a minister and became indirectly
tributary to his power as a preacher, but were not his
distinguishing gifts. It was his Puritan idealism that
dominated his Puritan realism, and this was the fountain
of his homiletic genius. It was the prophetic gift, the
sympathetic, the emotional, the image-making impulse,
that led him into the realm of the invisible and ideal,
and it was a gracious providence that led him, under the
guidance of his mother's prophetic soul, from all the
allurements of a lower order of life, where indeed he
might have been successful and useful, into the Christian ministry, where only all his best and most characteristic powers found their proper sphere.

In saying that Bushnell was preëminently a preacher
it is not meant that he was a preëminently popular
preacher. There are of course many sorts of pulpit
power, and no man's greatness and success as a preacher
may be measured by the number that crowd to hear him.
Many a pulpit mountebank is able to draw the crowd
and to achieve a superficial, ephemeral, and nominal
success. Bushnell did not value popularity in the
ordinary sense of the term, as Robertson did not. The

so-called common people did not listen to him with such
genuine intensity of emotional interest as they listened
to Mr. Beecher, and he had nothing of Beecher's popular
power.   But he was in some respects the superior of Mr.
Beecher as a preacher, certainly a much more desirable and helpful model for most preachers.   He had
most of the qualities of a great and impressive interpreter and advocate of religious truth, and no person
of even ordinary intelligence could listen to him without being attracted to him and strongly interested in
his sincerity and earnestness, his breadth of humanity,
his catholicity of spirit, his intellectual incisiveness, his
steady, orderly movement, his fresh and vivid conceptions, and the concrete style of his representation.
And no person of intellectual inquisitiveness, of love
of reality, of religious susceptibility, could ever listen
to him without strong intellectual interest, and often
without deep emotional and ethical and spiritual interest and profit.   Setting aside Mr. Beecher, whose distinctive qualities of genius have given him a unique
position among American preachers, Dr. Bushnell was
by far the most weighty and at the same time in
many respects the most attractive and suggestive and
forceful and helpful preacher of his day.   And as a
pastoral preacher he has in later days no successor,
Phillips Brooks excepted, who is Bushnell's peer, not
in intellectual penetration or grip or strength of mental movement, but only in quickening and suggestive
power and in practical helpfulness.

In estimating Dr. Bushnell as a preacher, and to do
this is the sole purpose of this discussion, it is necessary
to note more fully his equipment for the work of the

pulpit. Let us therefore undertake to investigate some of the sources of his power as a preacher. And if the discussion seems to have been anticipated, it is only in a general way, and may prepare us for a fuller analysis.

II

BUSHNELL'S HOMILETIC PERSONALITY

What Bushnell taught, the substance of his message, important as it is for our estimate of the significance of his career, is not the chief source of interest in him as a preacher. No worthy judgment upon his message even is possible, much less upon his significance as a preacher, without a basis in some knowledge of his strong and profoundly interesting personality.

1. His physical endowments and appointments were only in limited measure tributary to his impressiveness as a preacher. He was of medium stature, without bulk of figure, rather delicate in organization, yet lithe and full of nerve force. In early years he was something of an athlete and nearly to the end of life an enthusiastic pedestrian. In youth he was remarkable for his physical beauty. He had a handsome face and a straight, agile frame. But in later life he had lost the beauty of early years and was thin and bony. His voice had good carrying power, and his vocalization was easy and natural. But it was notable neither for strength nor richness, especially in later years. It was of medium tone, capable of great reach neither in depth nor height, and at last, owing to physical infirmity, wholly lacking in compass. It was not a sympathetic

voice, and lacked the power to stir strong, sympathetic emotion, and he was accustomed to use it in a simple, natural manner. He always uttered himself in free, downright, manly fashion, like a man of prevailingly intellectual habit, whose mind is full and must free itself, but rarely pouring itself out in impassioned utterance or attuning itself to the most delicate and tender emotions. It was the organ of his intellectual virility and common sense, rather than of his imagination or sentiment or feeling, and in ordinary use gave no sympathetic expression to his inward fervors. He had studied oratory in college, and Demosthenes was his favorite orator. But he despised elocution, regarding it as meaningless "mock oratory," and as he discusses in his commencement oration "Some Defects of Modern Oratory," one can imagine him in his characteristic rôle of critic. He cared for the rhetoric and logic of oratory, but not for its vocal aspects. The result was that he was a natural speaker and so far forth interesting, but lacked the oratorical training that did so much for Mr. Beecher. He carried the conversational type of speech into all forms of utterance, and in private intercourse he was one of the most brilliant conversationists of his day, superior even to Mr. Beecher in intellectual incisiveness and rugged energy of speech, but lacking Beecher's passion and pathos and flashing wit. The two men were alike in the simple, natural, conversational basis of their speech, but they parted company when they came to the high altitudes of emotion. Beecher soared, but Bushnell kept the "go afoot" style of vocalization. Bushnell's movements in the pulpit were not varied. They were energetic, even measurably intense. But during most of his life he was chained to his manuscript, and he must stand in one spot. There was not a great amount of gesture, and what there was of it was somewhat angular and ungraceful. But he was vigorous and had what calls itself the "magnetic" quality. His whole frame would at times respond to his mental and emotional intensity, while yet he held himself, as to his feet, to the one spot in which he had planted himself, as if in dogged resistance to any conceivable power that would undertake to dislodge him, — a sort of typical posture. There was an air of positiveness, sometimes almost of defiance, which reminds us somewhat of Robertson, in what he said and in the way in which he said it. It was the utterance of self-reliant judgment and strong conviction, and sometimes had the appearance of dogmatism and impatience of contradiction, — the speech of an honest debater, who is bent, not only on interpreting, but on advocating, the truth he has espoused, and on vanquishing its adversaries, whoever they may be. The manliness and courage of the man were manifest in every tone of his utterance and in his very attitudes and movements. "His preaching had," says his biographer, "in his early days a fiery quality, an urgency and wilful force, which in his later style is still felt in the more subdued glow of poetic imagery. There was a nervous insistence about his person and a peculiar emphasizing swing of his right arm from the shoulder which no one who has ever heard him is likely to forget." But with all his nervous intensity, his "verve" as the French call it, his poetic heat, he was always well-poised and self-possessed. The strong, steady mind and the sturdy will

held him in, whatever the stress of emotion.   His dress
was in harmony with the character of the man.   He
never dressed his profession.   He dressed the man.
There was a certain respectable negligence about it,
almost a homespun quality, in which he evidently had
a certain satisfaction and pride.   He avoided the clerical
mark.   His dress was like that of an everyday man of
affairs, and it proclaimed the man among men.   In
the later years of life his hair was long and shaggy,
always thrown back in a sort of wild disorder, and well
adorned a head massive at the top and with a bold,
precipitous front.   Taken as a whole, the physical
personality, the air of it and the dress of it, was suggestive of a certain noble freedom and self-reliance,
and dignity and self-respect.   His manners were wholly
unaffected.   He was a frank and friendly man, but he
had no surplus stock of respect or deference to the
opinions of any human being.   For mere opinions, as
such, especially religious opinions, he had scant respect anyway.   They have done great mischief in
theological controversy, these " gaunt notions, horning
and hoofing each other."   For his own opinions, indeed,
he had a good deal of respect, but he regarded them as
intuitions and moral convictions, and so to be cherished
on moral grounds.   He would with the utmost coolness
and *naïveté* contradict you to your face, if he did not
agree with you.   And yet you would not, could not, feel
that you were dealing with a man who was essentially
rude, for in the broader sense he was a gentleman in his
instincts and sympathies.   He was an iconoclast in the
realm of manners only because he was an intellectual
iconoclast.   The one supremely masterful thing about

his physical manhood was the eagle eye. There was a singular fascination about it. It held one as by a spell. When in later years, in stress of work and by reason of failing health, he was driven to occasional extemporaneous preaching, the forces of his physical manhood, although enfeebled by physical disease, were measurably liberated; and when at his best he made a stronger immediate impression upon his audiences than when chained to his manuscript, although there was no gain in the intellectual value of the sermon, and it is pretty sure that there would have been no permanent gain for his reputation or influence as a preacher, if he had followed the extemporanous method. But it is sure that the unchained eye enhanced the power of his oratory. It is evident, however, that Bushnell's effectiveness as a preacher was much less dependent upon the impressiveness of his physical personality than that of many of his contemporaries.

2. Bushnell's intellectual gifts, as already suggested, singularly fitted him for the work of the pulpit. Perhaps the most noteworthy characteristic of the mental aspect of his personality was his intellectual independence. It was an inheritance, and it was duly cultivated. He recognized the influence in his own character and career of his paternal grandmother, and he admired her freedom of spirit. She had tried the dialectics of Calvinism, and "had been so dreadfully swamped in getting her experience through the five-point subtleties that she nearly went distracted." Following her own independent spirit and relying upon her native sagacity and spiritual insight, she found a way out into the freedom of Methodism. Bushnell's antipathy to Calvinism

and his heroic faith in the freedom of the human spirit
may have been measurably an inheritance. At any
rate, he had from early years followed the natural bias
of an independent mind and had trained himself to look
inward and not to other men for guidance in the formation of his opinions. Here, in the realm of personal
reflection, he grappled with august and momentous
problems. He knows it as in large part his errand in
life " to find, to get a knowledge of and to get full possession of " himself. He undesignedly describes himself as a student of religion and of life in the following
words : " Some minds seem, from a very early age, to
have a strong adhesiveness to whatever comes in contact with them. When a subject enters the thoughts,
it is followed for hours, or perhaps days, with patient,
laborious meditation. In this way they come to an
astonishing maturity without much assistance from
books. Now these are the ethereal souls who are so
often described as reasoning without reflection and
embracing everything great by a constitutional energy.
Why, these men study more in their dreams than other
men by their midnight lamps." This "strong adhesiveness" and this habit of "embracing everything great
by a constitutional energy," are eminently characteristic
of Bushnell, and the terms are most felicitously descriptive of his peculiarities. He thus formed the habit
" from a very early age " of following the subject that
"enters the thoughts with patient, laborious meditation."
In this way he formed his own opinions. Even when
these opinions are in line with those of other men and
may have become the possession of many, they are
still wrought out in his own way and have for him all

the novelty of a strictly personal possession. He was more inventive than investigative. The self-reliance and grit of his homespun New England ancestors were perpetuated in his own intellectual independence, and, in his admiration for them, he recognizes them as kindred spirits. He had no use for any man "who could not stand straight and square upon his foundations, or who wriggled and twisted a body supported on weak, unsteady columns." This independence of spirit exposed him to the assaults of scepticism. He formed the debating habit of mind. All problems must be subjected to cross-examination and cross-questioning. But he expected no adequate solution of his difficulties by such cross-questioning. In fact, it was his spiritual intuition that demanded the cross-examination. His distinctive mental quality was insight. It led him to look straight into the heart of truth, rather than to take the long circuit about it. He was no insignificant logician. He reasoned with skill and force. But his characteristic gift was the penetration of the seer rather than the nimbleness of the dialectician. He meant to know realities, rather than to know about them. He saw quickly, as he felt intensely. He saw deeply, too, for the moral and spiritual activities take men into realms that are closed to the mere dialectician. It was this that saved him in periods of intellectual doubt. When the logical faculties failed to bring the solution sought, and when he recognized their inadequacy to the task, it was this habit of looking directly and steadily at the heart of great questions that gave intensity to his mental activities and relief to his moral and spiritual needs. The sermon on the " Dissolving of

M

Doubts " describes his habit of dealing with vexed questions.   It is the habit of a man who learns by looking.   He "hangs up" his questions.   He turns "a free
glance on them now and then as they hang."   He moves
freely about them.   He looks at them first on this side
and then on that, and then by and by, as he turns some
corner of thought in his inspection, he finds how quickly
and easily they open their secret and let him in.   What
seemed insoluble clears itself up in a wondrous revelation.   This is the method of the seer.   In it he becomes
"more deep-seeing."   In days when the preacher is
inclined to skirmish about the great facts and truths of
religion, rather than to grapple with them valiantly, it is
refreshing to come into contact with such a man and to
note the manly directness and vigor and lofty intellectual
courage with which he, single-handed, as if he had a
special call from Almighty God to do it, grapples with
the profoundest and most august truths and facts of
revelation.   Whatever one may think of his success in
the solution of his problem, or whatever one may think
about his method, one must at least admire his spiritual
and intellectual valiancy.   There is no skirmishing with
these problems.   No skirmish line is known in his intellectual tactics, no polemic fence and attack.   He
plunges at the objects of his intellectual grapple, as if
he has a life and death interest in them.   He hovers
about them until he is stirred by them.   Then he
seizes them with firm grip.   He looks them through till
he sees what should be told, and then he brings in his
report with a tone so honest, so real, with such ring of
truth about it, that no one will for a moment think of
doubting the worth of it all, however much he may

question the completeness of his vision. It was this
habit of immediate grappling with his problem that
developed that self-reliant, positive, strenuous, at times
seemingly arrogant, but always manly, temper and tone
that operated like a mental and moral tonic upon the
men of his time, making him the impressive and influential man among men that he was, one of the most
effective intellectual leaders of his day. And it was
precisely this quality that was tributary to his distinctive power as a preacher. It yields one of the most
distinguishing traits of his preaching, its declarative
quality. He was a good deal of an apologist in his way.
He knew the arts of the polemist and was even master
of the philippic. But it is his prevailing habit to state
the truth in a direct, positive manner, to promulgate it
rather than to reason about it. He tells what he sees,
not what he has excogitated in accordance with dialectical processes. He hints at the objects of his thought
by the use of analogies largely, rather than elaborately
elucidates them in logical order and form. Consequently
Dr. Bushnell was never a doctrinal preacher in the
sense of that term common in his day. He was eminently a didactic preacher. His sermons are freighted
with weighty truth. He was much more at home in
the discussion of a weighty subject than any preacher
of his day. His preaching had a more solid quality,
and aggregated a larger amount of important truth,
than that of Beecher or Brooks. All of these preachers
were ingenious in homiletic suggestion. They spoke to
the imagination and stirred an emotional interest in the
truths discussed. But Bushnell has the greater strength.
His themes always contain a strong religious truth

which is formally stated.   He must always have something large and important to discuss.   He therefore
takes a theme with a complex of thoughts, which is
capable of being thrown into the form of a proposition;
and it generally is thrown into that form, a form fitted
to the work of thorough exposition and discussion.
This puts the sermon at the very outset upon a strongly
didactic basis.   He is from the first committed to the
work of interpreting and supporting the truth enunciated.   If we look at the topics used in his discussion,
we find them to be preëminently the teaching topics, —
topics, that is, that are adapted to the setting forth of
the thought relations of the subject, topics that serve to
increase knowledge of the subject and perpetuate a
strong mental impression.   They are didactic phases of
the theme, which is complex in character as containing
a large group of allied thoughts.   And this whole complex theme-thought appears in the process of discussion.
The theme, however complex, pervades the whole sermon, and no one is ever at a loss to know what is in
discussion.   The progress is orderly and well-marked,
and the entire sermon has a noble unity and symmetry.
Other parts of the sermon disclose the same didactic
character.   The introduction is from the outset suggestive of the instructive quality of the sermon.   It is the
explanatory introduction, showing the connection between text and theme and bridging the way from the
one to the other.   The conclusion is practical in its character, yet it still perpetuates the didactic interest, furthering the mental impression already made, giving the
subject a new turn, showing the truth from a new angle,
and is almost always in the form of inference from

the subject discussed. The sermon is to a considerable extent Biblical. He was not an expository preacher
as Robertson was. But his preaching always attached
itself to Biblical religion, and he always discusses
his Biblical truth in a positive manner corresponding
to the declarative method of Biblical revelation. But
the point just here is that, although preëminently a
didactic preacher, dealing with the solid substance of
Biblical truth, his method of discussion is the practically
suggestive method. It is the declaratory, the affirma-
tory, the promulging, method that comes home suggestively to the experiences of men, adducing those
considerations that appeal, not to abstract thought, but
to common sense, common conscience, common feeling,
and common observation, and that touch the realities of
human life.

3. Bushnell's artistic gifts should be noted here, for
they were effectively tributary to his work as a preacher.
With Puritan robustness there was allied a delicacy that
was not the less Puritan when, as in his case, Puritanism
was at its best. His thought fell naturally into the
form and took the color that is furnished by the imagination. It is his theory, carried through life from college days, that revelation can be given only through the
imagination. At what time, in what ways, or under
what specific influences he was led to the position that
the human understanding is incompetent to deal successfully with the problems of religion, and that
consequently a theology or a philosophy of religion is
impossible, but that only such approximation is possible
as is furnished by the image-making faculty of the soul,
is uncertain. Criticism of the traditional theology not

only, but of its traditional philosophic basis, had already
in this country gained a hearing in his early years; and
perhaps the influence of Coleridge, whom in his college
days he found "foggy and unintelligible," but subsequently "lucid and instructive," may be recognized.
One of his Hartford friends says of him, "I have often
heard him say that he was more indebted to Coleridge
than to any extra-Scriptural author." By what specific
influence he was led to adopt the theory of the inadequacy of language to express and interpret religious
truth is also uncertain. Possibly the new historic and
literary spirit that had been awakened in the early part
of the century had wrought productively upon his artistic nature and had realized in him its earliest fruitage,
leading him to look upon the Scriptures as a form of
religious literature, rather than as a body of doctrine or
a "codex of legislation." Of this there are some indi-
cations, although they are somewhat obscure. But
however it came about, the positiveness of his conviction
touching this matter is sure. He was not very consistent in his repudiation of theology and denial of its
possibilities, as has already been suggested, for he had
a theology of his own and was a firm believer in it.
Nor did he apply his theory of language very consistently, for it is an instrument for setting forth his own
theological conceptions, and although it had not scientific precision, it had an accuracy of representation that
was adequate to the purpose of expressing with singular
lucidity often the most occult and difficult theological
conceptions. In fact, he played fast and loose with his
theory. Failing to recognize a relative permanence of
significance in the secondary stage of language, that

has long since passed the early and representative stage of its meaning, he was accustomed, after the manner of Coleridge, to deal with its original and etymological significance, thus involving the discussion in the network of his own fancies and throwing confusion into it. But it must be confessed that, after all, this was tributary to his attractiveness and force as a preacher. This use of the representative faculty not only conditioned his method of conceiving and of interpreting the truth, inclining him to the use of the analogical method of interpretation, but it colored his diction. In this lies the attractiveness of his style, which has the qualities of descriptive clearness and concentrated strength. It leads him often into fancifulness, but it never fails, even in his most insubstantial imaginings, to hold our interest, even though it may not command our judgment. There was a time when he came to a new literary awakening, which was not altogether unlike his later ethical and spiritual awakening, and in this we may detect the influence of Coleridge. He began, as he tells us, with the plain "go afoot" style of Paley. But after reading Coleridge's "Aids to Reflection" for a whole half-year, he got a new idea of the power of language. It was its power of figurative representation, and as a result he says, "My powers seemed to be more than doubled." Among the distinctive characteristics of modern preaching is its temperate use of figurative language. On the one side, we have a reaction from the theological, philosophical, and dialectical type of preaching, with its preponderance of abstract thought and prevalence of abstract terminology, in favor of a type of preaching in which feeling and imagination have free play. This

results in an increase in the use of figurative language.
On the other hand, we see a reaction from the exuberant use of figurative language that characterized classical rhetoric. Classical oratory appealed largely to the
emotions, and the discussion of rhetorical figures was a
disproportionately important part of the older treatises
on rhetoric. It was the figurative type of language that
appealed to emotion and passion. Modern rhetoric
deals more with the intellectual aspects of language.
It lays stress upon the importance of intellectual con-
vincement. It accentuates the didactic element. This
results in a temperate use of figurative language. The
modern orator uses but relatively few figures of speech,
and modern works on rhetoric abridge the discussion of
figurative language. Figures of speech that are adapted
to the excitation of high-wrought emotion, like apostrophe, vision, the stately figure of hyperbole, and many of
the grammatical figures that were prominent in classical
rhetoric and in the oratory of the seventeenth and eighteenth centuries, are less frequent. The figures used by
the modern orator are largely with reference to making
the subject discussed clearer and more forcible. They
are largely figures of resemblance, and are verbal rather
than grammatical, belonging to vocabulary rather than
to syntax. The metaphor, which is tributary to clearness and force, is more common than the simile, which is
adapted to the more stately, ornate, and elaborate style,
like that of Jeremy Taylor. This suggests the prevailingly didactic character of modern preaching, and at
the same time its freedom from the prosaic dulness of
the old dogmatic type of preaching. Dr. Bushnell's
style of preaching is an illustration of this in an eminent

degree. His rhetorical figures are few in number and
not very varied. Metaphor and simile — and that the
condensed simile, with metonymy — are the chief figures. The figures of passion are rare. There is but
little exclamation and exaggeration, and no high-flying
apostrophe or vision. His figures are natural. They
grow out of the thought, and there is nothing strained
or artificial about them. But they are strong and impressive. His use of the imagination appears in his
vocabulary. It is this that secures color, imparting to
his utterance a warmth and semi-poetic glow, suggesting
more than is asserted. His vocabulary has not the
range and variety of Mr. Beecher's. He has not foraged so widely in different fields of knowledge for
treasure wherewith to enrich his vocabulary. It is,
however, the vocabulary of the preacher, which in the
nature of the case must be a somewhat limited vocabulary. For, however widely the preacher may range in
his studies and investigations, — and Dr. Bushnell did
not range very widely, — he must put the result of his
knowledge and culture into the language of common
life, at least into a type of diction that will be readily
apprehended by the common people. The result is
that the sources of the preacher's vocabulary are likely
to be less manifest than those of men in other professions. There is, however, a great difference in preachers in this regard. Some disclose the sources of their
vocabulary more readily than others. It is one of the
characteristics of Dr. Bushnell that he puts the mark of
his own personality upon the product of his knowledge
more fully than most preachers. He shows, therefore,
the results of his training and culture quite as much in

the facility with which he handles his themes, in his penetration and grip and range and general strength of mental movement, as in his diction. But there is one noteworthy quality in it that may well receive attention. It is the descriptive vocabulary. It is not ornate, nor highly pictorial. It is soberly descriptive. It represents the objects of thought as they appear to the imagination. It is a descriptive quality peculiar to himself. His mark is on it. His theological terms are descriptive. He scrupulously avoids all technical theological terms. He seems to have almost a morbid dislike of them. He puts the thought that is behind the term into some word descriptive of it. Regeneration, for example, he described by the term "naturalization." This is a manifestation of his analogical habit of mind. It sometimes leads him astray. He undertakes, for example, to use the English word "atonement" in its etymological sense of at-one-ment. In thus describing or undertaking to describe the truth of the atonement by the analogy of the original English word, he loses or ignores its real significance as it has appeared in the history of theology. What is true in his use of theological terms is also true of his use of philosophical terms. All such terms are changed into popular descriptive terms. His vocabulary indicates familiarity with nature, art, trade, and industry, and he uses the terms that are brought from these departments with great force and accuracy. His diction is largely the language of energetic movement, that contributes force to his style. He uses the preposition or the adverb in connection with words that suggest physical action, in describing the objects of his thought. He has us "shaken out of our prayers."

Our "crust is broken up." "God turns us about and
beats us back." We "stay by our evil mind." The
"church slides into the world." Such a style has
movement and life. There is an interesting blending of
the reflective, the practical, and the poetic in his preaching. The thought is that of an original, reflective mind ;
the subject, the method, and the aim are practical; the
style is semi-poetic. This yields a blending of elements
that are tributary at once to interest and effectiveness.

4. His ethical gifts still more manifestly fitted him
for preëminent pulpit effectiveness. His most impressive ethical quality, perhaps, was personal will force.
He bore the mark of it in his entire personal bearing,
his attitudes, movements, gestures, tones of voice, and
the glance of his eye. His whole life, from its beginning to its end, bore witness to it. He was constitutionally independent, self-asserting, and fearless. He
belonged to a race from which this ethical forcefulness
came to him as an inheritance. It was a strength tempered by delicacy and grace, but it was preëminently a
strong race. The same manly courage and tenacity of
purpose which he showed in fighting his own doubts
showed itself also in facing the contradictions of men
in defence of his faith and conviction, in his grapple
with the great problems of existence and the great facts
and truths of Christian revelation, and in his last long
fight with disease and finally with death. As far back as
1837, when he was only thirty-seven years old, he spoke
of the threatening disease with which he struggled
all through his professional life, as hanging about him
and of his fear that it would get a deeper hold of
him. It was a manly fight under great burdens, and it

is amazing that under such physical limitations he should have accomplished so much. He kept in good cheer, often making light of his burdens and exhibiting an oversensitiveness about his physical weakness even up to the last, refusing sturdily to accept the proffered assistance of others to support his tottering steps. He would "stand on his own legs" to the end. This force of will he threw into his preaching. It was one of the great elements of power in his oratory of which altogether too little has been made in men's estimate of him. There was a strong contagion in his downrightness and positiveness. It was an intellectual and moral tonic. He carried men even against their will. He subdued them by the force of his personality; men rebelled against his teaching and antagonized his influence and shouted an alarm against him, only to find themselves vanquished in the end, it would be difficult to tell just how. They quarrelled with him and tried to suppress him, but they never succeeded in silencing him or in putting him down. Friends were alienated from him and years of distrust and heartburnings followed; but they yielded their wills at last to the force of his personal manhood, and he won back their hearts, while they may have refused to yield mental assent to his teachings. That he held his own, not only in his own denomination, but in his own church, and was not immolated by his enemies, was due quite as much to his masterful handling of himself and of other men in days of detraction and misrepresentation, as to the support of wise and large-minded men to whom all honor is due for defending the freedom of Christian teaching among the Congregational churches of the state of Connecticut.

Bushnell was not understood. His method was new to the men of his time. He was breaking away from the old path and breaking out a new path for the theology and the preaching of New England, and men did not take kindly to it. His method is now a commonplace, and largely through him a free possession of the American pulpit. But the dogmatic and dialectical method held the field in his day, and men who cherish such method as sacred do not understand the poet and mystic who invades their precincts. Men of routine and of the established order, who have no vision, stand in dread of the iconoclast. Men sought to bring Dr. Bushnell to book, but when they laid hands on him, and he grappled with them, they felt the muscle of an athlete, and they became shy of trying conclusions with him. He did not prefer to fight. He was not so " strenuous " as to love fighting for his own sake. He shrank from it, in fact. He was much more intent on establishing the truth, as he understood it, than on fighting down error. But he had the fist of a pugilist. He was ready for any man at any reasonable hour and in any rational method of combat, and when pushed to it, he handled weapons that were a terror to his adversaries. Like Robertson, he was a born leader of men. Considering the time into which he was cast, when men of light and leading had become dissatisfied with the traditional defences of religion and had begun to discern from the high summits of their observation the methods of a new day ; considering his own high altitude, standing on his own solitary peak, with the vision of the new dawn in his face ; considering his own intellectual inquisitiveness, his keenness of insight, his literary instincts, his independence of spirit and his indomitable courage, — it was impossible that he should not be a theological iconoclast. He did a revolutionary work, and he has had a larger following than even he ever could have dreamed of. His influence has been so strong that to-day he has his innings, and it has been so silent that the men who are now domesticated in a new order hardly realize what they owe him. Men who do not accept all of his results, and it is not necessary that any man should do this, accept substantially his method and his spirit and know their worth for the pulpit. It is hardly too much to claim that upon the more thoughtful and cultivated and better-trained men especially, as well as the truer and more genuine spirits of the American pulpit, he has had a stronger influence even than Mr. Beecher. The above-named qualities of his personality, the physical, intellectual, artistic, were all dominated and fused and fired by the energies of his masterful will. And it was this combination that yielded one of the most notable qualities of his preaching, namely, its vitality. His preaching is alive all through. There is a vitality in his style that bears the mark even of his physical intensity. It is vital with the movement of vivid imaginative representation and with strong emotion. It is intellectually alive. We feel the presence of a strong, virile mind. The ruling thought of the sermon vitalizes the whole organism. There is no let-up in the tension of mental energy. It is sustained force. The subject is grasped as with the energy of life, and into it is poured a flood of ethical and emotional and spiritual force. Here are the words of a man who means what he says and all he says, and nothing other than what he says, and has felt the power of what he says; else who could say it as he says it, or who feel it as we feel it? It is singularly real. No second-hand religion or theology here, and no half-conviction or professional emotion. The organism of the sermon is fresh with life. It is charged with the force of the personality of the preacher. No homiletic hotchpotch here. The style has the vitality of intellectual clarity and accuracy, of ethical, emotional, and spiritual force, and of imaginative suggestiveness. This vitality discloses itself in his intellectual productiveness, notwithstanding his lifelong struggle with physical infirmity. His mind was always at work. Subjects were perpetually crowding in upon him. They were so numerous that they must wait, be put aside, "hung up," for future investigation. He was never hard put for something to say. He knew nothing of the agonies of mental and moral poverty. This same vital quality disclosed itself in the rapidity of his mental movement. His quickest work, he says as far back as 1839, is his best work. Not because it was quickest, but because it was the outcome of a mind intensely active and that took vigorous hold of subjects that came before it, so that the accumulated results of past hours of thought came rapidly to fruitage. It showed itself in his quick, pungent, vivacious answers to questions which, anticipating the modern question-drawer method, were dropped into a box at the door of his church lecture-room and which were sometimes answered impromptu from the desk. It showed itself in his conversation, in his talks at the club, in which he was recognized as *facile princeps*. It was an event much to be coveted and long to be remembered to hear him pour himself

out in his fulness when he was at his best.   Few men
have matched him in the art of pungent colloquy.   This
vitality, perhaps, gave him a drawing towards the West,
where he mistakenly imagined his work might be better
appreciated, an impulse which he never wholly lost.
And yet New England was his proper sphere.   It is
altogether doubtful if elsewhere Bushnell would ever
have found a basis for the wide-reaching influence he
has exerted.   The thought of the age was almost,
although unconsciously, ready for him, and New England was the true centre for the exercise of his intellectual leadership.

5. It remains to consider the religious element in his
personality as related to his power as a preacher.   Bushnell, like Robertson, was gifted with capacious and refined religious sensibilities.   In either case it reached
the measure of religious genius.   In either case it was
an inheritance.   It both cases it was nurtured under
the favoring conditions of evangelical piety from early
days, and the fruit of it remained to latest years.   If
Robertson's piety was the more emotional and affectional and his early evangelicalism of the more pronounced type, Bushnell's was not the less real and
enduring.   Bushnell early developed a more distinctively intellectual and rational type of religious character
than Robertson, and it was more distinctively ethical as
a form of religious experience.   It was, therefore, more
closely allied to what called itself in his early days " the
religion of nature."   The early conditions of his life
tended to foster a certain ethical austerity, and the
inquisitiveness and independence of his mind tended to
the development of the rational element in his religion.

But from the first he was at heart a mystic, and no
form of rationalism or of moralism could claim him.
Even in childhood he had not only the poet's but the
mystic's eye for nature, and he reached out into fellowship with it "in a sense of the divine beauty and maj-
esty" that allured him.   It is interesting to note that
it was in the atmosphere of the college that he "was to
think himself out of his over-thinking, and discover how
far above reason is trust."   It was by following the
mystical tendency which was native to him that he was
led, when a tutor in college, to exclaim: "I am glad I
have a heart as well as a head; my heart wants the
Father; my heart wants the Son; my heart wants the
Holy Ghost — and one just as much as the other."   And
here was his anchorage ground and the stay of his
religious life.   He was not inclined to the work of the
ministry.   He had studied law and was preparing to
enter a law office at the West.   He had something the
same struggle with himself with respect to entering the
ministry that Robertson had.   With Robertson the difficulty was largely a sense of spiritual unfitness and the
attractions of a more active life that appealed to his
imagination.   With Bushnell it seems to have been the
attractions of the legal profession.   This was in line
with his questioning and debating habit of mind, with
his previous studies, and with his interest in public
affairs.   The influence of his religious difficulties may
also be seen here.   In either case it was a letter that
decided the question.   In the case of Robertson it was
a letter from a neighbor.   In the case of Bushnell it
was a letter from Yale College.   Both of these princely
men entered the ministry oppressed with a certain sense

N

of unfitness. It is a very noteworthy fact that many men, who have proved themselves to be, as we say, " born preachers," men who in all ways were fitted for the work of the ministry, men most devoutly conscientious and spiritually minded, and who have exerted a most powerful influence in their day, have had this shrinking sense of unfitness. The instances are numerous. It is noteworthy, too, that in every case — and in these two cases preëminently — they have risen superior to it, and the very shrinking seems to have been a condition of the greater power. Bushnell had something the same struggle with mental difficulties that Robertson had. It came earlier than Robertson's, but they met and vanquished their difficulties in much the same way. They met them on moral and religious, not on speculative, grounds. It was in 1829 that Bushnell came to Yale College as tutor, where he remained for two years. He was a member of the church, had been religiously trained at home, and for four years had lived under the Christian influences of the college, but he came a doubter. He was, as we have seen, constitutionally a questioner. His intense intellectual activity kept him perpetually agitating difficult questions. His religious inclinations, sympathies, and habits brought this activity to bear upon religious questions. His self-reliant nature led him to undertake the clearing up of these difficulties in his own way, and he took but few into his counsels. During his tutorship there was a religious awakening in the college. He was at first unmoved or seemed to be unmoved by it. At last, however, he began to see and feel his responsibility as a teacher, for he had, and knew that he had, a strong influence over his pupils.

The result was that he invited some of the young men whom he most strongly influenced to his room, and then and there he told them the position he proposed to take. "The result was overwhelming;" they all broke down together. It was the turn of the tide for him as for them, and it was an hour big with import for the pulpit of New England. Its most commanding religious genius and one of its brightest ornaments had been won. It is a profoundly interesting story. And it might be worth while to pause here and note the value of a strong moral basis for the Christian life. Bushnell was conscious of the processes of his religious develop-ment and he clearly traces the four stages of it.[1] The first is the period of natural religion, when he was led "socially and by force of the blind religious instinct of his nature." The second was the period of ethical religion, when he "was advanced into the clear moral light of Christ and of God, as related to the principle of rectitude." The third and fourth were the periods of spiritual religion. They are those periods in which Christ was revealed more perfectly and through him the nature and character of God as self-revealing love in sacrifice. At the time above mentioned, Bushnell was evidently emerging from the first into the second stage of his religious development. Here was a man who was held by his conscience. This seemingly was the chief thing that anchored him, till God in grace could do his larger and better work within him. It was good, strong anchorage ground and God held him to it and by it till with Fatherly grace He could pour fresh light and life into his large, open soul. This ethical element in his

---

[1] "Life and Letters," p. 445.

religion was always present. It tempered his emotions and had a strong influence upon his thinking and preaching. It was this ethical experience of religion largely that fitted him to deal with men who were troubled with intellectual difficulties. He lays down two rules that governed him and should govern every man. First, perfect honesty in the formation of opinions and principles of action. "It is one thing," he says, "to take a position and use reason to defend it, and another to use reason in selecting a position. In the one case reason obeys the will; in the other, will obeys the reason." Another rule is never to swerve in conduct from honest conviction. "Decide because there are reasons for deciding, and then act because the decision is made." By these rules he governed his whole life. Therefore, the rational and ethical elements in his religion are always present even though they may often appear under highly mystical forms. His sermons have the strong rational and moral ring of a man who is true to the core of life. Another suggestion from the early experience of Bushnell is the value of the religious revival of the right sort in the rescue of men from scepticism. He was not a believer in the revival method for the ordering of church life, and took strong ground against it, although he participated in revival movements and some of his most effective extemporaneous addresses were made in connection with them. And his own experiences demonstrate the power of a great religious awakening in a time of intellectual dislodgment to save sceptical men. This religious awakening influenced him by taking hold of his moral nature, and the influence is noted by him in an autobiographical reference in a sermon preached in Yale College Chapel entitled, "The Dissolving of Doubts."[1] Now, this experience lies back of and is seen in its indirect influence on his preaching. Of course it is not necessary that every man should have just this sort and measure of experience in order to become a helpful preacher, although in Bushnell's case it is questionable whether he would ever have reached his full measure of power without it. But in general it is pertinent to suggest that it will be a dark day for the church, if young men, who find themselves perplexed by the problems of religion and theology and have the manly sincerity to acknowledge their perplexity, are not to be treated with large-minded and large-hearted Christian generosity and tolerance, as Dr. Bushnell was not treated; a dark day if Christian thoughtfulness and studiousness and moral sincerity are to be discredited in a pulpit that originated in Christian liberty — and can justify its existence only on the basis of an ever enlarging Christian intelligence.

It was fifteen years after Bushnell entered the ministry before the mystical, which is the more distinctively spiritual element in his religious nature and experience, was fully manifested. It was then that he entered upon a higher type of religious life. And it is in connection with this experience that he gained, as he himself tells us, new conceptions of the significance of Christ, and this became the basis of new conceptions of the character of God. From this time on to the end his religious life was constantly deepened and enriched. He lived ever more completely as in the abiding presence of God.

[1] "Sermons on Living Subjects," Sermon IV.

This was the period when all the wealth of his mystical poetry and poetic mysticism developed.

The influence of his religious development is discoverable in the distinctively Christian quality of his preaching. It is an interesting and somewhat suggestive fact, that many of those modern preachers, who have been much perplexed in faith, and who perhaps have for a time been distrusted by many of their brethren and permanently distrusted by others, have after all been the men who have preached Christ with unusual power and persuasiveness, and have in reality been among the most helpful preachers of their time. The man who, like Bushnell, has struggled for his Christian faith, and has won his standing-ground as by the hardest, is likely to cherish it with a peculiar sense of preciousness. Such a man will be content with no by-play in his preaching. He must get back to the great central realities of a living Christianity. We find this in Bushnell's case. He always discusses what is of vital importance to the Christian life, and he always has a distinctively Christian theme. His sermons of the specifically evangelistic type have never been published; of his power, therefore, as a preacher to the heart and conscience with reference to immediate and decisive evangelistic results, we have probably no adequate impression from those in our possession. The published sermons are of the pastoral sort. Of these, consisting of three volumes, more than nine-tenths are from New Testament texts, and all of the sermons, even those from Old Testament texts are specifically Christian in substance and tone. They are sermons for edification, speaking to the Christian intelligence of the hearer and reaching the practical life through intelligence, but they also bear the trace of a heart strongly moved by the truths presented. We are told that his utterances at the Lord's Table, and at the services preparatory to it, were utterances of deep Christian feeling and that these were occasions of great uplifting. It was then that he poured out his whole heart upon his people. His prayers were remarkable for their depth of feeling, their spiritual power, their freedom and simplicity and directness. He prayed as one who lives in the conscious fellowship of God. The higher world was to him the real world, and he bathed himself in its atmosphere as in his native element. As with every great preacher from Paul, Augustine, and Luther down to the preachers of our own day, it was this mystical element in his religion that was predominant. He was a Christian pantheist and lived in God as in his own proper dwelling-place. The influence of his religious personality is seen in the intense reality of his preaching. Nothing second-hand nor conventional here. No saying of things because it is orthodox or proper or prudent to say them. The utterance is laden with moral and spiritual conviction. The ethical and spiritual life quickened his intellectual life, and inspired all his intellectual activities. It is a rare instance of the effect of profound religious experience in awakening the mental manhood. The late President Porter in his memorial address upon Dr. Bushnell directs attention to the influence of his religious life upon the development of his individuality. It awoke within him a new manhood. He suggests also that it gave great zeal and ardor in his work as a pastor, and fitted him, as

few men were fitted, to meet the mental difficulties of
thinking men with respect to the problems of religion
in his day.

III

BUSHNELL'S HOMILETIC THEOLOGY

It is not in line with the writer's purpose in this chapter that he should attempt an interpretation of Bushnell's
theology, — much less that he should attempt either a
criticism or a defence of it.   It is only necessary to consider it, as it relates itself to the substance, tone, and
method of his preaching.   Some things that might and
should be considered in this connection, have already
been touched upon in the previous discussion, but will
perhaps have additional consideration from a somewhat
different point of view.

That Dr. Bushnell had an adequate scientific conception of the problems of theology will doubtless generally
be questioned in our day by those who are most competent to speak upon the subject.   But that he had pretty
definite and positive conceptions of his own about these
problems, and especially about the great central themes
of Christian theology, which he sacredly cherished, will
of course be questioned by no one.   He was not careful to
put these conceptions into rigid forms of definition, nor
had he any faith in the permanent value of theological
definition, but he had pretty clear theological conceptions that interpreted to him the significance of his
religious feelings, convictions, and experiences.   His
theology lies back of his preaching, and no preacher of
his day preached his theology more fully than he.   He

had no theology, and would have none, that he could not preach. As a merely speculative interest it had but little value for him. He even denied that it had any value as a mere product of speculation, save for intellectual gymnastics. It was, in fact, the work of his life to relate theology to experience. This is perhaps the chief reason why his theology has made such an impression, and why men have been so much interested in it. It is not wholly their interest in the personality of the man, nor in his forceful and suggestive literary style. It is true that we are so strongly interested in the man, and in his cogent and attractive manner of expressing himself, that he easily solicits our interest in what he thinks and says. But it is a more vital and personal interest than that. His thinking interests us because it practically concerns us. It relates itself to our own needs, and to many of our best life experiences. His theology, therefore, may be called homiletic theology, — theology that can be preached because it touches the realities of human experience. Dr. Bushnell may have been subjective and measurably unscientific in his thinking, but that he was a brave, forceful, and useful religious thinker, almost every one in our day will acknowledge. To show that religion has significance and value independently of any particular form of intellectual experience of it, and to interpret it not in terms of speculative thought, but in harmony with the facts of ethical and spiritual experience, and to bring the facts of experience that lie below the speculative understanding to the task of verifying the claims of religion, and to show that as facts, they are thinkable and reasonable, — this was the work of his life. This, therefore, must be our starting-point in estimating his theology.

Under what combination of influences or by what particular agencies he was led to abandon his early naturalistic and rationalistic basis of thought upon the problems of religion, and " to think himself out of his overthinking," is not wholly clear. The development of this sceptical attitude toward the intellect as the organ of religious knowledge, was a somewhat occult process. Doubtless we may discover in it his own originality and independence of character. It is evidently connected with his own ethical and spiritual development, by virtue of which he is set in reaction against the dominance of the dogmatic and rationalistic method that overvalues and one-sidedly uses the processes of the speculative understanding in theological investigation. It probably stands connected, too, with those influences of early years, whatever they may have been, that led him to adopt the theory that language, as to its nature and function, is an organ of representative thought, rather than of exact scientific thought, and this is probably connected with the rapid development of the imaginative side of his nature. It should be remembered, however, as already intimated in another connection, that criticism of the then existing theory of religious knowledge had already begun to do its disintegrating work. It was already undermining the philosophical foundations of theology. Ethical and spiritual idealism was gaining ground. Bushnell knew this movement, although he did not know its sources, nor its full import. He saw more clearly, however, than most of the men of his time saw, and probably than any other man in the Christian min

istry in this country. He saw but little, yet it meant
much. The man of vision, who lives on the mountain
top, catches lights that flash from other distant and
higher peaks, which the men who linger in the valley
below do not catch ; and though it be but a flash, it is
light, and it has vast significance for the seer. Bushnell could not have been altogether ignorant of what
was going on without as well as within himself. He
was, indeed, an independent thinker, but he was not without dependence upon greater thinkers. Men of light
and leading like Coleridge pointed the way, and he was
quick to follow, for it seemed to him the homeward
path ; but he followed in a strikingly independent way.
He thought that some things which other men had
already excogitated, were his own independent product,
and they were in a sort. But he had company on his
new path, although he was unconscious of his companionship. In ruling out metaphysics and dialectics from
theology, and in finding anchorage in ethical and spiritual experience, Bushnell is doubtless a pioneer in this
country, and, as has been well shown, anticipates much
that has become a somewhat common possession, and that
bears the general name of Ritschlianism, which is itself
simply a not very remote product of Kant's and Schleiermacher's thinking ; for there is nothing here the raw
material of which is not furnished by those great thinkers. This conviction, which ultimately came to him as
a new discovery, that religion is the basis of all theology
and furnishes to reflection all of its materials, and that
it is to be interpreted according to its own facts as ethical and spiritual experience and not according to abstract,
speculative processes or theories, gives character and

direction to his own theology. In considering the change that passed upon his theology, in which his ethical, religious, and artistic development had so strong an influence, we should not forget the value to him of his earlier rationalistic experiences. As a rationalist and an adherent of the religion of nature he had learned two things: he had learned to think and he had learned to doubt, and the lesson was of great value to him in after years. In the processes of his early independent thinking he came to question the church doctrine of the Trinity, and, in connection with this, the traditional conceptions of the person of Christ. It was not the current theology but the current Christology that was first challenged. His conception of God modified as his conception of Christ modified. His theology was in an important sense a product of his Christology. The Christ that had been presented to him did not seem to satisfy either his intellectual or his spiritual or ethical needs. With great intellectual and moral courage he therefore sets about the task of finding a Christ who should satisfy his higher needs, and here the brave thinker, the honest doubter, and the devout believer join hands. He did not save his orthodoxy, but his religious faith was saved by attaching itself to a Christ that met all his spiritual needs, the living Christ who is the complete revealer of God, and in whom alone we can know God. With this new knowledge of Christ there comes, as already suggested, a new knowledge of God. God is known to him and interpreted not through speculative thought, as the young rationalist would know and interpret Him, but as He is discovered in Christ and as He becomes inwardly revealed through the sense of kinship with Him which

comes through fellowship with Christ. Thus God becomes a real, living, pervasive presence, the background
of the universe, immanent in all its processes, and discloses Himself in immediate knowledge. This is the
basis of his conception of the revelation of God. It
appears in his " Nature and the Supernatural." Nature
and man are parts of one great whole. The supernatural is constantly playing into and through the order
of the world, and this conditions his conception of the
miraculous. God is the ever present reality, and never
ceases to work as a supernatural force in the world of
nature and of humanity. In the modification of his
Christology his soteriology underwent a corresponding
modification. A new conception of the person of Christ
involves a new conception of the work of Christ. But
it also took connection with new conceptions of the
character of God and of His revelation to men. The
same general conception of the divine character and
revelation that appeared in " Nature and the Supernatural " appeared also in his " Vicarious Sacrifice." God
in Christ has come into living and abiding relation with
humanity, and sacrifice is but the necessary outcome and
disclosure of the fact that God is in the human race in
the order of redemptive love. This leads him to reject
what calls itself the forensic conception of the atonement, but not necessarily the truth that is expressed by
it, as he himself subsequently practically acknowledged
in the supplement to " Vicarious Sacrifice." But supreme stress is laid upon the moral force of the atonement. There is no Christ for us, that avails with God,
who is not the Christ within us as a living redemptive
force. And the Christ within us avails with God pre-

cisely because he does God's work within us and brings us into the likeness of God. No one has ever presented Christ more cogently or more attractively as a moral force in the very life of humanity, present there as a power of ever fresh renewal for the human race. And no one has ever grasped the conception of a race redemption more strongly or exhibited a loftier faith in the "outpopulating power of the Christian stock" in the future processes of human development. In all these theological changes we see the working of the strong, independent mind that is not afraid to challenge traditional beliefs, of the vigorous ethical nature, of the devout and pious heart, and of the mystical imagination. It yields for him a theology which he is sure can be preached and which he is equally sure men need to hear.

Bushnell's theology never appears in his preaching in technical form, nor is it here in a formal manner at all, but its substance is here pervasively. And it is this that secures for his preaching a fundamental and comprehensive character, so that it aggregates a great amount of strong and edifying thinking. He seizes the principles that underlie practical working Christian truth, and presents them in such way as makes them available for life. His preaching discloses his purpose to get theology at work. Hence the mingling of the didactic and the impressional, of the intellectual and the ethical and emotional, of the truth as we are to think it and the truth as we are to live it. It has solid thought and strong feeling and conviction. It deals with living men and with real needs, and not with things remote from common human life. It is full of insight, rationality, reality, and persuasiveness. It will live because it contains so much that men need to hear and want to hear when they know their real wants.

Bushnell's reaction against abstract and dogmatic theology and against speculative processes in dealing with the phenomena of religion, had for one of its results a higher estimate of religion as a historic reality. His views of revelation were modified. God has not revealed Himself in a body of doctrine but as a personal, living, historic presence. Consequently his supreme interest is in the historic Christ. To know Christ is of supreme importance, for to know Him aright is to know God aright. It is no wonder, therefore, that his Christology was the first thing to be set right. This secures a Christo-centric quality to his preaching. It attaches itself to the historic Christ. It is Christological rather than theological. It is theological only in the sense that the character of God as revealed in Christ is a subject that is often brought to our attention. He knows chiefly the God who is revealed in Christ, and his Christology is his theology. There are more discourses in the volume entitled " Sermons for the New Life " that have a theological centre than in the other two volumes. But these relate largely to the government and providence of God as seen in the light of Christ, and to the way in which we come to the knowledge of God. " Every Man's Life a Plan of God," " Spiritual Dislodgments," " The Spirit in Man," " The Hunger of the Soul," " The Reason of Faith," " The Capacity of Religion Extirpated by Disuse," are sermons that touch upon these questions, and they are among the strongest and most impressive sermons of

the volume. But most of the sermons in this and all
of those in the volume entitled " Christ and His Salvation," are distinctively Christological. As being based
on historic religion, it follows that his preaching is eminently Biblical. His themes are always taken directly
from Scriptural sources, sometimes by felicitous processes of suggestion, but they always have a fresh
Scriptural flavor. They contain the raw material of religious thought as it emerges in the fresh forms of the
Biblical records, and never in the formal doctrines of
the church. Citations of individual Scripture passages
are not abundant in his discussions. He deals rather
with the trend of Biblical teaching, and the Scriptures in
their bold outlines are brought to the support of his discussion. There is never lacking such Biblical defence
of the truth in hand, and not infrequently there is a
distinct Biblical topic giving the Biblical contribution to
his argument. As having for its chief object the presentation of Christ in his living relation with men, his
preaching does not to any considerable extent touch
upon his external or extra-world relations ; and as interpreting Christian truth with supreme reference to practical life, it is prevailingly anthropological and ethical.
It is not " the way of salvation " as objectively given in
Christ, so much as salvation as a power to subdue man,
and as a power, when appropriated by man, to bring
him into fellowship with God. It deals with the human
soul and has an interesting psychological quality, and it
deals with the individual soul, not with the collective
life of the church. There are but few sermons that
touch the church at all. They deal with the higher
ranges of human experience. The ethical quality of

his preaching, which, by examining the themes of his
sermons in all these volumes, especially the last entitled "Sermons on Living Subjects," will be found to
be predominant, is distinguished by the fact that the
principles of the ethical Christian life are discussed,
and hence that it takes a didactic or expository form.
One of the topics of the discussion also deals specifically with the practical moral bearings of the subject,
and the conclusion of the sermon rarely fails to use the
subject discussed for the realization of practical results.
By greatening the significance of the truth discussed,
he will all the more effectively impress it upon the
moral life of the hearer. And yet the entire sermon,
however didactic its character, has an elevated moral
tone and aim. It follows from all this tendency to interpret the truth to the Christian intelligence of men,
and then to apply it to practical edification, that he was
preëminently a pastoral, as distinguished from an evangelistic, preacher. The class of truths discussed and
his manner of discussing them are not in general adapted
to the evangelistic aim and method. The motives with
which he deals also are motives that centre in religion
largely as a present reality. His preaching is for edification rather than for conversion. The motives urged
are rational, ethical, and spiritual and presuppose an
already existing Christian mind. And yet there is a
tone about his preaching, there is a cogency in his
handling of great Christian themes, as is illustrated in
the sermon, "Christ Waiting to find Room," that is well
adapted to evangelistic impression, and such sermons
must strongly have influenced those who did not pro-
fess and call themselves Christians. Many of the truths

o

discussed touched the very heart of the Gospel, and they must have won the moral and spiritual allegiance of men. But this at least is true, that this sort of preaching which greatens to the mind and enforces upon the heart and conscience the august truths of redemptive religion, is the best possible ground-laying work for evangelistic preaching.

CHAPTER V

PHILLIPS BROOKS

I

THE CHRISTIAN HUMANIST

It is not difficult to fix at the outset upon what is most distinctive in the character of Phillips Brooks It is the breadth and wealth of his humanity Using the term in a somewhat comprehensive sense, he may be called the great Christian humanist of his generation. He came to the world with a great human soul, and he bent all his energies to the task of interpreting and ennobling human existence. The total impression left by his biography by Professor Allen is that we are here in contact with the most human of human beings, from whom nothing that belongs to humanity can ever be foreign ; and this impression heightens and intensifies all previous impressions from whatever source. To account for him, therefore, must be a matter of interest. Genius — and not the less, but even the more manifestly, religious genius — is always the gift of God. We cannot, therefore, reach of course the full secret of this superbly built specimen of New England manhood. But some things are clear, and perhaps the clearest thing, and the most noteworthy, is that he was the consummate flower of nine generations of cultured Puritan stock. We are

given to know that on the one side he inherited the
Puritan's high sense of the worth of humanity, his large
estimate of its possibilities of development, his recognition of the sacredness of the individual soul, and his
enthusiastic devotion to its highest welfare. This was
the spring of that lofty idealism that passed into an
optimism that was unmatched in his generation. On
the other side he inherited the Puritan's sturdy common
sense, his outlook upon the earthly and temporal interests of men, his aggressive and enterprising devotion
to all that belongs to the ordinary relations of life, his
love for the concrete and tangible, his aptitude for
practical affairs, and his personal reserve and pride of
individualism.   As we have seen in the case of Beecher
and of Bushnell, so in this princely product all that was
best in the Puritan stock, in its idealistic and practical
aspects, disclosed itself.   Without this Puritan "enthusiasm of humanity" no adequate estimate of this largely
and symmetrically moulded man is possible.   Such a
man could not be compressed within the limits of a
narrow provincial ecclesiasticism, nor twisted into line
with a narrow institutional Christianity.   He belonged
to the church catholic.   He had a sort of prenatal com-
mitment to that theory of the church which recognizes
its free self-development from within under the organizing agency of the Holy Spirit.   Yet he was not a
Congregationalist.   He was baptized in the Unitarian
Church.   He may have been influenced by the intellectual freedom and the moral earnestness of Unitarian-
ism.   But he was not a Unitarian.   It was the Episcopal
Church to which his parents migrated when he was four
years old that nurtured his subconscious and later con-

scious life. That this church was his early religious
home, and that the mark of its nurture was upon him,
will always stand to its honor. Its evangelical piety
left an indelible impress upon him, as that of the evangelical branch of the Anglican Church upon Newman
and Robertson. Let it be confessed that it is matter for
devout gratitude that he was nurtured in this evangelical school. Here was one of the sources of that religious love for men that enhanced so greatly his power
as a preacher. But it was too narrow a school for him,
as it was for Robertson. As by inheritance, as by his
bias to intellectual freedom, by the impulse of his large
intelligence, which induced him to get behind the historic forms into the larger catholic principles that lie
behind this school, and by all the preponderating influences that were brought to bear upon him from without, he was a Broad churchman. But he was a Broad
churchman only in so far as this section of the Episcopal Church represents the church of idealized and
redeemed humanity. And it may be justly claimed
that, despite the influences of these two schools, he
was not, in the larger estimate, a product of his church.
He belonged to a broader world than any branch of
it represented. He was not an ecclesiastic. He was
indeed loyal to his church, but he was free from many
of its limitations. He had but scant respect for an
institutional Christianity, that does not recognize the
kingdom of God as broader than the church. In a
reasonable manner and measure he accepted church
authority and found a way of justifying it, but he
regarded the dogma of apostolic authority as a fiction
He loved the church because it represented ideal human-

ity, and he found its strength, not in its alleged apostolic order, but in the saintly lives of its members, not in the sanctity of an office but in sanctity of character. Within the liturgical and canonical exactions of his church he exercised his freedom, in this sense of freedom, even rejoicing in these exactions. But a formal, institutional Christianity had no value for him, and he cared but little for the ecclesiastical assembly, having a greater relish for the associations of human friendship than for what seemed to him the pettiness of ecclesiastical debate. He freely affiliated with men who were beyond his ecclesiastical boundaries. All this because his impulses were humanistic rather than provincial or ecclesiastical, and because the church represented to him the sacredness of humanity.

Coming to his student life we find disclosed this same broad, human spirit. It is easy to read too much into the early studies and products of his student-life, but we may find much here that was really distinctive of the man. We find here a student isolated from the boyish sports of life, but eager for the knowledge of men and things, with a dislike for what is abstract and in the formal sense philosophical, with strong bias for history, biography, and literature, with pronounced literary tastes, and disclosing the same affluence, and the same descriptive qualities of style that characterized his maturer years. He belonged to the old Harvard of the humanities. In the preparatory school and in the college, he acquired a good working knowledge of the classics of which he availed himself in subsequent years. He worked rapidly and had time to follow his bent for literary culture. He exercised the freedom of self-direction, following his own impulses or instincts as he foraged among the college libraries, appropriating with avidity whatever came within his reach, laying the foundation for a better appreciation of the literature of his own day by mastering the best products of the literature of the eighteenth century. He always went below the surface of things and tried to get at their inner meaning. But he was as averse to metaphysics as Bushnell was, and as ignorant of philosophy in the formal sense of the word. He was, however, not indifferent to nor ignorant of those fundamental philosophical principles that are necessary to the interpretation of life, with which it was the necessity of his mind to grapple, and he absorbed them, as many another thoughtful man has done, from the intellectual atmosphere in which he lived or from the literature with which he became familiar. In later life he was something of a student of Lotze. It is evident that Lotze appealed to his humanistic tendencies. We may surmise that what interested him chiefly in his philosophy was the prominence of the ethical and æsthetic elements in it, the stress laid upon value-judgments in dealing with the problems of human existence, and its recognition of personality as belonging in its full significance only to the being of the Absolute. He was especially interested in the lives of great men, Luther, Cromwell, Mohammed. The larger the personality the greater his interest; this was his point of interest in Carlyle. His ready responsiveness to what is human found illustration in his college career. He is a product of the old Harvard curriculum. All the great masters in the modern pulpit have been products of a curriculum in which the humanities were supreme.

If the modern curriculum of elective miscellany can turn out a better product for the Christian pulpit, it will doubtless be seen and acknowledged in due time. Turning to the influences that ultimately determined his choice of the Christian ministry, we find them somewhat obscure. The consciousness of eminent oratorical gifts could hardly have been one of them, for in college he gave no promise of being an orator. Perhaps his freedom from a sceptical habit of mind may have been a favorable negative condition for the choice, for he was not a constitutional questioner like Bushnell. Ancestral and personal piety have, of course, their place in the problem. The ministry as a sphere for the expression of the didactic, ethical, and artistic impulse, which was strong within him, is to be considered. But in early years he had a dread of submission to authority, and cherished the impression that the ministry would limit the free development of his powers, and this, with the dread of provincialism, caused him to hesitate. And so one fancies that at last the decisive thing was the conviction that after all the ministry furnished the largest and completest sphere for his devotion to the interests of humanity. At any rate, we are assured by his biographer that he saw the mistake of his early estimate, and that he came to the ministry with the conviction that it was the best sphere for the exercise of all his powers; and he succeeded as but few have done in vindicating this judgment in his own ministry.

We find the same characteristic tendencies in his student life in the divinity school. Here he begins to grapple in dead earnest with the great problems of life. He was faithful to the curriculum, although a

critic of it, and seems to have received a strong impulse in the direction of intellectual freedom, at the
same time continuing subject to the same sort of evangelical influence which he had found in his home.
But he ranged widely and with amazing eagerness and
wealth of result beyond the courses. He led a somewhat retired life, and plunged into the heart of a broad
student world. As by a sort of divination, or hunger of
soul for what he needed, he seized upon what seemed
to belong to him. He apparently made no special
mark in technical theology, whether in dogmatics or
in exegesis. He was especially interested, however, in
historic theology. Of the church Fathers he was a
thorough student, and we may trace the influence of
Origen, and back of him of Philo and of other church
Fathers, in the allegorizing habit which characterized his
preaching. He always gets behind the historic form
of truth and seizes the back-lying principle suggested;
and this habit of looking at truth through the imagination, which was in part at least the result of his study
of the Fathers, was made very prominent in his
preaching throughout his entire career. But beyond
the theological studies he ranged more widely, probably, than any student of his day. He had a gift and
a love for the classics. He was especially interested
in the classical dramatists, from whom he was learning the Greek interpretation of life, and at the same
time he became absorbed in modern English literature.
It was in the theological school that he resumed an
earlier habit of keeping note-books, in which he gave
expression to thoughts which crowded upon him from
his reading and study, and which in the form of illus-

trations, hundreds of them, appeared later in his sermons. These notes, whether in the form of literary impressions or of personal thoughts, or of suggestions from others, are full of salient characteristics, — his catholicity of spirit, his largeness of outlook, his sense of the practical utility of truth, his enthusiasm for life, his reflective habit, his gift for personification. They disclose the results of his historical and literary studies. He is beginning with nature and man, with the earthly and human, not the divine. In all this and in his eager admiration for all that is humanly great and good we see the humanist. It is the intellectual development that impresses us, and there is almost nothing that indicates profound evangelical piety. He seems, indeed, carefully to exclude all such utterances of pious feeling as we find in the early letters and writings of Schleiermacher. We behold a large independent nature, that is subjecting itself to a great variety of human impressions, that is feeling its way out into human life, and is developing freely from within along lines that disclose his most distinctive impulses.

It was in line with his humanistic tendencies that he should love the city more than the country. He had an artist's eye for scenic beauty, and it quickened his poetic impulses; but he loved more the crowded city streets, where he could feel the rushing tides of human life. He was a born city pastor, and could sympathize with Thomas Guthrie, who criticised the sentiment, "God made the country, but man made the town." Providence, therefore, had in reserve for him a city parish, and it must be regarded as rare good fortune that his first pastoral contact with human life should have been among the people of the Philadelphia of years ago. Not less fortunate was it that his later, rather than his earlier, ministry was in Boston. Nor is it less a matter for thankfulness that he entered upon his ministry just before the opening of the Civil War. It was a time of great distress, but of mighty inspirations. Many a minister was lifted above himself by the greatness of that conflict, and found in it the incentive of all that was most effective in his ministry. It awakened and evoked the greatness of Phillips Brooks. It challenged all his noblest enthusiasm, all the passion of his patriotism, all his courage, all his freedom, all his philanthropy and humanity; and he threw himself into the conflict, preaching with a fiery patriotism, like that of Schleiermacher, that mightily stirred the souls of men, bringing to bear on the platform, no less than in the pulpit, all his vigor of thought, of imagination, of emotion, all his force of will, all the wealth of his most human experiences, stored up for just such use, upon the great questions that were in issue. Here was well laid the foundation for a great career. Later years may have witnessed in many respects more important service for the church and the world, but none were marked by greater intellectual brilliancy or more popular effectiveness than those years of the Philadelphia ministry that lie behind the twenty-two years of the greater Boston ministry. It was a proof of his clear discernment, as well as in accord with his deepening ethical and religious experiences, and in line with all his best human impulses, that he should have recognized the changed conditions of the ministerial problem when he went to Boston. In Philadelphia he was called to deal more largely with associate life, and to grapple with great public problems. In Boston, where the problems of religious thought were more exigent, he recognized himself as summoned to deal more specifi-cally with individual life, to become the interpreter of life to the individual soul. And here we see the same large humanity placed at the service of men who are struggling with the contradictions and confusions and doubts of human life. It was in this Boston ministry, a ministry of great power in ennobling men's concep-tions of the world and of life, that he proved himself to be the great pastoral preacher of his age. Here it was his choice vocation to interpret men to themselves, to tell them things about themselves they did not know, to explain things of which they were only half conscious, to ennoble them in their own eyes, to humble them in their imperfections and sins, to interpret the humanity of Christ and the divinity that is possible for man. Everywhere and always it is the same great soul, clear and broad in its intellectual apprehensions, sturdy in its moral devotions, tender in its human sympathies, that is giving itself, with increasing sense of the fellowship of God and of His Christ, to the higher interests of men. In his intercourse with friends we see increasingly the large- and tender-heartedness of the man. His letters have not the moral sobriety of Bushnell's nor the intellectual brilliancy of Robertson's. But in their ardent affectionateness they remind us somewhat of Schleiermacher's. In all his relations with his friends we note an increasing hunger of heart for human companionship. It was an increasingly lonely life, and he lived more and more in the affections of his friends.

One may venture the suggestion, and indeed the biography leaves the impression, that, while he never felt the vocation to a celibate life, as Newman tells us he did from the age of fifteen years, it may have been the increasing conviction that he was called to be the shepherd of many souls, and that in this calling he belonged too exclusively to the many, to sanction the venture to limit his affections by domestic life.

In his relations with sister churches beyond the borders of his own communion; in his interest in the problems of education, of politics, of reform, of philanthropic enterprise; in his conception of religion, of theology, and of the church and the ministry; in his literary culture; in the anthropological influences that disclose themselves in his literary style, notably in his genius for rhetorical personification, in which it seems to be a necessity to put a human soul into the objects of his thought, — one finds the trace of the great Christian humanist, the great human friend, the great human churchman. His religion is human, his theology is human, and it becomes the better divinity because it embodies what is human in the heart of God. It is this large humanity, touched by the power of Christ, cherished and enriched by fellowship with Him, that contains in large measure the secret of his power over men.

This gives us our point of view. In furthering our investigation it is necessary to go into a closer analysis of his personality, his theology, and his preaching. We will consider, then, the man, the message, and the method.

II

THE HARMONIOUS PERSONALITY

The significance of a harmoniously developed, symmetrically trained, and religiously consecrated personality for the work of the preacher no one has ever
discussed more forcibly or persuasively, or perhaps
realized and illustrated in experience more effectively,
than Phillips Brooks. It is the personal element in
his preaching that is largely the secret of its power.
Its value is not so much in its contribution to our
knowledge of the great truths of religion, not so much
in the originality of his thinking or in the weight of his
thought, as in his personal appropriation of Christian
truth and in his interpretation and enforcement of it
as the vital experience of a great soul. It is the self-
revealing, manly sincerity of it, its downrightness and
straightoutness, its fervid intensity of conviction, its
sympathetic identification with the hearers' needs, its
interpretation of what is most human that awakens
the slumbering echoes of the soul, its outpouring of the
vast wealth of his inner life, — it is this that makes the
unfailing impression. In personal intercourse he exhibited a Puritan reserve that seemed to warn men
back from the sanctuary of his inner life. In the private records of his growing intellectual life there is but
little that is self-revealing save the ferment of an awakened mind. But the preaching is always self-revealing.
Here we find the whole man. The place where men
find God is the place, he thinks, where they should
find the preacher too; and in finding him in the ful-

ness of his self-disclosure, they may the more readily find God.

What most impresses us in his personality is the harmonious blending of all its elements. Professor Allen has reminded us of the profound impression which the character of Lincoln made upon him. What was true in Brooks's estimate of Lincoln's character was eminently true, he thinks, of Brooks himself. It was the fusing of the processes of a great mind with the emotions of a great heart, and the energies of a strong, steadfast will that seemed, as a result, to leave no salient points of greatness. It was as if Brooks found a sort of self-interpretation in Lincoln. We are also reminded of his estimate of the character of Christ, in whom the qualities are so blended that no one thing is obtrusively prominent, or rather so prominent is the condescension, which is the negation of all obtrusiveness, that all other elements of greatness are dwarfed in the apprehension of common men. So closely identified are the intellectual and ethical with the spiritual elements of His personality, that men do not think of Him as the master mind that is subduing the intelligence of the proud modern world, or as the master will that is bringing every knee to bow to Him. And one would think it almost a profanation to speak of Christ as the great Plato or the great Alexander of the kingdom of God. He is not so much the world's great religious thinker and organizer as the compassionate, comforting man of sorrows. And yet it is precisely the great intelligence and the strong, steadfast will that give adequate significance to the consecrated heart. Something the like may be said of the personality of Phillips Brooks himself.

There is, indeed, a gradual and progressive development of the elements of his personality. They of
course do not all emerge simultaneously into manifestation or blend in unity at the outset. The early period
has been regarded as characteristically the period of
mental development. The early products of his reflection disclose the bent of his mind. Ethical and spiritual
qualities are less prominent. There is no such expression of the moral striving of the soul or of intense
religious feeling as we find in the youthful Schleiermacher. He begins with his beloved human world and
life, that speak to him with all their wondrous, fascinating
suggestiveness, and he will sound their depths, if may
be, with the plummet of his intelligence. His mind is
going forth in its eager quest to find the meaning of their
wondrous realities, and in his search he comes back
again, as from the vantage-ground of new experiences,
to the God and Father of his childhood days and to
the Christ of his early love and devotion ; and already,
before he enters upon his sacred calling, he has come to
a fresh sense of the meaning of life, a new recognition
of the meaning of Christ for his own life and for all
human life. And this awakening to the greatness of
Christ as the interpreter of God and the interpreter of
all life, and this new conviction that all truth and all life
should be made consecrate to Christ, left their impress
upon his entire ministry. If in the early period the
mental development was prominent, as is generally the
case, and in the mid period the ethical, in the completion and crown of his development we have the outpouring of the great heart, whose tides of emotion have
been gathering volume from the first and all through

the experiences of his life. And so from the first we see the unifying process. The thinker is the man of action, and the shepherd's heart inspires all noblest thought and achievement in his devotion to the welfare of men.

The physical equipment was symbol of his soul; and the rush of his speech was typical of those mental, moral, and spiritual energies that were fused into unity and came forth in a stream of fiery intensity. The physical stature and proportions, towering and sym-metrical; the manly attitude, poise, and bearing, free and unconscious in its grace ; the large, dark eyes, mirth-ful, yet serious, speechful of all moods of inner intensity ; the well-set, expressive lips ; the radiant countenance ; the full, strong voice, not well managed, but full of feel-ing and of force, — all this was fit organ for the inner manhood that struggled to put itself forth in advocacy of the truth he had appropriated and assimilated in the love of man and for the uplifting of his life.

In mental as in physical stature he was large and well-proportioned, and in mental movement facile and forceful. The quality and measure of his productive-ness bear witness to the wealth of his intellectual life. The notes that represent his mental development at the age of nineteen or twenty are remarkable for their insight, inventiveness, and maturity, and already disclose the man of genius. He had not the intellectual strength of Bushnell, nor the intellectual penetration of Robert-son, nor the subtlety of Newman, nor the analytic skill of Mozley, nor the dogmatic forcefulness of Liddon ; but in intellectual inventiveness and productiveness he was almost the match of Beecher. He was not a close

P

but a broad thinker.   In technical Biblical knowledge he had no large equipment, but he was a most ingenious and suggestive interpreter.   He made but little use of logical processes in his discussion, but he knew the laws of thought and ordered his own harmoniously.   He disliked abstract thought, but he had keen insight into the inner relations of religious truth.   He had the Puritan common sense that chastened his idealism and tempered the fervors of his emotion.   He managed the affairs of his great parish with discretion, was a wise and effective bishop, and would have been called, had he consented, to leadership in the administration of two great universities.   He had the impulse and the gifts of the teacher, and might have held the chair of church history or of Christian ethics.   He was not without critical acumen, but he had in preponderance the creative imagination of the true preacher, and preferred the processes of mental suggestion to those of mental elaboration.   What distinguishes his mental movement, therefore, is the dominance of the imagination, and because of the strength of it he early disclosed his inclination for the literary and poetical, rather than the scientific or philosophical, interpretation of life.   His lines of mental movement do not lie in the realm of causality or of contiguity in thought, but rather of consanguinity.   It was the analogical rather than the logical mind, the mind that looks at things in their resemblances, that readily discerns family likenesses. Following the lines of mental association, occasionally the line of causality or of contiguity of thought, but much more frequently, indeed almost always, the lines of resemblance, he steers for the fundamental fact or principle that underlies the various realms of reality or of experience upon which he touches and that holds them all in the unity of a controlling law. There is a poetic or semi-poetic, as well as a scientific and philosophical, use of the imagination. Science and philosophy group the materials or the phenomena with which they deal under family likenesses; they classify them under general laws. Generalization of a legitimate sort in any sphere is in fact, though it may not be in name, a process that corresponds to the method of science and philosophy. Any process that lays hold of the truth in its fundamental principles and wide-reaching family relations may be called in a limited sense a process that has philosophical value. Even in the generalizations of science and philosophy the use of the imagination is necessary, but of course they are based upon critical judgment. The preacher uses the imagination more fully and freely in laying hold of the fundamental and regulative principles of human life and experience and of the great facts and truths of revelation. This was the method of Phillips Brooks. Hence he was an interpreter. For what is the interpretation of life or of revelation, but the classification and generalization of facts, truths, or experiences, the gathering of what is individual under some general principle or law? The significance of any experience, truth, or fact is known only by its family resemblances. Phillips Brooks's habit of dealing with general religious principles was a sort of philosophic process applied to the teaching of religion. His prevailing didactic method was analogy. If sometimes in the imaginative suggestiveness of his treatment of the subject in discussion he threatens to lead us too far afield

into the realm of fancy and of sentiment, his strong
common sense, his balanced judgment, and his literary
sanity are pretty sure to rescue him, and, although his
thought may be highly poetical in its remote resemblances, it is still marked by a certain moral sobriety
and manly strength that appeal to the intelligence of
the hearer. Hence he may be called, even in an
eminent degree, a didactic preacher. In England he
was regarded as eminently such, and he always won a
hearing from the educated and cultivated classes. He
never debated, never argued his subject, and never
appealed to external authority. If he discusses a doctrine like that of the Trinity, it is not the church form
of the doctrine that engages him. It is his purpose
rather to detach the fundamental principle that contains
the life of the truth, and to show that it meets our
human needs and finds vindication in our life experiences. His didactic methods are among the most
interesting peculiarities of his preaching.

Considering the prominence of the imaginative element in his equipment, there are not wanting those who
estimate his artistic qualities as most characteristic. His
æsthetic endowment and outfit were certainly notable.
But a close analysis of his character will always disclose a preponderance of the ethical over the æsthetic.
In his apprehension and regard, beauty is always subordinate. But he well understood, and he well realized
in the harmonious blending of his own faculties, the
close alliance of the ethical and æsthetic. His own
lofty idealism was at once ethical and æsthetic. It
embraced the lofty conception of a moral good and a
moral beauty that are blended in inseparable unity.

His conceptions of God, of Christ, of humanity, of the individual soul, are profoundly ethical, but they are strongly æsthetic, for they embody conceptions of supreme beauty. For him the Supreme Being must be the realization of a moral perfection that is absolute moral beauty. His world-view is moral and æsthetic. Good is the source, good is the goal, and good is the process of all things; and this supreme good is the divine order and beauty of a universe that is sublimest art. All life, in its ideal reality, and it was chiefly in its ideal reality that he would behold it, is supremely true, supremely good, and supremely glorious. Therefore he loved life, like a Greek, as a thing of beauty. It was the necessity of his nature to live in the higher interpretations of life, to idealize the universe, because he believed that at heart the true, the good, and the beautiful are one. This artistic quality in his nature disclosed itself in his tendency to personify nature under forms of poetic beauty. He was himself no insignificant poet, and he had the quick artistic sense for all its products. He gave but little heed to form in his own poetic products; but his literary form in the sermon, which he treated as an instrument whose supreme value is in the end to be realized, will, by its affluence, grace, force, and spontaneity, perpetuate his influence. He was a competent critic of architecture, and Trinity church in Boston is in part the witness for his artistic sense.

His moral qualities are given in the bent of his nature, but they were fruitfully nurtured by his profound reverence for the moral significance of life. For him all life, conscious or unconscious, must have a moral goal, and all existence is known only in its end. Even the existence of God has an end beyond itself and is supremely moral. Will is the centre of the divine, as of all, personality, and the moral end of God's existence is to "fulfil himself" in the revelation of His holy perfections to His rational creation. The moral significance of Christ's existence on earth and in the heavenly world is to complete the realization of the ideal of the divine in man, to disclose what is human in God, and to complete the work of restoring kinship between God and man. The end of all human existence is the realization of the ideal of moral completeness. With Goethe he held that the end of life is to live in the realm of the true, the good, and the complete. The material universe itself, as the revelation of God, can have only a moral goal. All its forces are pushing it on to the "far-off divine event," and the event as "divine" can only be the good. ❡ It is the glory of God to reveal his fatherhood. It is the glory of Christ to reveal the kinship of the divine and the human. It is the glory of man to disclose his sonship with God. It is the glory of the universe to complete itself as the kingdom of God. It was this world and life view that nurtured his moral manhood and furthered most fruitfully his moral development. This in large measure accounts for the supreme stress he lays upon personality, and his aversion to all that is merely abstract and impersonal. His world must be alive with personality, for this only realizes the moral ideal of existence. Hence his reverence for personal freedom. It is the moral glory of man, as of God, that he is free, for only in freedom can he realize the moral ends of his existence; therefore he guarded most sacredly his own freedom. That he was accustomed to

hedge himself about with a reserve that seemed to warn
men against intrusion seemed a half-conscious recognition of the sacred rights of his personality. He reacted
most strenuously against the fatalism of degenerate
modern life, for it fails to recognize moral freedom as
the chief glory of manhood. It is this conception of
manhood that accentuates his love of intellectual freedom, his jealousy of all encroachments of arbitrary
authority, and his submission to rational and moral authority as the condition of the realization of a larger and
truer freedom, and the more complete accomplishment
of the moral ends of existence. Tolerance is with him
only a recognition of the freedom of the soul in the
realization of its moral and intellectual tasks. In order
to accomplish the moral ends of his own existence he
must be free, and other men within their own spheres
must be equally free, hence also his reverence for the
truth as a moral good and as tributary to the moral ends
of life. Truth is not an end, but an instrument. It has
moral worth; it is tributary to life. Life is the end;
truth is the means for realizing that end. Doctrine has
value only as it builds character and regulates conduct.
To be is the supreme end; to know, a subordinate end.
Hence the speculative intellect can never become an
adequate organ of knowledge. Knowledge is a virtue
only as it relates itself to the will, hence the increasing
emphasis put by him upon the moral factor in men's
lives and upon the religion of obedience. Knowledge,
sentiment, imagination, feeling, all are subordinate to
the obedient will. Not less earnestly, but more wisely,
than Newman did he proclaim, and with increasing
urgency, that it is the end and the glory of man's

existence to know and to do the will of God.   Because
of this moral conception of life was he an optimist.   The
freedom, the spontaneity, the reality, the cheerfulness,
joyfulness, exuberant hopefulness, and resistless enthusiasm of his spirit were only in part the gift of nature.
It was his moral optimism that kept him, as it kept
Schleiermacher, in perpetual youth.   He knew the dark
side of life, but, like Emerson, he refused to linger with
it.   He must find an ideal world behind the dark and
sinful realities of life, and so bright was it in his vision
that it irradiated the darkness and the sin, and they were
lost in the "glory that excelleth."   It was this steady
uplift of soul that strengthened his will and held him
steadfast to his purpose to give himself to the ennobling
and enriching of the lives of men.   Hence the practical
character of his preaching; truth for the sake of life;
life for the sake of realizing the supreme moral ends of
existence.   The whole substance, the entire tone and diction, of his preaching bear the mark of this optimistic
view of life and of his supreme purpose to help men
interpret their lives aright, and to realize the final purpose of their existence.

Behind his ethical optimism was his spiritual idealism;
behind his faith in the good and his devotion to its ends,
his faith in God and fellowship with Him; behind his
ethical virtues, his religious virtues; behind the moral
ideal of life, the religious ideal.   His world was the
world of spirit.   God, as the ground of all things, the pervasive presence in all things, and the goal of all things,
is the supreme reality.   That vision of soul, that sense
of the invisible and eternal, we call faith, was one of his
choicest gifts, and it was nourished by all the choicest

sources of his culture, and all the great experiences of
his life. The faith faculty enlarged, and he lived ever
more increasingly "as seeing Him who is invisible."
And the faith that is vision is also the faith that trusts
and lives in fellowship with its object. It was this that
was the spring of all his choicest sympathies, not his
contact with humanity, not the literature that fertilizes
a great human heart, but a sense of moral alliance with
God, a sense of identification with Him. The great
human heart, turned Godward in the consciousness of
oneness with Him, found its message, and made him
prophetic in his utterance. Then, as from the fountain
of eternal inspiration, it turned itself manward and
uttered itself forth with a power of conviction and per-
suasion and comfort and inspiration that was unmatched
by the preachers of his generation.

III

THE HOPE-BEARING MESSAGE

When we speak of a preacher's message, we commonly have in mind the truth he interprets and advocates with such sympathetic earnestness and strength
of moral conviction that it seems somehow to suggest
that the man has a special call from God to utter it.
It presupposes such appropriation and assimilation of
the truth by the preacher that it becomes a personal,
mental, moral, and spiritual possession. It also presupposes such insight into the needs of one's fellow-
men, such devotion to their higher welfare, and so
strong an inward didactic and ethical impulse, that he is

constrained, as by a sort of divine compulsion, to communicate the truth to them.   This is substantially what we mean when we say that the truth is given as a message, and that the preacher is summoned as a messenger to proclaim it.   And this is what we call the prophetic gift.   It does not fully realize all that is contained in the Biblical conception.   But this is what we mean by the modern prophet.   The prophet is the man who is conscious of an inner constraint so to communicate the truth that it shall be a compelling power in the souls and lives of other men.   All religious truth, therefore, that is really preached becomes a message.   But it is only the truth that is charged with the energy of personal life, and that aims at the reproduction of itself in the personal life of other men, that, for the preacher, has the character of a message.   From this point of view it may be said of no modern preacher more truly or more worthily than of Phillips Brooks, that the truth he brought was a message, and of none may it be said more appropriately than of him that he had the prophetic gift.   Phillips Brooks did not have much to say about his message, and did not claim the consciousness of a supernatural call to be the messenger of God to men.   Such a claim would doubtless have seemed to him pretentious and unreal.   To him the divine call was no ghostly and exceptional thing, remote from the genuine experiences of common human life.   To him it was the simplest and most natural thing in the world that he should feel constrained to tell men what had become so mighty a force in his own soul.   He held that it is, in fact, the vocation of every man, each in his own way, if he only knew it, to bear witness to the truth that is in him and that not to know this as life's vocation is a deplorable ignorance, and that not to actualize it is a deplorable wrong. All men should feel impelled to communicate the grace they have received. All men should have a message for their fellows. Every man in whose heart is the apostolic message and who has the gift and the grace to give it to others is in apostolic succession. This man of prophetic and apostolic gift and grace handled the truth that was in him as if it were his message; and this consciousness of a mighty inner constraint to bring the truth to men, as if he were bringing a message, contained implicitly the presupposition that his truth was a gift from God for the sake of his fellow-men, and that he was called to be God's messenger.

But there was a good deal of truth held by him that did not appear in his message. He knew more theology than appeared in his preaching. The general public has but little knowledge of his teaching of religion in the class room. One fancies that he may have followed in the class room very nearly the same general method that he followed in the pulpit; and yet he would doubtless recognize the necessity of a more careful exposition of the forms in which the theology of his church was expressed, and of vindicating the truth thus expressed in the court of Christian intelligence. His work in the class room, therefore, may have been in some respects different from his work in the pulpit, for teaching is not preaching. But it is evident enough that the stock of his preaching was conditioned by the form and measure of his own experience of the truth. For him experience was primarily and practically the norm of all truth that may be presented to men in the form of a message. In the pulpit he therefore interpreted only what he could advocate as essential to religious experience and as regulative of religious life. For preaching must be a message of moral conviction and of spiritual sympathy. Hence his preaching dealt with the great practical realities of Christianity. They appeared in a great variety of forms, and with great wealth of illustration; but they were the ever recurring, simple, fundamental realities of a Christianity that is life. This conception of the preacher's vocation conditioned his attitude toward the theology of his church. It was a conviction that took possession of him in the early years of professional study, and constantly strengthened in the later years of professional life, that it is not the preacher's function to assume on the one side the attitude of the critic, nor on the other side the attitude of the advocate of the theology of the church. Apparently the theology of the evangelical school in which he was educated never had a very strong hold of his intellectual life. His own intellectual virility and independence gradually reacted against it; and the encouragement he must have received from his large-minded teacher of dogmatics in the divinity course set him forward doubtless still more determinately in the path of intellectual freedom. However this may be, it is clear enough that intellectual independence was a necessity for him. And it is a matter for profound gratitude that the evangelical piety in which he was nurtured outlived the disintegration of the evangelical theology in which he had been educated, and that, as in the cases of Schleiermacher, Robertson, Beecher, and

Bushnell, it remained to the end. But if he must assume an independent attitude toward the theology of his church, he must not become its critic. The attitude of the preacher is first of all the attitude of the interpreter, and then that of the advocate, of such back-lying truths as interpretation finds useful for practical life. It is the preacher's calling neither to throw doubt upon the theological formularies of the church, nor to defend them as a theological partisan. He was, therefore, neither a radical iconoclast nor a dogmatic confessionalist. The creeds of the church are not necessarily inerrant, and are not to be accepted as final statements of the theology of the church, nor are they to be set aside as valueless for Christian faith and life. He held stoutly to the Protestant position of the right of the individual soul, and especially of the right of the teacher of religion to validate the truth in experience, and to determine how far the symbols of the church express the truth that is essential to the soul's well-being. But Professor Allen has directed attention to the fact that, notwithstanding his passionate love of intellectual freedom, he was, in the process of his religious development, increasingly convinced that "sympathy," not "liberty," is the word that most adequately suggests the proper attitude of the Christian preacher, for it "expresses the chord that binds the human race."[1] He knew that the individual Christian consciousness is largely a product of the historic consciousness of the church. If it is possible for the individual soul in its freedom to enlarge the boundaries of the truth it has received from tradition, it is not the less true that the collective consciousness of

[1] "Biography," Vol. II, p. 486.

the church lays the foundation for that enlargement.
Hence his position that the creeds of the church contain
a substantial body of truth, which it is the preacher's
calling, neither on the one hand to challenge or deny,
nor on the other hand unconditionally to defend, but
rather to interpret, and by thus intelligently and sympa-
thetically interpreting, to detach the inner substance of
the great truths which contain that message which becomes tributary to the continuous development of the
life of the church. This position, which he seems to have
reached with relative independence of others, reminds
us of Robertson, and is in general the Broad churchman's
position. It has its difficulties. It doubtless results in
a certain vagueness of theological definition and even
of conception, and it taxes the skill and sometimes the
candor of the preacher. But it is difficult to see how
otherwise the interests of tradition and of freedom can
be conserved, or, in a word, how the collective and the
individual Christian consciousness can be harmonized.

To interpret the theological views of Phillips Brooks,
as they appear in his preaching, is not an altogether
easy task. They, of course, do not appear in scientific
form and they bear the mark of his exuberant rhetoric.
They are characterized by the vagueness and indeter-
minateness that are doubtless admissible in a rhetorical
and popular presentation of the truth, but which are,
nevertheless, sometimes tantalizingly elusive. But the
task is not an impossible one, although confessedly the
effort may seem inadequate.

In stating some of the chief aspects of his message,
let us begin with his conception of religion. Religion
is human. It is the most human thing in man, for it has

its indestructible source in his spirit, which is the most distinctive characteristic of his manhood. Its incentives are indeed from without, but its substance, its essence, is within. It may be evoked from within; it cannot be brought from without. It may be stimulated; it cannot be created. It belongs to man as man, and he is normal, he is truly human, only in so far as he is religious. The irreligious man is by reason of his irreligion so much the less a man. Nothing therefore is added to the man when he becomes religious. It is no ghostly experience, but as truly human as the most familiar experience of the soul. In it the soul only appropriates its own best ideal, and enters upon the harmonious development of all its powers. This is not new. It is, in fact, one of the commonplaces of the religious intelligence of our time. But it is the rediscovery of an anthropology and a theology that are, after all, not so very old. It is a truth that demands constant emphasis, and no modern preacher has more persuasively enforced it or more intelligently interpreted it than Phillips Brooks. He seems to have no definite psychology of religion, and gives no scientific definition of it, nor is it necessary that he should do so, for his representations are worth more than definitions. Religion is a talent, a faculty or combination of faculties of the soul, a state of consciousness, an activity, a relation or complex of relations of the soul, but what it is and how to locate it is not always easy. The locality varies. It is now here, now there. It is now this, now that. It is not primarily thought, although religion cannot be divorced from thought. It is not in the imagination primarily, although the imagination becomes one of its most important organs. Sometimes it appears in the conscience, sometimes in the feelings and affections, and it is never fully at home outside the will. But for the most part religion is not located at all. It is not quite correct to speak of one part of a man's nature as being religious and another part as unreligious or non-religious. Man is religious in the totality of his nature. There is an intellectual element in religion. We are commanded to "love God with all the mind." He had thorough respect for the intellectual factor in religion and laid much stress upon it. There is an æsthetic element in it which realizes itself in artistic form. Religion is the soul turning in all its functionings toward the personal Invisible and Eternal. And as religion had better not be located within, so it had better not be located without. Of course he would freely acknowledge that determinate times and places and persons and events and experiences have a specific religious significance. Not, however, because they hold religion as a monopoly, but because they are associated with religion as a specific interest. But the prevailing representation is that, in its true conception, all life is religious. In its true conception the universe is the temple of religion. "Religion," he says, "is nothing in the world but the highest conception of life." All life, all time, place, person, events, experiences, are in their ideal significance religious. The profane, the sinful, is just the failure to realize this significance. Here we have the Broad churchman, and such we may almost say Phillips Brooks was constitutionally. He reacted vigorously against the localizing of religion, and had no sympathy with High Church religious provincialism. Of course he could

not and would not deny that God can and does reveal
Himself at one time, or in one place or person or event
or experience more fully than in another.   Surely he
would not deny that religious experiences may be conditioned by local and temporal associations, or that when
so conditioned religion becomes specific.   But it was
religion as a universal interest that dominated his conception, and his appeal to men, that they consecrate the
whole soul and body with all their powers, and the
whole life with all its activities, to God and to His kingdom, was one of great worth and power.   But he might
well perhaps have qualified his message sometimes, and
have recognized more fully the pedagogic significance
of religion as a specific interest ; and if he had been, like
Robertson, as close and discriminating as he was broad
in his thinking, he very likely would have done so.

As in his conception the soul in the totality of its powers is religious, so the soul in the totality of its activities becomes the organ of religious knowledge.   And
here we have the modern psychologist, and the modern
advocate of the religion of experience as contrasted
with the religion of authority.   It is this rich and fruitful conception of religion that contributes so much to
the message which reveals men to themselves and
awakens their manhood to its higher possibilities.

As being truly human, religion therefore is natural.
The unnatural thing is irreligion.   He who has not come
to the knowledge of himself as religious is abnormal.
Even what we call the supernatural element in religion
is natural, in so far and in as much as it harmonizes
with the constitution of the soul.   When God comes to
awaken the soul and to evoke its latent religious sus-

Q

ceptibilities and capacities he does it no violence.   The
response of the soul is as natural as the response of
nature to light or air, and failure to respond is abnormal.

And as being human and natural, religion is simple.
The fundamental things are always simple.   All the
primal activities of the soul are simple, and religion
belongs to these primal and normal activities.   What is
more simple, or more human and natural, than love or
trust or reverence or obedience?   These are the primal
and the simple activities of the soul, and they contain
the elements of religion.   Turned Godward and Christ-
ward, they are religion.

Although religion is subjective in its elements, it is
not in its development a purely human product.   As an
endowment, it is human ; as an experience, it is divine.
As bedded in our nature, it is God's gift through creation ; as dependent on Him for its incentive and for its
full content, it is His gift through grace.   We do not
first know Him ; He first knows us.   In establishing our
relations, the initiative is with Him.   He first comes to
us, He first loves us, and in the language of Dr. Bushnell, " Loving God is but letting God love us."   No Calvinist ever more strenuously insisted than he did upon
the " priority of God."   A purely self-wrought religion
is for him a contradiction.   At best it would be only a
form of ethics.   Most urgently does he proclaim the
freedom of man and defend the humanness and naturalness of religion as a truth that ever needs enforcement ;
but it is, in fact, the burden of his message that religion
is realized as a mutual, conscious relation between God
and man only because God has the initiative in its
realization.   Religion on man's part is a relation of

conscious dependence on God, but it is realized only
because God makes Himself known as a creative and
sustaining energy.   If religion is realized as a relation
of conscious subjection, it is because God makes Himself known as a moral authority.   If it is realized as a
relation of moral alliance, it is because God makes Himself known in loving sympathy as the Father of spirits.
In a word, only because God moves upon the soul in the
processes of His self-communication do we ever come
to the knowledge of our relation with Him which is the
experience of religion.   Hence while all men are constitutionally religious, they are experimentally such only as
they are recipients of the self-revealing grace of God.
Hence revelation and religion are inseparable.   And as
there is no "natural religion" save in the sense that
all religion is natural, so there is no "revealed religion"
save in the sense that all religion is revealed.   The distinction therefore between a certain type of religion that
may be called "natural" and another type that may be
called "revealed" is an unreal distinction.   All religion
is at once natural and supernatural, natural in endowment, supernatural in incentive ; and the distinction between religions is in the sort and measure of revelation
they embody.

This revelation of God which is the inspiration of
religion is the revelation of His personality, of Himself.
Revelation is not truth and religion is not knowledge.
Revelation is a divine activity upon the soul that discloses the presence of God, and religion is a resulting
life.   But such a self-communication of God involves
the disclosure of truth, and the very idea of God in its
Christian form is a product of revelation.   Hence the

preacher deals with a given content of truth.   This
truth involves conceptions and facts about God.   God
is not only immediately self-revealed to the individual
soul, He also comes mediately to the soul through the
religious consciousness of others — through a community
consciousness ; and this religious consciousness of the
race is a product of divine revelation in all ages.   The
Bible is a record of this self-revelation of God in other
ages to a certain favored section of the race.   The highest form of this revelation is through the historic Christ.
The Bible therefore is preëminently the preacher's book.
He laid great stress upon the personal factor in preaching, but he laid proportionate stress upon the factor of
truth which is fixed for us in Scripture.   Hence he was
himself a Biblical preacher, not in the same way that
Robertson was, nor as Bushnell was, but not less than
either in the fibre and tone of his preaching.   He
appeals to the native intelligence of men, but the stock
of his preaching is not rationalizing reflection.   He
appeals to the human conscience, but the appeal is not
a rationalistic moralizing.   He speaks to the imagination
and the sentiments and the emotions of the heart, but
the basis of his preaching is not subjective mystical
sentiment.   He appeals freely to all the faculties of
the soul, he throws himself out upon the most ordinary
experiences of men in the real world, but he uses experience only to confirm the truth of revelation and above
all the revelation of God in Christ.   Thus, while life
interprets truth, truth interprets life.   He highly values
and freely uses the Old Testament, finding in its dis-
closures of God a fruitful source of knowledge, and in
its records of religious experience a source of strong

incentive ; but he is preëminently a Christian preacher,
finding in Christ the divine revelation in ideal form.
Authority in religion does not depend on the infallibility
of the Bible.   The Bible is not authority, but only a
record of the source of authority.   Authority is found
in those compelling truths and facts that find an echo
in the moral and religious nature of man, and above
all in the mind of Christ or in His full personal manifestation, and Biblical authority is ultimately the authority of Christ.   And His authority consists not wholly in
the self-evidencing power of His truth, but in the validating power of His complete personality.   We know
Him for what He is, and then we believe Him in what
He says.   We take His truth, not only because it is self-
vindicating, but we take many things on His authority,
and trust Him when we cannot see and follow Him
where we cannot go alone.   Thus experience and revelation, or the subjective and objective factors in authority, are harmonized.

The God who is revealed in Christ is intensely personal.   All the energies of his own intense personality
and above all the energies of his own sturdy moral
nature impelled him to the recognition of God as a free
moral personality.   God is not known by reflection.   He
is already given as a basis for reflection.   He is known
primarily through that subconscious process by which
we transfer our own knowledge of personal will to
what we recognize as the ground of all things.   It is
the necessity of our own consciousness of freedom to
ascribe free personality to the world-ground.   We thus
subconsciously come to know God through ourselves.
Tradition and reflection confirm what is already given.

That God is also revealed in a historic person like Christ greatly intensified and enriched his conception of His personality.   This centre of God's personality is will.   Will is centralized energy.   It is an energy that turns back upon itself.   The divine personality is conscious centralized force.   But the will of God is also a loving will.   Hence it reaches beyond itself. The divine personality is a loving personality.   Love is social.   It is creative, outreaching, self-revealing, self-giving.   God is fatherly in His very nature.   He is personal will, but more ; He is a diffusive, a pervasive, all-loving energy of life.   In his outreaching fatherly love, He is creative.   In the very act of creation, as even the Buddhist teaches, there is a certain sacrifice of self-giving.   Self-sacrificing love is also the principle of redemption.   That word " Father " as applied to the God of love, is no unmeaning term.   It suggests that there is something human in God.   The divine is the human carried into the infinite of rational and moral perfection.   It is this God of fatherly love that comes into personal contact with every human soul.   God is immanent as a living, loving presence, not only in all forms of the material universe, but in every soul of His rational and moral creation.   The divine centrality and the divine ubiquity, the supreme will, the supreme love, not ourselves, yet nearer to us than ourselves, for "in Him we live and move and have our being," — here we have in its most attractive and persuasive form the modern theistic pantheism.

Because of the kinship between God and man an in-carnation of the divine in the human is possible, and the incarnation in Christ is not only a historic fact, but, as involving a reconciliation between God and man, and a permanent moral alliance between them, it is the great central fact of theology and of history, and contains the mightiest motive for the Christian life. Of the very few theological or ecclesiastical terms used by him, this is of most frequent occurrence, and this indicates its importance in his theological thinking. Of the person of Christ he has no definition. His definitions are only representations. His Christology is vague, as all modern Christology is, and perhaps must be. It is the character of Christ with which he for the most part concerns himself, and with His person only as related to His character. In His personality He is ideal humanity. What each human being in his own limited measure was made to be, that was Christ in His complete measure. But although truly human, sharing the humanity that is common to us all, He is still uniquely human, and this uniqueness is not apparently in the sinless perfection of His humanity alone, but in the fact that it is a divine humanity. He shares the nature of God so far as the nature of God is akin to the nature of man, and thus He unites the humanity of God, so to say, with the humanity of man. But although we have here no well-defined ontological Christ, we have a most exalted conception of His person; and of his supreme reverence for Christ he has left a most vivid impression. For all phases and for all interests of human life, Christ with him has absolute significance and worth. So central is Christ in his thinking, so central according to his apprehension is Christ in the entire record of revelation, so central in all human life, life finds in Him so completely its expression and interpretation, that it is quite the necessity that all the experiences of humanity shall somehow fall into relation with him.   A passage to which the reader is referred in the sermon entitled "The Conqueror from Edom,"[1] one of his most interesting and forcible sermons, will illustrate his conception of the universality of Christ in human thought and life.

Since the incarnation is in his thinking the central reality, his soteriology is conditioned by it.   The atonement, therefore, must be conceived from the point of view of the incarnation.   It is not, therefore, a transaction between a Christ and a God who stand outside of humanity, but who are revealed in and are identified with humanity, and the efficaciousness of the atonement is not in the sufferings of Christ, but in the obedience of His holy will.   The reconciliation of God and man is not a forensic transaction dealing with ideal relations, but an actual participation of man in the righteousness of God, a view with which the church has become familiar, but which, in his early years, as advocated by Bushnell and Robertson, was strange and unwelcome.

The church doctrine of the Trinity he did not, at least in the pulpit, criticise or deny, nor yet did he defend it in its formulated aspect as an article of theological belief.   He always got back to the vital principle that is bedded in the doctrine, and that has available worth for the Christian life.   He was accustomed to find in it an expression of the vast wealth and variety and of the inexhaustible fulness of the divine nature.   And as thus presented it became in his hands immeasurably attractive.

[1] Vol. I, p. 40.

Kinship of nature between man and God means that man is the child of God. The New Testament representation that man becomes the child of God by identification with Christ is based upon the already existing fact that he is such by nature. If he were not God's child by nature, he could never become His child by grace. Christianity does not create, but only declares, the fact, and furnishes the requisite provision for its realization. In coming to Christ we come to ourselves, as in coming to us, Christ "came to his own." Sin on its negative side is a failure to realize one's sonship with God; on its positive side, it is refusal to accept and actualize the fact. The terms in which he characterizes sin are in general not theological or ecclesiastical, nor are they always in line with Biblical representations of it; but they suggest phases of it that are profoundly realistic and impressive, and set the dark reality in a new aspect. Sin as a delusive self-estimate; sin as folly in refusing to be what one was made to be; sin as a meanness in choosing a lower life than God meant for one; sin as a wrong done the soul and fellow-men and God, and hence guilt, — all this is most vividly set before men; and his Lenten discourses, in which he deals with the darkness and degradation of sin, are among his most searching and impressive discourses. With him it is not so much the sovereignty of God as His fatherhood, and not so much the servantship, as the sonship of man that gives significance to the dark reality of sin. Regeneration, conversion, sanctification, are the beginning and the completion of the process by which one comes to the recognition of one's self as a child of God, and lives agreeably to the fact.

The terms in which he describes the church also are not theological or ecclesiastical. It is conceived from the humanistic point of view. The church is idealized humanity. It is God's thought of redeemed humanity, in process of actualization. It is what man as man was meant and made to be, and is to become. The empirical or historic church does not, as in the language of theology, consist of the elect, or of the regenerate, or of the baptized, but of those who have come to the recognition of the true meaning of their humanity, of those who recognize and accept the ideal of their manhood, and are trying to live out their human lives as the true children of God. Baptism is the symbol and the pledge of the restoration of, and the consecration and the introduction to, a true manhood. The Supper is the symbol and the pledge of the real fellowship of the true children of God.

His view of the great future was full of hope and joy. How otherwise could it be, with his lofty idealism, that refused to find the key to the mysterious processes of the moral universe outside the fatherly grace of God? He believed in and he lived in the kingdom of redemption. The kingdom of this world had vanished, as it were, from his prophetic vision, and he saw only the kingdom of God. The God who is the source of all things, and who is in all things, is pushing all things onward to the far-off goal of righteousness and peace and joy. This optimistic cheerfulness and hopefulness colored all his estimates of the empirical world. He refused to linger with the dark side of life, counting it a sort of immorality to do so. He looked beyond the perversions and corruptions of men, and beheld them as in process of rectification, in the divine order of the kingdom of God. It was surely impossible that so severely ethical a mind as his should have accepted or tolerated the brutality of modern favored nations in their exploitation of inferior races for the purposes of commercial and political supremacy. One cannot imagine him as sanctioning the iniquitous imperialism that boasts of the "manifest destiny" to supremacy of the Anglo-Saxon race, that baptizes slaughter and ravage in the name of philanthropy, and calls it the work of "benevolent assimilation." But he believed that "good will be the final goal of ill," even though it be through the wrath and brutality of man, and that the God of vengeance is still the strong, conquering God of grace. He could not have failed to see that the political party with which he had been allied in the early years of his ministry had already, before the close of that ministry, apostatized from its noble ideals and traditions, and his keen ethical sense must have been outraged by the hypocrisy, and the general moral degeneracy of many of its leaders; but he never broke with it, and did not ally himself with the movement of political independence that sought reform. He believed in the good which he thought still remained, and looked for reform from within. He was always looking ahead for the good that is to be. The future somehow has in store things that will be different, and things that will be better than the things of the past. He lived as upon the verge of brighter days and of larger glories of the kingdom of God. And this transcendent optimism he transferred to the mysterious future. He was committed to no dogma of the future life, and was wise and most serious in all his discussions of eschatological questions, but he cherished the hope, and indeed lived in the joy of it, that redemption will reach to the ultimate limits of the human race, that God will not be baffled in his purpose of universal grace, that He will "make his pile complete," and that all men will come to ultimate righteousness and blessedness.

These are some, only a few, of the items of a message of great power and beneficence. They are in substance not new, but they are made new by the genius of the preacher, and speak with new persuasiveness from his lips. They may be of no great scientific value for the reflective life of the church. But they are very simple and they are fundamental; and they are transcendently precious to all such as need in special the voice of hope, as they struggle to live out their human lives in the midst of the contradictions and confusions and bewilderments and burdens of the world; and they are presented with a rhetorical forcefulness and attractiveness, with a wealth of suggestiveness, with an infinite variety of forms of representation, and with a strength of personal incentive, that is well-nigh matchless in the pulpit of his age.

IV

THE ILLUSTRATIVE HOMILETIC METHOD

In his "Yale Lectures on Preaching," perhaps the most valuable of all recent contributions to homiletic literature, Bishop Brooks has left on record his conception of the nature, the function, and the method of the sermon. In theory as in practice the sermon is for him only an instrument, and as such it must accomplish two things : it must interpret and it must persuade ; it must edify and it must inspire. A characteristic peculiarity, therefore, of his method is the interplay of the expository and the persuasive elements in his preaching. The first impression upon the hearer or reader will perhaps be that the emotional and impressional, or the rhetorical, element predominates. But a closer inspection shows that after all the basis of his preaching is didactic.

In determining the class to which any preacher belongs we must take into consideration the type of religious truth with which he deals, and the way in which he handles it. As regards the substance of Bishop Brooks's preaching we readily note two things : the first is that he deals with a distinctively Christian type of truth, and presents it in its relation to our entire life. No part of our complex nature, mental, physical, social, as well as emotional, ethical, and spiritual, is remote from his touch. He did not preach much about Christ in the sense that he did not frequently make the person, character, or life of Christ a definite theme of discussion. But all his preaching has a distinctively Christological centre. His preaching, therefore, is not subjectively rationalistic in its character. What calls itself "natural religion" has no place in it. All that is truly Christian is with him natural. Christ is the true interpreter of nature, and what is truly natural cannot be far remote from what is Christian. But he deals with Christian truth in its broad, generic principles. Isolated truths have no significance for him. He deals with it in its wide-reaching relations and traces it in many realms of reality and of experience. These two qualities in his preaching fix in general his place and class. He is preëminently an interpreter of Christian truth. The didactic preacher deals with principles; the Christian preacher discusses those principles from the distinctively Christian point of view.

But looking a little more closely, we shall see the form which these qualities in his preaching take and the school of didactic preachers to which he belongs. His teaching is not prevailingly Biblical. He is a topical preacher, unlike Robertson, never preaching expositorily and rarely textually. Nor is he a doctrinal preacher, for with the formulated doctrines of the church he never deals. Bishop Brooks did not belong to this relic of a past generation. He was not an apologetic or polemical preacher. Nor is his method argumentative. For abstract, formal methods of proof he cares not, and he quotes no authorities. He combats no one and spends no time in contrasting what he believes with what other people believe. His method is that of proclamation, — the affirmative, declarative method. He reasons much, but argues little. His mental movement is not logical or dialectical, but intuitional. But his declarative method has often the force of argument, and more than the persuasiveness of argument, for he appeals to the incontestible facts of human experience. Nor does his preaching take the historical or biographical form. Brooks has nothing of Robertson's analytic skill in the handling of historical and biographical material. He illustrates liberally from such material, but the sermon never takes the historical or biographical form.

It hardly need be said that the evangelistic element is not prominent in his preaching. He is a pastoral, not an evangelistic, preacher. That he deals to a con-

siderable extent with those truths that are adapted to
the work of conviction and conversion is evident, and
that his preaching left a strong impression upon the
feelings and moral convictions is equally clear.   But his
method of presentation is better adapted to the production of gradual and permanent results in character and
life rather than to the work of immediate conquest.

It is the rhetorical and impressional quality of his
method that distinguishes him as a didactic preacher.
He is a singularly persuasive interpreter of truth.
There were more distinctively intellectual preachers
than he.   Mozley was such, Robertson was such, and
so was Bushnell.   But neither of them reached his
mark in vivacity of thought and attractiveness of diction.
There is more that is striking in his preaching than in
that of any of his contemporaries.   Yet his thought is
not the less substantial that it is put in a rhetorically
suggestive manner.   He affects no profundity, but he
strikes quick and often deep into the heart of things.

Let us now look at some of his salient qualities as an
interpreter and advocate of the truth.   In no way can
we discover so readily what is distinctive in any preacher
as by noting his didactic methods, or the methods by
which he gets his thought before his hearers.

Analytic skill is prominent in Bishop Brooks's method.
The entire sermon is a process of analytic discrimination.   It generally starts with an analysis of the text
by means of which it is brought into relation with the
theme.   If, as is sometimes the case, the sermon starts
with some general reflection upon a particular phase of
the subject which is already in the mind of the preacher,
it is always harmonized with the text by some process

of analysis, and thus the proper point of departure from the text is secured. The discussion is an analytic process by which the inner elements and relations of the subject are made apparent. Not infrequently the entire development consists in an analysis of those traits and those motives by which human character is disclosed. In such analysis but few preachers excelled him. His humanistic interests and his study of human character and life are constantly manifest. But his preaching is constructive as well as analytic, and the organizing and vitalizing quality of his mind is readily apparent. Nothing is left unrelated and in fragments. The process of dissection is tributary to the work of unification. He takes hold of a principle and carries it strongly and steadily through, so that it appears pervasively in every part of the sermon. About the central thought the sermon is wrought into a vital unity, and analysis is only tributary to the process of synthesis. The omnipresence of the theme secures proper significance for all the processes of analysis.

His favorite expository method is analogy. The subject of the sermon is generally secured from the text by some analogical process, and it is this analogy that furnishes the starting-point. It is often a remote and poetically suggestive analogy, and therefore quickens the imagination and stimulates curiosity. But although it is a metaphorical analogy and not adapted to the uses of argument, it is still didactic analogy. It throws light upon the truth in hand. It suggests its reasonableness, and it becomes a solid basis for discussion. By the aim which he has in view and by the virile method of his discussion, his poetic analogies are taken out of

the realm of fancifulness. They at once present the
truth in a clearer light and render it the more attractive.

Closely connected with the analogical basis of the
sermon, and as in fact a part of it, is the general view of
the subject that is presented. As already indicated, he
always deals with a general principle. He gets away
as rapidly as possible from what is specific and historic
in his text into some general truth that is somehow
suggested by it, and that has a common family relation
with it. The strongly didactic character of the sermon
appears to best advantage here. It passes from what is
individual and local and provincial into what is universal. It deals with what has fundamental and generic
validity. The general principle makes the individual
and particular instance clearer and more real, and what
is individual and local finds new significance and value
in what reaches so widely beyond it. This generalizing
of the thought excites curiosity at the outset. The
juxtaposition of somewhat remotely related thoughts,
yet not so remotely related as to seem far-fetched and
grotesque, stimulates interest and puts the mind upon a
search. The hearer listens with eager attention because
he will have the matter cleared up. If it is well cleared
up, *i.e.* if the analogy is successfully carried through the
different phases or spheres of its application, there is a
resulting intellectual satisfaction and a corresponding
strength of emotional and ethical impression. A certain
weight and impressiveness is given to any truth by
being brought under a general law or principle. In
the light of the general principle, we see new light in
what is specific. The individual fact or truth stands,
not in its own light alone, but in the light of the broader

R

principle that covers it.   There is always a certain lack
of weight and impressiveness in the discussion of any
truth unrelated to the broader truth that includes it.
It is this grasp of broad principles that accounts for
Phillips Brooks's success in making the claims of religion seem rational and natural and real.   It is at once
a didactic and a persuasive method.

But the sermon does not linger and is not lost in
what is general.   The process of the discussion is always
from the general to the particular, from the generic to
the specific.   If the sermon were to linger in the realm
of the generic, it might indeed be successful teaching,
and the preacher might show that he has a philosophical grasp of his subject, but he would fail as a preacher.
For it is the function of the preacher to interpret and
enforce what is specific by relating it to what lies back
of it.   It is the blending of the generic and specific that
results in getting the whole subject clearly and impressively before the hearer.   The particular case, as belonging to the realm of experience or observation, brings
out more clearly and forcibly the general principle, and
the general principle makes the particular case the more
impressive, as showing that it falls under a comprehensive law.   Here, too, we recognize the interplay of the
didactic and persuasive elements in his preaching.

The deduced or inferential thought is another factor
in his didactic method.   The deductions are not formal;
the preacher's mind moves with great rapidity from
premise to conclusion, from principle to inference or
application.   It is done in an altogether informal, vivacious manner, and, in a way, reminds us of Dr. Thomas
Guthrie.   Some one remarked to Sir William Hamilton

that Guthrie's preaching was defective in logical quality, and he answered, " It is the very best sort of logic ;
there is but a step between the premise and conclusion."
All this has a certain argumentative force, without being in argumentative form.   Brooks is constantly making general statements from which he runs rapidly out
into inferences.   Some of these deductions are of the
broad, general sort.   They always come in rhetorical,
never in logical, form.   They are just such inferences
as we are always in a quiet, unconscious way making.
We always carry the force of the primary thought into
what comes from it.   A deduction has the weight of
what is behind it.   This is the strength of the syllogism.
Many of our preachers' deductions are popular, incom-
plete syllogisms.   Take the following examples from the
sermon that may be entitled " Spotted Lives,"[1] " When
we remember what a source of strength the purest reputations in the world have always been, what a stimulus
and help, *then* we have some idea of what the world
loses in the fact that almost every reputation becomes
so blurred and spotted that it is wholly unfit to be used
as a light or a pattern before the man is old enough to
give it any positive character or force."   That is, we
infer the world's loss from early spotted reputations by
reminding ourselves of the opposite, *i.e.* the strength
that is contributed to the world by unspotted reputation.
From the value of good reputations we infer the world's
loss from bad reputations.   The sermons are crowded
with these inferential thoughts.   He deals a good deal
in spurious inferences, directing attention to the way
men of the world think and talk about the affairs of

[1] Vol. I, p. 176.

life. Take this passage in the same sermon:[1] "You
talk about the corruption of political life, that seems to
have infected the safest characters, and the answer is:
'Oh, there is nothing strange about it; no man can go
through that trial and not fall. No man can live years
in Washington and be wholly pure.'" Here is a syllogism. (1) The safest, *i.e.* the strongest and purest,
characters are least likely to fall; (2) but the corruptions of political life infect even these safest characters;
(3) consequently *no man* can go through the trial and
not fall. No one can live a pure life in Washington.
That is, in the opinion of a certain class of men political
corruption is inevitable. This is an example of that
"fatalistic habit of mind" which he so strenuously antagonized. Note the following:[2] (1) Social life cannot be elevated and ennobled; (2) but one must go into
social life; (3) consequently, he who goes will be con-
taminated. That is, we are not to blame for what we
cannot escape; no man can go into the world and escape its spots, therefore we are not to blame because
we are spotted.

Perhaps his most obvious, most common, and most
effective method of addressing the intelligence and convictions of men is the appeal to experience. It is this
appeal that contributes clearness and force to his preaching. Sometimes he may assume that what is exceptional
in experience is common. He not infrequently assumes
that a high grade of experience belongs to ordinary men.
In this his idealistic and optimistic tendencies remind us
of Schleiermacher, but on the whole he succeeds in hit-
ting upon what most men recognize as something, or like

[1] Vol. I, p. 177. [2] *Ibid.*, p. 178.

unto something, they themselves have thought or felt or
observed or done.   At any rate, this is the appeal, the
appeal to what men know, or should know, the appeal
to life.   The personal form of appeal is common, and it
comes largely in the interrogative form.   It is so obvious
in all his sermons that it is not necessary to linger with it.
It is apparently the leading aim of his preaching to make
men's sense of the significance and value of existence
more real and more intense, so that they may be lifted
into the height of more noble feeling and be impelled
to more practically useful living.   And in doing this he
constantly appeals to what is purest, noblest, ideally
best in men.   Bushnell will make the truth more real, so
shall life become more real.   To clear the truth from
the unreality with which it has become invested is his
task.   Brooks will make men's lives more real, more
cheerful and useful, hence his immediate appeal to life.
Thus shall the truth become more real.   Bushnell interprets life in the light of truth.   Brooks interprets truth
in the light of life, and here largely lies his convincing
and persuasive power.

In this connection his literary style may well be considered.   It might be shown by careful analysis that the
literary quality is admirably adapted to the didactic interest of the sermon.   But perhaps it is more obviously
tributary to the persuasive and impressional interest.
His vocabulary is that of a man whose thought moves
in the realm of concrete reality, of a man who has dealt
with life rather than with abstractions.   There is a
marked anthropological suggestiveness about it.   It is
the diction of a man who has studied human nature and
human life.   Three qualities are prominent in his liter-

ary style.   Naturalness is one.   It is the naturalness of a man whose mind is fertile and full, who utters himself with the simplicity of intellectual abundance and with the vivacity of natural feeling, who likes the colloquial forms, and who has the freedom of a large vocabulary. Clearness is another quality.   It is the clearness of a man whose thought is perspicacious, because it deals so largely with the life of men, with what is familiar to them in experience.   What is relatively remote from them in thought is brought near to them by being associated with what they constantly see or feel.   It is the perspicacity and the perspicuity of the illustrative preacher.   The aphoristic form of the sentence becomes tributary to this quality, likewise its concreteness. The contrasted thought, and still further the expanded thought, is another element.   Iteration is a quality of style tributary at once to clearness and impressiveness. The following sentences remind us of the rushing style of Newman : "I have been powerful; I have turned the currents, and made the world different; I have been useful; I have made the world better ; I have been honored ; I have made men regard and love me."[1]   The periodic sentence is not common.   The loose sentence prevails, and the blending of the two, by breaking up and changing the form of the sentence, becomes tributary to clearness.   The occasional long, periodic sentence, by its cumulation and climax, is not without its contribution to perspicuity.   The colloquial style is clear because familiar ; and the connectives that bind the clauses together are tributary to the same result, because they keep the continuity of thought.

[1] "Keeping the Faith," Vol. I, p. 58.

But force is, perhaps, the most striking quality. Vivacity is an element of force, and the elements of vivacity are many. Variety in the architecture of the sentence is one. The use of the historic present is another and is very common. The direct personal address is another. The rhetorical interrogative, the inversion of the sentences, the figurative vocabulary — all these are elements of force. The vocabulary is that of a man who has the most vigorous conceptions of whatever his mind touches, a vigor that seems to spring from his own vivid consciousness of personal force, who, in the fulness of his own conscious life, attributes life to all things, who looks at all things as in vital, organic relations, and who inclines to personify everything. It is this that imparts the lively, pictorial quality to his style. Everything is in movement: " Life blooms," " Darkness rolls on toward the light." His figurative diction is primarily for the purpose of illustrating his thought, not merely for emotional or æsthetic effects. Therefore he rarely uses the figures of exaggeration that appeal to the emotions. His figures fall easily and naturally into line with his thought, and are a product at once of its fulness and of its imaginative vivacity. He never goes out of his way for imagery that will impress us with its novelty. His most remote and subtle thoughts seek simple, concrete expression. Mental acts he likes to represent in the language of physical movement, as if in process before our eyes. Personification is, perhaps, his most striking figure. He projects the life of his own personality outward upon everything, and the objects of his thoughts live like personal beings before us. One fancies that this hypostatizing habit, a product of his own imaginative genius, was richly cultivated by the church Fathers.

From the whole, then, we may see that in theory, as in practice, the sermon for him as an end to itself, or as a work of art, has but little value. It must have a pre-vailingly ethical rather than artistic significance. The chief question is its fitness to its object. If the man is enriched, the sermon will fairly well take care of itself. He is not an advocate of lawless homiletics, and he was careful and methodical in his own preparation. Clear-ness and definiteness of structural outline he advocated and fairly well realized in his own preaching. Yet the sermon is of supreme value only for what it can accom-plish; and a strong didactic and ethical impulse to com-municate the truth with reference to the practical interests of men's lives is the basis of his, as it must be of all first-class, pulpit talent. This regnant purpose, inspired by a great human sympathy and a great longing to help men in the struggle of life, holding in line all his imagi-native activity and concentrating all his mental fulness and productiveness upon one point, left its mark upon his rushing, wealthy, vital, multiform, manly, and often careless, product, and did its work. The very affluence of the sermon attests its instrumental significance. It is opulent in material and never runs dry. It is an over-flow plump up to the end. It seems to say itself. The intellectual and emotional vitality of the preacher is manifest at every turn, yet it is the product of great diligence and of most conscientious effort. He keeps himself full and flowing, and his productiveness is due to most painstaking literary and homiletic training. But something that moves his whole soul he will always have to say, and then it will say itself in a simple, straight, natural way. He apparently selects his theme before his text, at least not infrequently, and in fact advocates this as being likely to yield for the preacher a freer and wider range. In his own case it doubtless proved tributary to a larger productiveness and effectiveness; but it is not a principle that is universally valid, for many a man's productiveness and effectiveness are dependent on limitation rather than on range. The practical quality of the sermon also, its eminent helpfulness, bears witness to its instrumental significance. One cannot imagine him as engaged in the work of sermon preparation without a strong and definite purpose to help as many of his fellow-men in the struggle of life as he may be able to reach. Of all the objects at which the sermon may well aim, he lays most stress, and the primary stress, upon the immediate needs of the congregation.

As illustrating his conception of the sermon as an instrument, its unconventional and unstereotyped form is also in evidence. Because it is fountain-full and conscious of its object, it develops itself freely and naturally and therefore variously. He has a certain general regulative method for handling his subject, and it bears his own mark. We have an explanatory textual introduction or general reflections on the theme already in mind, connected with this textual matter, thus setting the text in relation with the theme; then an analogy caught from the text that furnishes a basis for the discussion. This secures a generalized thought which is the theme. The principle contained in this generalized thought is then taken out into various realms of experience and is particularized. Everywhere in the discussion we have con-

crete illustration, and at the close the truth discussed is
brought into immediate relation with the personal Christ,
who in some way actualizes the truth in hand and furnishes the requisite incentive for its realization by the
hearer ; and the note of cheer and hope rings clear at the
end.   This in general is his method.   But the flow of
the individual sermon is free, and he has no stereotyped
form.   He advocates unity in the various elements of
the sermon and acts upon it.   But there is no formal
combination.   The elements flow into each other, are
freely and naturally blended, and there is no sermon
building, but a growth ; and the growth is so natural that
no two sermons are altogether alike in method.   Even
the somewhat negligent movement of the sermon indicates that the form is always wholly subordinate to the
substance and aim.   This free handling not infrequently
results in a certain disharmony.   Sometimes it is a structural or a logical, and sometimes it is a literary or rhetorical, negligence.   Sometimes he understates his theme
or overstates it.   Sometimes he fails to discuss what it
contains and should discuss, or he discusses what it does
not contain or what is too remotely related to it, and he
cares too little for climax in the order of his thought.
Yet these defects from the point of view of technique are
all overborne by the vitality and wealth of the sermon.
They are logical defects that do not seriously limit the
rhetorical effectiveness of the product, or they are literary or rhetorical defects that do not compromise its
practical effectiveness.   The not infrequent negligence
in diction suggests that the preacher is supremely intent
upon what he says, and the manner of saying it is a
minor consideration, and the very negligence may bring

him a little nearer the average hearer.   Naturalness, clearness, and vivacity of style are not always a pledge of exactness.   The style of Bishop Brooks is too rapid, colloquial, and concrete for technical exactness.   The popular preacher need not be a very exact preacher. Yet it must be acknowledged that, illustratively and suggestively, our preacher succeeds in saying what he means to say and conveys his meaning with accuracy of result, even when his terms fail to stand the critical tests.   It is an unconventional type of diction, colloquial, free, and familiar, nothing pedantic, stiff, or stilted, often homely and always realistic; it is honest, idiomatic English, and the Anglo-Saxon element is abundant.   There are sometimes awkward phrases, bad combinations in syntax, and sentences that are needlessly pleonastic and redundant. There are not wanting those whom he fails greatly to interest because they regard him as "wordy."   Yet a more careful inspection of his thought justifies the exuberance of his style, and again it must be said that the sermon overrides all defects, and they are lost in its superabundant life and force.   And any man who would know better what it is to be a helpful, pastoral preacher, a real preacher, full, simple, earnest, unconventional, the preacher of an imaginative, suggestive, and ethical mind, who cares chiefly to make the truth effective, who is bent upon getting it at work in the minds and hearts of men, who would fuse and fire the truth with the energies of a manly human soul, may well give himself with diligence to Phillips Brooks.

CHAPTER VI

JOHN HENRY NEWMAN

I

THE ANGLICAN MOVEMENT

IT may, on the face of it, seem an anachronism to undertake to find a place among representative modern preachers for a reactionist like John Henry Newman. He was an ecclesiastic who looked upon human life wholly from the restricted churchly point of view, an ascetic in his personal habits, and a celibate by conscious calling; a dogmatist, who was fanatically devoted to tradition, authority, and the dogmatic method, and who, aside from his literary impulses, seemed to be wholly bereft of any share in the modern humanistic spirit. But this, after all, is a superficial estimate. The movement he represents has a place among the important developments of modern life. Many of the productive influences that were at work during that period lie behind the Oxford movement, were shared by Newman and his chief associates, and his career can be understood only in connection with them. Against many of these influences, political, theological, and ecclesiastical, as they appeared in the liberal school, he was strongly, even violently, reactionary. And it is this reactionary, or negative, aspect that monopolizes superficial attention. But the Oxford movement has a positive as well as negative aspect, and it is this that furnishes the only adequate explanation of Newman's singular but very interesting career. It is necessary, therefore, at the outset to look at what lies behind this movement and at its relation to Newman's life.

In its primary intent the Anglican movement was a positively religious movement. Whatever one may think of its agencies and methods, there can hardly be a doubt as to its object. In his "Apologia pro Vita Sua," [1] Newman claims that it was "a spiritual awakening to spiritual wants," that the leaders were in line with the religious necessities of their age, and that while they were "superior to the age," they were yet "carrying out its higher points." Results in some considerable measure vindicate this claim. For there can be no doubt that in many ways the religious life of the Anglican church was elevated by it, and that, false as were many of the principles enunciated, and extravagant as were many of the methods pursued, it has had for its result the conservation of important religious, theological, and ecclesiastical interests. The rapidity and extent of the movement indicate that somehow it found response in the conscious religious needs of men, or awakened a sense of need of which they were not conscious. It is claimed for it, and there is no reason for doubting the correctness of the claim, that within four years after the initiative, in 1833, it had spread over all England, and that too despite the fact that "the 'Tracts for the Times' went straight against the whole course of the church of England for the last three centuries."

[1] Page 140.

The unorganized character of the movement is also in evidence. It had no effective leadership in the modern sense of the term. Its supporters were advocates rather than organizers. Newman, the most prominent figure and the dominating force among them, was, according to his own confession, wholly deficient in organizing and administrative ability. He was introvertive and sensitive and shy. " He would have shuddered at the very thought of founding a sect or creating a schism," and " the natural gentleness which shrank from giving pain " and "a dread of the trials which faith itself might have to encounter in the storms of life " may, perhaps, in part account for his lack of initiative. Pusey also, who brought to the movement the prestige of high position and a great name, was a thinker and a scholar rather than a man of action. Whatever may be the final verdict as to the value of Newman's work during those days of agitation, and whatever our estimate of the rationality of his principles and the sanity of his methods, it is not probable that the earnestness and sincerity of his piety will be successfully discredited. He may have been fanatical; he may have from the first lacked balance, as his brother Francis charges ; he may at times have been arrogant, as his mother and sister seemed to think ; he may have been self-deceived, as there is abundant ground to suspect, for with respect to this very question he says, " Who can know himself ? " He may have been secretive, may have involved himself in seemingly irreconcilable contradictions, and in stress of battle may have sometimes fought wildly ; he may have been ambitious for intellectual and spiritual domination : but that he was dishonest, as Kingsley practically charged in his famous onslaught upon him, and as his own brother broadly intimates, that his motives were at bottom other than sincerely religious, will not be readily credited by any man who has ever felt the power of his passionately earnest soul. To elevate the religious life of the church was manifestly his steadfast aim. To effect this he believed it necessary to restore, what he assumed to be lost, a sense of the sacredness and authority of the church, so that it may become a greater power in men's lives. He had been trained in the evangelical branch of the church, as was the case with some of his most prominent associates. Whatever may have been the character of the religious teaching and nurture of his home, with respect to which his brother and his brother-in-law Mozley seem to differ, he himself has made it certain, as a matter of record, that his early life was powerfully influenced by the writings of Scott and of Romaine, and others who were numbered among the Evangelicals, men whose earnest piety and whose fame were the pride of that school. It was the "unworldliness" as well as "intellectual independence" of Scott, to whom he "owed his soul," that attracted him. During the early part of his Oxford career he was numbered among the Evangelicals, and, according to the testimony of Mr. Gladstone, who was at Oxford with him, the fact was placed to his discredit. Within four years of the beginning of the movement he seems to have been more of an Evangelical than a High Churchman, although he was already diverging from the Evangelicals upon the doctrine of apostolic succession. But of the degeneracy of the Evangelicals at that time there can be but little doubt. Mr. Mozley's account of

St. Edmund's Hall,[1] the headquarters of the Evangelicals during Newman's residence at Oriel College, may be the exaggeration of an opponent, but with all due consideration for partisan feeling, it leaves the impression of intellectual degeneracy and of defective social conscience. They were noted then, as they have been since, for missionary zeal, but the tone of their piety was emotional and sentimental, and had very likely a touch of cant. Their preaching dealt largely with the cross of Christ, and less with his person and character. They laid much stress upon the doctrine of election, upon Christian assurance, and upon the depravity of human nature, and they were intolerant of those who differed from them in opinion. It is not difficult to detect the ground of Whately's contempt for them, and of Robertson's subsequent strong ethical reaction against them, and this may also in part account for Newman's break with them. But high Anglicanism was not in much better condition. Its type of piety was formal and conventional, its preaching was insubstantial, its parochial work was perfunctory. There was abundance of conventional almsgiving, and but little ethical and religious devotion to the welfare of men. To awaken the whole church to a new religious life was without doubt the aim of the Oxford movement of the last century, not the less really, although in a very different way, than the movement of the preceding century.

No powerful movement of the human spirit can be an isolated movement. The Oxford movement had an artistic or literary as well as religious significance. Newly awakened religious sentiments were associated with

[1] "Reminiscences," Vol. I, p. 242 ff.

a new movement in the realm of the feelings and of the imagination. The Oxford movement was one of the remote and indirect results of those revolutionary movements in thought and life during the previous century that had mightily stirred the souls of men. These movements were now finding expression in new literary forms. The world and life had new significance. The reality and the ever abiding, vitalizing presence of God in His world had taken new hold of men's convictions. He was no longer a remote spectator of His world, and the world was no longer a machine. It was charged with new life, and it spoke to men with a new meaning. A side of man's nature had been suppressed and robbed of its rights, and now it had awakened and was exacting reprisals.

In Germany this literary movement had appeared at the close of the previous century in the form of Romanticism. Carlyle was making the British public familiar with some of its chief representatives in the world of letters, — Goethe and Novalis and Jean Paul Richter. They represented the secular aspects of Romanticism. Schleiermacher represented its religious aspects. In England the movement appeared in the early part of the last century. It took the form of a more subjective, more meditative, but also a more passionately earnest type of literature. It was the literature of a new type of subjective experience, as the literature of the former period had been more objective and formal and passionless and respectable. Byron marks the transition between the two periods. Coleridge and Wordsworth represent it on its secular side, having also strong affiliations with the church upon which they made a

s

powerful impression. It was through them that the emotions and imaginations of the choicer spirits in the church were stirred. Keble appears as the poet of the "Christian Year," and Newman is awakened to a new artistic as well as religious life. Keble and Newman are not disciples of Coleridge and Wordsworth, but apart from them these promoters of the Oxford movement can hardly be conceived as existing. Much that lies behind the English Romanticism of this period finds no place in these men. They were narrow and provincial, and lacked the large humanistic spirit that belonged to the men who influenced them. They thrust the new emotions and imaginings that had been awakened within them into archaic realms, and brought out in new forms what was old. What seemed new and modern in the literary work of these men was also old. The symbolic, the quasi-sacramental significance of the material world was an old thought of the church Fathers. It was a master thought with Wordsworth, but it won fresh significance in the hands of Keble and Newman. Butler had appropriated one phase of it from the church Fathers, and it gave a new didactic significance to the principle of analogy. Keble appropriated it from Butler; and Newman from Keble, as he had interpreted, enlarged, and enriched it in new poetic forms. It stirred the powers of his imagination and led him to interpret, not the world and humanity in terms of new poetic thought, but the old doctrines of the church in new dogmatic forms. Newman's genius in vivifying the past by the power of his imagination was altogether unique. In connection with this quickening of new literary life there came revived interest in the artistic aspects of worship, the outcome of which is the later ritualistic phase into which the original Oxford movement passed, and in which it lost itself. There was also a revival of interest in ecclesiastical architecture and in other products of church art, especially as they had appeared in past ages in Germany.

In connection with this quickening of the religious imagination and consequent reaction against the old rationalistic and deistic methods of thought, there came a revival of the historical and critical spirit. In the liberal school represented by Whately, Arnold, Thirlwall, and Milman, the historic method displaced the dogmatic, and critical investigation was substituted for dogmatic assumptions and traditional apologetics. Newman had been associated with Whately at Oriel and was under his influence. From Whately he learned the art of correct and discriminating thinking. Under this influence Newman, prior to 1827, was drifting in the direction of liberalism. He was inclined to abandon the dogmatic for the historic method and the method of common sense. Liberalism he defines as "a denial of the dogmatic principle." It is a substitution of the historic for the dogmatic method. Newman's definition of liberalism is correct. When, however, later in life he defines liberalism as agnosticism and indifference, and charges it with holding the position that "there is no positive truth in religion and that one creed is as good as another," he becomes reckless. The real difference between his position and that of the liberals, *i.e.* between the dogmatic and liberal position, with respect to the significance of church doctrine is that, in the one case dogma is the source of religion, and in the other it is only the product of religious reflection. When he abandoned liberalism and became a defender of dogmatism he took the position that there can be no religion without dogma. The historic spirit, however, Newman shared, as did all his associates. There was revived interest in the study of the Fathers, and the " Library of the Fathers " is one of the best products of the Anglican movement. In fact, it may be called preëminently a historic movement. But the difference between the liberal and the reactionary school was that the latter were not willing, thoroughly and consistently, to apply the critical method in historical investigation. The former applied it freely, but only with such success as was possible at that early day. Whately was a logician, but he did not believe in applying the methods of logic to theology. He believed strongly and intelligently in historic criticism, and applied it to his investigation of the teachings of Paul. Arnold applied it in the secular sphere to his investigations of Roman history, and in the spiritual sphere to Old Testament ethics. Milman applied it to Latin Christianity, and Thirlwall to scholastic philosophy, and advocated its elimination from the theology of the church. Newman was afraid of it. He used history in support of his dogmatic assumptions, refusing to apply the critical methods to his investigation of historic material. This is the point of divergence between the liberals and the reactionists. The latter came to the Fathers from the dogmatic, not from the critical, point of departure, and they thus sought to bolster their theories of the church and its doctrines.

In connection with this historic movement there was developed among the liberals a new conception of the ethical aspects of Christianity. Whately and Arnold are strong advocates of Christianity as an ethical system. Arnold was led to apply it to political and social problems. It is this ethical conception of Christianity that stands behind his Erastianism, and behind his interest in the social problems of his day. The advancing democratic spirit, that has since so fully developed in England, furthered Arnold's movements. It was Arnold who foresaw that " Labor will meet with reënforcement from the philosopher, philanthropist, and statesman." And Maurice, Kingsley, and Robertson are the successors of Arnold, and of the early liberal school known as Broad churchmen, in the application of the ethical principles of Christianity to social and political conditions. Against all this and against the free application of the methods of historic criticism as they were applied by the liberals, Newman vigorously reacted. It is sufficiently evident that Newman was afraid of such questions, or, at least, of the results of a free application of the methods of historic criticism. The critical method was destructive of the dogmatic method. His brother Francis charges that Newman was indifferent to all questions of moral reform, and we may well believe it, so far at least as these questions were disassociated with his own conception of the proper ecclesiastical method of dealing with them. In a kind of moral fright, therefore, Newman drew back as from an abyss of subjectivism and secularism. He thought he saw that the Evangelicals were playing into the hands of the liberals, and he abandoned them. Liberalism is "the halfway house to atheism." The state authorities are under the influence of the liberals; they seek to bring the church into subordination to the state. Newman supports the autonomy of the church as its only basis of security. Thus he more and more deeply intrenched himself in devotion to the dogmatic method, and the end was Rome.

It was impossible that, with the religious, literary, and historical movement, there should not have been associated a movement of thought still more fundamental. There was, at that time, a process of change in philosophical conceptions. Mr. Hutton, in his monograph on "Cardinal Newman,"[1] indicates Newman's philosophical attitude. He believed "that the philosophy which (like Locke's in modern times) insisted on what is called evidence that a revelation was divine before reposing any trust in it, was the kind of philosophy which would have undermined all the greatest spiritual movements that the world ever experienced, and extinguished all noble enthusiasm in the very moment of its birth." These are weighty words, and they seem faithfully to indicate Newman's philosophical attitude. It is evident that he had already abandoned the empirical philosophy of his day, upon which the defence of Christianity had been based, and that he had felt the need of a more spiritual type of philosophy. The empirical philosophy was behind the deistic conceptions of the universe and the rationalistic methods of defending Christianity. In a very interesting passage in the "Apologia,"[2] wherein he quotes the substance of an article published by him in the *British Critic* of 1839, two years before the appearance of Tract 90, entitled "The State of Religious Parties," he refers to the reli-

[1] Page 173.   [2] Page 138.

gious, literary, historical, and philosophical influences under which the leaders in the Anglican movement had been working. In referring to the philosophical influences, he speaks of Coleridge in the following striking language: " While history in prose and verse was thus made the instrument of church feelings and opinions, a philosophical basis for the same was laid in England by a very original thinker, who, while he indulged a liberty of speculation which no Christian can tolerate, and advocated conditions which were often heathen rather than Christian, yet after all instilled a higher philosophy into inquiring minds than they had hitherto been accustomed to accept. In this way he made trial of his age and succeeded in interesting its genius in the cause of catholic truth." These words remind us of the divergent methods in which great fundamental truths may be applied. They recall to us the divergent schools of thought into which men who claim to follow Kant and Schleiermacher have separated. It is no more strange that Friedrich Schlegel should have taken the principles of Kant and of Schleiermacher over into the Roman church than that Newman should have carried Coleridge and Wordsworth there. It is evident that Newman knew from personal experience the " all-corroding, all-dissolving scepticism of the intellect in religious inquiries." He knew the philosophic scepticism that denies the competence of the speculative intellect alone to pronounce authoritatively and finally upon the august problems of religion and theology. Unfamiliar, probably, with the revolution in the theory of knowledge that the latter part of the previous century had witnessed in Germany, he had followed Coleridge in assuming the

position that it is the human soul in its moral and spiritual activities that becomes the organ of religious knowledge, and thus becomes the point of attachment for an
objective revelation, and finally the point of attachment
for objective church authority. The application which
Newman makes of the subjective principle as containing
the true doctrine of faith in external church authority
is, of course, wholly unsatisfactory and inconsequential.
But it is perfectly clear that he has already appropriated the subjective principle, and that, up to a certain
point, it moves step by step with the philosophy of
Christian experience. The process by which, at last, he
found a refuge in the church of Rome by yielding to his
scepticism with respect to the competence of the speculative intellect in the realm of religion, which found no
adequate counterweight in the subjective principle of
ethical and spiritual experience, may appear farther on.

Perhaps enough has been said to indicate that the
Oxford movement, although reactionary with respect
to the theological and political movements of Newman's
age, was nevertheless based on, and supported by, influences and agencies that are distinctively modern.

II

NEWMAN THE ECCLESIASTICAL DOGMATIST

When Newman entered the Roman church he went
home. It was a plunge as into his native element.
The transition was an "absorption." He enters as with
a shout of exultation and triumph. The restlessness
and confusion of uncertainty vanish, and his entire sub-

sequent career indicates that it was a joyful emancipation. Even his literary style discloses the influence of
the change. We may wonder that a man of his intelligence and culture and training could have made such
a surrender of himself. But after all it was not strange.
It was the necessity of his position and the legitimate
issue of many years of dissatisfaction and unrest. It
was not a supernatural call, or a " miraculous admission
into the Roman communion " as his superficial brother-
in-law grotesquely suggests. There was nothing ghostly
about it. Nor, on the other hand, is it necessary to assume that he had all along been dishonest. He was
indeed, as he tells us, conscious of no doctrinal change
when he entered the Roman church; but this does not
mean that there was no change at all save in ecclesiastical relations. But confessedly the change, whatever
it may have been, was not very important. He was, in
fact, already substantially upon Romish ground without
being fully aware of it. He had tried to believe that
the Anglican church was the original, apostolic catholic
church held in bondage to the state, which to him represented the unconsecrated kingdom of this world. By
the bent of his nature, by all its leading tendencies, and
by the influences and circumstances of his life he was
in a sort precommitted to the dogmatic position of the
Roman church. Newman was a born ecclesiastic, as
Brooks was a born humanist. To him, as his brother
suggests, "the church was everything," as to Brooks
humanity behind it was everything, and the church
nothing apart from its significance for humanity.
Newman looked out upon and estimated life from the
ecclesiastical point of view, as Brooks from the human-

istic point of view.   To Newman the world was a wholly depraved and lost world.   To Brooks it was indeed a sinful, but also a redeemed world.   Newman looked too exclusively upon its darkness, and found in life only a miscarriage of justice and goodness and truth. Brooks looked through it upon the glory of its ideal reality, and found in it already the kingdom of God. To Newman the world has significance and value only as related to Christianity, organized as the catholic apostolic church, whose mission it is to rescue and dominate the world.   To Brooks it has a significance and value of its own for the life that now is as well as for that which is to come, and the church as the organ of Christianity is only the partial, and is destined to be the ultimate, complete realization of that which belongs ideally to the world as the kingdom of God.   If we look closely into Newman's characteristic tendencies and into the circumstances, influences, and experiences of his life, we shall find the material for the building of the ecclesiastical dogmatist.

One may easily suspect that he was, in a sort, subconsciously committed to Romanism by the dominance of his imagination.   He was a man of exceedingly delicate æsthetic susceptibilities.   He inherited a highly artistic temperament, which as poet and musician he cultivated from early years.   He was born into and he lived in the realm of the imagination.   The invisible was always to him the real.   The "Apologia" is an interpretation of the processes by which he was led into the Roman church, and a skilful defence of his integrity and consistency.   It is a rare piece of psychological analysis, and has all the interest of a modern psycho-

logical romance. This early development and dominance of the imagination are here made apparent, and
Newman seems to recognize it as a subconscious influence determinative of his subsequent career. He
was an idealist of the most extravagant type. His
sense of the invisible was a genius. There are "two
and two only supreme and luminously self-evident
beings, myself and my Creator," he says.[1] In this
supreme self, and God-consciousness he is early inclined to a "mistrust of the reality of material phenomena." The visible world is at best but a complex
of symbols of invisible reality. His "imagination ran
on unknown influences, on magical powers and talis-
mans." "I thought," he says, "that life might be a
dream, or I an angel and all this world a deception,
my fellow-angels by a playful device concealing themselves from me, and deceiving me with the semblance
of a material world." It is apparently easier to believe
in angels than in men, in God and in soul than in the
material world. It was this "childish imagination"
that he carried into his religion. It intensified his conviction of the reality of his conversion, "of which," he
says, "I am still more certain than that I have hands
and feet." He finds significance in the fact that at ten
years of age he had marked the sign of the cross, and
had drawn the likeness of a necklace upon his first
verse-book. His brother notes as significant his early
remoteness from ordinary life, his introverted habit of
mind, his fastidiousness, and later on his inclination
toward Virgin worship. He notes also the influence
of Romanism upon his imagination as seen in some of

[1] "Apologia," pp. 54–56.

his grotesque utterances at St. Mary's during the last days of his connection with the Anglican church. It is to such an imagination that the Roman church with its antiquity, its imposing claims to apostolicity and divine authority, its treasury of saintly merit, and the artistic splendor of its ritual, powerfully appeals. He confesses that in those years of preparation for his mission, which he had long cherished, — and to such a temperament the consciousness of a mission seems native, — the Roman church with its venerable shrines and noble churches much impressed his imagination and touched his heart. It was this vivid image-making power that intensified his faith and made real its object, so that he believed, not only with all his heart and conscience and will, but with all the force of his imagination. Such a man may easily lose the balance of his powers, and this explains, perhaps, the lack of poise of which his brother speaks. Such a man may even become a fanatic in his superstitious credulity. For what is superstition or fanaticism in religion but just this one-sidedness and dominance of the imagination that result in loss of balance in the activities of the soul? What is extra-belief but gratuities of belief imposed upon the mind by the tricks of the imagination? So strong was Newman's conviction that feeling and imagination should have free play in the religious life that he became a sort of advocate of fanaticism and superstition. "In one of my first sermons I said, I do not shrink from uttering my firm conviction that it would be a gain to the country, were it vastly more superstitious, more bigoted, more gloomy, more fierce, in its religion than at present it shows itself to be."

These words may be interpreted as a rhetorical license
which must be permitted the preacher, but the truth
is that Newman would not regard what he advocates as
superstition or bigotry at all, but the reasonableness of
a dogmatic faith.

It was perhaps in part his religious imagination that
predisposed him to the ascetic life. From the first he
was inclined to asceticism. He never mingled in the
sports of childhood. He was sober and secretive and
inclined to solitude. He tells us that at the age of
fifteen the impression was borne in upon him that he
was called to a celibate life, and that before he was
thirty it had become a settled conviction. At Oxford
he led an abstemious life. He fasted often and never
at any time indulged in luxuries. He was fascinated
with the idea that his religious life was to be one of vigorous self-denial. And what he imposed upon himself,
he inculcated upon others. It cannot be denied that
for him the Christian ideal was the ascetic ideal. The
Christian life is the contradiction of the worldly, self-
indulgent life, and it must be exactingly and painfully
self-denying. In such self-denial and self-imposed
hardship there is merit, and the merit is one of the
legitimate motives in the striving for it. It is a privilege, winning large rewards, to share the sufferings of
Christ. By disobedience to the law of cross-bearing
the worldly Christian forfeits the unspeakable privilege
of suffering adversity, which profits the soul and honors Christ. Penance is a Christian virtue, and penance
is with him the representative term for repentance.
Repentance is not simply sorrow for sin and turning
from it, but it is the penance that "adds what sin

deserves."[1] Kingsley misapprehended Newman's doctrine of the economic method of interpreting truth according to the fitness of the recipient to appreciate it, a principle that is recognized by all writers on Christian ethics, as Newman showed. He misinterpreted his sermon on "Wisdom and Innocence"[2] as advocating untruthfulness. But he was not mistaken in charging that the discourse on "The Apostolic Christian "[3] advocates the ascetic life as the normal Christian life. The more carefully one reads this discourse, the stronger the impression becomes that Newman intended to exalt the ascetic life as the only worthy type of Christian life. It is clear enough that this is the life he would have all his hearers adopt as best realizing the Christian ideal. He speaks of the "picture which Scripture gives us of true Christian life," and insists that we must all "attempt to measure our own life by it." And this idea of a "Christian life as set forth in the Scriptures is something very definite." Then he proceeds to describe it as an ascetic life. The monk and the nun are our modern Scriptural Christians. "What are the humble monk and the holy nun and other regulars, as they are called, but Christians after the very pattern given us in Scripture?" "Who but these give up home and friends, wealth and ease, good name and liberty of will, for the kingdom of heaven? Where shall we find the image of St. Paul or St. Peter or St. John, or of Mary the mother of Mark, or of Philip's daughters, but in those who, whether they remain in seclusion or are sent over the earth, have calm faces,

---

[1] "Apologia," p. 59.   [2] "Sermons on Subjects of the Day," XX.
[3] Ibid., XIX.

and sweet, plaintive voices, and spare frames, and gentle
manners, and hearts weaned from the world, and wills
subdued?" Beautiful, saintly lives no doubt they are.
But we have here the realization of the essentially
Romish conception of an ascetic separateness from
the world as the mark of a normal Christian life.
Newman's message of the unworldly life was an
important one for his age. He made a strong and
salutary impression upon self-indulgent Christians in all
communions. But the form in which his message came,
its severely ascetic note, robbed it of much of its legitimate power. Let it be remembered that the words above
quoted were uttered while he was still in the Anglican
church, and they contain a premonition of the issue of
the conflict in which he had been engaged. Yet he
lingered two years longer in the church. The volume
containing this discourse was issued after he had re-
signed his position at St. Mary's, and while he was still
awaiting developments. The discourses all bear directly
or indirectly upon questions that were then in agitation,
and they all advocate a type of character and of life and
a type of ecclesiasticism that find their fullest exempli-
fication in the Roman church. They are an advocacy
of the ecclesiastical conception of life, and proclaim
his rapid advance toward the Roman communion.
Practical religion is living for the life to come, as worldliness is living for the present life,[1] — a conception that
contains only a half truth. The presence of God is
found only in the church; when God leaves the church,
it becomes weak and beggarly like the world.[2] Because
God is found only in the church, it only is the kingdom

---

[1] Page 81.   [2] Page 104.

of God. His conception of the world as an unredeemed
world, and as wholly without God, is extravagant and is
disheartening. In all these sermons, as in the " Parochial and Plain Sermons," not less than in the " Discourses to Mixed Congregations," preached after he
entered Rome, the prevailing theme is the ruin of the
world, and the church is summoned to rally for the
spiritual conquest of the world, and to show that to
be a Christian is not an easy thing. He criticises the
effort to make religion cheerful. We must take our
feast with bitter herbs. Persecution is the note of the
church, perhaps the most abiding note of all. Apparently, therefore, the only normal condition for the church
is that of persecution. There is constant lamentation
over "the present state of the Holy Church." In the
present distress he advocates " living by rule." [1] His
praise of the saints is indiscriminate. It is highly
idealistic, and is accompanied with perpetual dispar-
agement of everything modern. His illustrations, save
in the way of admonition, are never drawn from modern life, but are always scriptural or ecclesiastical.
The idea of " sacred habit," is a frequently recurring
idea. " If we claim to be the church, let us act like
the church, and we shall become the church." By faithful devotion to outward church duties, God " will vouch-
safe to bless it, and to make it a means of teaching us a
deeper reverence and a more constraining love, and will
draw us on into the very bosom of catholic sanctity and
the very heart of catholic affection, by observances and
prayers, which in themselves are little worth, and excite
the jeer or the criticism of the worldly and profane."

[1] Pages 25, 117, 261, 272.

Surely in all this we have the utterance of one who has the heart of an ecclesiastic, which is ever drawing nearer to its proper home.

Newman's constitutional and habitual conservatism is another note of his essentially ecclesiastical mind. Against all forms of liberalism, political, ecclesiastical, or theological, he was from the first strenuously opposed. If during the early Oriel period, under the influence of Whately, he was inclined to or tolerant of it, it was but a transient phase and had no permanent significance for his life. He was always interested in politics, and "his politics occupy an earlier place in the memory of his pupils than his theology."[1] He has been called "a lord chancellor thrown away." This doubtless with reference to his genius for diplomacy. In his constitutional tendencies as well as in his theories he would have been a Tory chancellor. If he had become, as might have happened, tutor to the Prince George of his day, he would have been a Tory tutor and might have figured as the future king's counsellor. Even in boyhood he was the antagonist of democracy and the defender of royalty and despotism, and seemingly on no other ground than that of a sort of fanatically conservative respect for power as such.[2] The Oxford movement was as hostile to political as to ecclesiastical and theological liberalism. Its promoters were all Tories and defenders of hereditary privilege. The democratic spirit was gaining ground. It disclosed itself in the aspiration of the unprivileged classes to rise in the world. There was a great quickening of worldly aspiration and ambition.

[1] " Reminiscences," Vol. I, pp. 34–36.
[2] " Early History of Cardinal Newman," pp. 6–10.

T

Liberal movements were furthered by this aspiration and at the same time they promoted it. It was against this that the Oxford Tories reacted. Against Arnold especially, with his Erastianism, there was violent opposition. So bitter was Newman that he questioned whether Arnold could be a Christian. Because of the attitude of the Liberals Newman, like the Tory church-men of to-day, was soon convinced that, for its own security, the church should be separated from the state.

This habit of mind conditioned his conception of the church. He could conceive of Christianity only as a community organized as a visible apostolic church, in which centres a divine authority, and he could conceive of no religion as possible but the religion of dogma. From the age of fifteen this had been his conception. A religion of feeling and sentiment is a delusion and a snare.[1] Accordingly the principles for which he contended were first, the visible apostolic church with its authoritative bishops, its sacraments as channels of grace, and its discipline of penance, and secondly, the authority and validity of dogma as against the anti-dogmatic principle of liberalism. How he defended his attitude toward all forms of liberalism on theoretic grounds we shall see farther on. Just now the point in hand is his conservative habit of mind, that of itself precommitted him to the religion of dogma and to the church which is the supreme embodiment of privilege and authority.

A love for intellectual preëminence, not to say domination, is another characteristic of Newman's ecclesiastical mind, which led him ultimately to the proper sphere for

[1] " Apologia," pp. 95–96.

its realization. There is, indeed, no evidence that Newman had a vulgar ambition to make for himself a name
as a church agitator and reformer. He certainly had
no ambition to develop a sect or organize a party in the
church. If that had been his object, his procedure
would have been different. And yet it was impossible
that a man of his force of personality, of his zeal for
what he held to be true, especially of his dogmatic habit
of mind, into which so much of personal will entered,
should not have had, it may be an unconscious or half-
conscious, passion for dominating the minds and consciences and wills of others. Indeed he himself
acknowledges that he had a strong desire to influence
others. "While I was fighting for the Anglican church
in Oxford," he says,[1] "I was very glad to make converts, and though I never broke away from that rule of
my mind (as I may call it) of which I have already
spoken, of finding disciples rather than seeking them,
yet that I made advances to others in a special way I
have no doubt." He acknowledges also the correctness
of the charge that he was "fierce" in his methods of
agitation, and this suggests at once the passion of the
advocate. Newman was not a mere interpreter of the
truth. He put strong conviction and force of will into
his advocacy. He was not willing to let the truth work
its own way in the minds and hearts of others. He put
his own will into his faith, and he would press the wills
of others into the service of their faith. He was an
investigator, but he carried his dogmatic precommittals
into his investigations, and became a personal advocate
in the very processes of his investigation. He wished

[1] "Apologia," p. 247.

to win intellectual and moral ascendency over men.   In this he resembles many other great theologians of the church.   It is a mark of the theological and ecclesiastical mind.   It is the necessity of the dogmatist to identify his own personality with the truth he advocates. Nor is this altogether a matter for reproach.   Any man who is intense in his convictions and strong in his opinions will wish to win the allegiance of others to the truth he cherishes.   This passion for intellectual supremacy is inseparable from Newman's consciousness of a mission.   He returned to England in 1833 with the strong conviction that he had a work to do there. His brother charges that he makes himself and his friend Froude ridiculous, without seeming to know it, in adopting the words of Achilles as his motto : —

> "Now that I am coming back to battle,
> You shall see the difference."

It was Newman's opinion that every man should make up his mind by the time he is thirty years old what his life work shall be.   He had evidently made up his mind what his own task should be.   It was easy for him to influence men.   He was a man of most fascinating personality.   He impressed men by the strength of his sympathy, the earnestness of his convictions, and the force of his will, rather than by the reasonableness of his opinions, or the soundness of his judgments, or the clearness of his insights.   He was an exceedingly interesting and impressive teacher.   As a preacher, he won a hearing by the distinctively religious character of his message, which appeals to the higher needs of men, by the passionate intensity of his advocacy, and by the

force and grace of his diction, rather than by any skill
as an orator.   In private intercourse he was at his best,
and young men gathered about him as about an oracle.
Powerful as was his influence in the pulpit, his most
effective work was through the press and in the class
room and in the social circle.   He was not unconscious
of his power, nor did he fail to use it consciously.   Why
should he not have used it thus?   No man, especially
no man of such power as Newman possessed, can reasonably be asked to deny himself the right and the
privilege of seeking ascendency over the minds and
hearts of men in the advocacy of what he regards as
vital to their welfare, provided always that it be done
honestly.   Whether Newman advocated views that were
consistent with his ordination vows as an Anglican
clergyman may be questioned.   But that he was honest in his advocacy and regarded his position as tenable
will not be generally questioned in our day.   Newman's brother charges him with inordinate ambition
and with a loss of moral balance in carrying out his
schemes of ambition.   It was an unfraternal and unseemly exhibition that he made of himself, in so doing,
and especially in waiting till after Newman's death
before he did it.   One suspects that when Newman is
charged with arrogance and with lack of humility of
spirit he is not altogether correctly represented.   The
dogmatic attitude doubtless always has the seeming of
arrogance.   Estimated by the highest rational and
moral standard it is arrogance, and the high Anglican,
both as an Englishman and as a churchman, has vast
capacity for such arrogance.   But we must estimate
Newman as a man from the basis of his personal dis-

position, not from the basis of his dogmatic position and dogmatic method.   It is above all discreditable that Francis Newman should draw aside the veil that hides the sanctities of home, and should quote his sister's words of criticism: "John *can* be most amiable, most generous.   He can win warm love from all his friends; but to become his friend the essential condition is that you see everything along his line, and accept him as your leader."   One fancies this to be a correct estimate of Newman.   But it suggests the infirmity and the narrowness of the dogmatist and the offensiveness of the dogmatic method, rather than the arrogance of personal ambition.   But the point in hand is that it is precisely this passion for intellectual and moral ascendency, which belongs to the consciousness of a dogmatic mission, that is the mark of the ecclesiastical mind.

But it is Newman's attitude toward religious truth which, more clearly than anything else perhaps, illustrates the predominance of the ecclesiastical mind. His theory of religious knowledge, of religious certainty, is one of the most subtle and obscure and perplexing problems of his career.   It is a psychological phenomenon, which, when once apprehended, throws light upon his procedure, and clearly indicates his precommittal or predestination to the Roman church.   There is in it a singular blending of scepticism, of dialectic, of piety, and of credulity.   Newman was fundamentally and characteristically a dialectician.   He was the most subtle and exhaustive of reasoners.   He penetrated deeply into the intricacies of a subject and was sure to discover all its difficulties.   Being of a religious turn of mind, it was a necessity that he should bring this subtlety to bear upon the problems of religion. He believed in and advocated the use of reason in religion. In his case it served a double use. He used his reason to defend his position. This, perhaps, was the chief impression made upon the minds of those with whom he discussed religious questions. His subtlety and unconscious facility in reading his own ideas into a discussion is seen in his "Development of Christian Doctrine," in which he undertakes to apply the modern doctrine of evolution to the development of the dogmatic system of the Roman church. It is a painful exhibition of a subtle, dialectical mind dealing with what we in our day regard as relatively insignificant subjects and insignificant difficulties. But it is also an interesting exhibition of facility in using reason to defend an already won position. It is this tendency which his brother has in mind in characterizing the method of his reasoning. Give him his premises, make any concession to them, and he will bring you to confusion. This is the mental habit of one who uses his reason to defend his position.

But Newman also used his dialectic in preparing the way for the selection of his position. He had much to say about the negative and preparative value of logical processes. But their chief value in his apprehension was to show the impossibility of arriving at truth by such processes. As Bushnell thought that the chief use of metaphysics is to demonstrate that metaphysics is impossible, so Newman thought that the chief use of the speculative reason in religious investigation is to demonstrate its futility. It cannot verify or vindicate religious truth. Newman was an intellectual sceptic.

From the rationalistic point of view he was an agnostic. Reason is of value in furnishing preparative proof. But the chief thing proved is its own incompetency. His ultimate attitude was that there is no halfway house between atheism and Romanism, although he had tried for a long time to find such a refuge in Anglicanism. Much has been said about his sceptical attitude with respect to the problems of religion. Atheists even have claimed him as a sort of ally because he regarded human reason as incompetent to furnish adequate evidence of the existence of God. There is nothing strange in this sceptical attitude. It is, in part, due to the natural workings of his own highly speculative mind, by reason of which it was impossible for him to obscure the difficulties that gather about any important problem. The more important the problem, the more difficulties he saw. But it is, in part, also the outcome of the disintegrating processes to which the theory of knowledge had been subjected by the philosophic criticism of a previous period, the results of which had crept into his thinking during the early period of his Oxford life. He had familiarized himself with sceptical writers who discussed the problem of religious knowledge. He tells us that when he was fourteen years old, he "read Paine's tracts against the Old Testament, and found pleasure in thinking of the objections which were contained in them." He, at the same time, read Hume's essay on the miracles and he was familiar with Gibbon. His brother-in-law, Mozley, tells us that he had sceptical books about him during the Oxford campaign, although he kept them carefully locked up and concealed from his pupils. He had early adopted Bishop Butler's principle that "probability is the guide of life." He gives an interesting statement of the matter in the "Apologia." The most that the logical understanding can do for us in investigating the problems of religion is to give us probability. In a profoundly interesting and illuminating account of his own intellectual processes, he speaks of "the all-corroding, all-dissolving scepticism of the intellect in religious inquiries." It can never land us in the realm of truth. Normal reason, indeed, would reach the truth; but the reason of man, outside the church, the unredeemed reason, is fallen and depraved. And he boldly declares that "every article of the Christian creed, whether as held by Catholics or Protestants, is beset with intellectual difficulties, and it is a simple fact that for myself I cannot answer those difficulties." He cites as examples the doctrine of the Trinity and of Transubstantiation.[1] Of the latter he says, "It is difficult, impossible to imagine, I grant; but how is it difficult to believe?" One may believe what one may not even imagine! Not even the doctrine of the divine existence can stand before the corroding processes of the intellect. In vain do we rely upon anything that is human for assurance; reason, education, even Scripture itself, cannot stand before the onset. The only power that is "adapted to be a working instrument in the course of human affairs for smiting hard and throwing back, the immense energy of the aggressive intellect," is a power "possessed of infallibility in religious teaching." Thus the intellect gives us no certainty. But Newman was a man of religious necessities, and it is the impulse of piety to find some basis of assurance. Where,

[1] Pages 232, 265-291.

then, shall it be found? It is not necessary to enter upon a thorough analysis of Newman's theory of knowledge. It is set forth with full elaboration in his "Grammar of Assent" and is briefly touched upon in the "Apologia." What is the basis of certainty in religion? We have some standing-ground in ethical and religious experience. The testimony of the Christian conscience and heart has value. In the discourse entitled "Grounds for steadfastness in our Religious Profession,"[1] he speaks of the self-evidencing power of religion, and declares that no traditional religion avails without its personal appropriation in experience; and he finds no contradiction between this position and the position that religion is dogma and comes to us with the note of external authority. In the "Apologia" he writes: "If I looked into a mirror and did not see my face, I should have the sort of feeling which actually comes upon me when I look into this living, busy world and see no reflection of its Creator. This is to me one of the great difficulties of this absolute primary truth to which I have referred just now." Then he adds, "Were it not for this voice speaking so clearly in my conscience and my heart, I should be an atheist."[2] The speculative intellect cannot find God, but He reveals Himself in the human heart and conscience. Here apparently we have the validating power of religious experience. We might infer that the moral and religious nature are an adequate organ of religious knowledge. But this is by no means his position. This would presuppose faith in the subjective principle that

[1] "Sermons on Subjects of the Day," XXIII.
[2] "Apologia," pp. 264–269.

would ally him with Luther and with Protestants. We must, therefore, look farther. As the reason gives us no absolute certainty, so neither does the heart nor conscience. There is no basis of certainty in any form of mere subjective experience. The mind must be compelled to make a venture by the pressure of the will. Belief is a venture of the mind under the dominance of the will. It is not secured and certainty is not won till the will is surrendered. We "will to believe." And here appears the application of Butler's theory of probability as interpreted by Keble. It was this notion of the living power of faith, this resolution to believe where the evidence furnished is only probable evidence, that he got from Keble, as he himself tells us. But it is not to the experiences of the heart and conscience, not to the persuasions of our moral and religious nature, that we are to will to surrender. We will to submit to an external authority which speaks to us as with the voice of God. This is not an irrational surrender, without a basis of evidence. We are predisposed to believe by the experiences of our inner life. But we need more than this. The church comes to us with its claims of authority. We examine these claims in the light of such evidences, external and internal, as are furnished us, and we find them in harmony with the needs of our own souls and lives. This does not give us certainty. It is only probable evidence; but we yield because the persuasions of the heart and conscience, together with this external evidence, are stronger than our intellectual uncertainty. Having willed to believe, we reach assurance. We can thus believe even when all the ordinary experiences of life are opposed to our belief, and such

belief is a moral obligation. In the problems of religion, therefore, private judgment must be surrendered.
The right of private judgment may indeed be exercised
in forming our estimate of the results of religion in the
lives of bodies of men, but this is a very different thing
from exercising such judgment in determining the validity of Christian doctrines.[1]

It was because he could not find in the Anglican
church all the notes of an objectively authoritative
church, viz. apostolicity, catholicity, and autonomy,
that he wavered so long. This is the explanation of
his uncertainty and of the seeming contradictoriness
of his position. The Anglican church may be apostolic, but it is not catholic, and in subordination to the
state can never be autonomous. Upon the authority of
such a church he could not rest. He must find a church
upon which he can rest with absolute certainty. The
charge of moral timidity in all this process, as well as
the charge of mental suicide and of moral confusion
and contradiction, has some basis. His career presents
the singular spectacle of an extreme of intellectual
scepticism that was offset by an extreme of religious
credulity. Contrast Luther's bold appeal to the attest-
ing power of the moral and religious consciousness and
to the witness of the spirit in the heart. Luther com-
plained that the Roman church robbed the Christian of
his assurance, and he boldly appealed from the church
to Christian experience. Newman finds no basis of certainty in any form of subjective experience, rational,
ethical, or spiritual, nor in the voice of the Spirit within
the individual soul. But he finds it in a church whose

[1] "Sermons on Subjects of the Day," XXIII, p. 359.

preposterous claims have been refuted by historic criticism, and which, if ever validated at all, must be validated by a reason whose processes we are taught by Newman at the very outset to distrust. It was this attitude toward the problems of religion that naturally led him toward the Roman church.

The outward circumstances of Newman's life and the personal influences brought to bear upon him were also tributary to the ultimate result. It is as if all things were in combination to work out the one predestined issue. Influences seemingly the most contradictory wrought toward the same end. Those who agreed with him stimulated and encouraged him, and those who were hostile to him only intrenched him the more firmly in his position. The Evangelicalism in which he had been nurtured, instead of drawing him farther from the goal, seems almost to have started him toward it. His committal to the religion of dogma at the age of fifteen was clearly the outcome of the prevailing conception of Christianity as a system of doctrine. He never thoroughly grasped the conception of Christianity as primarily a disclosure of personality, and as only secondarily a revelation of truth. Nor had he formed the true conception of dogma. With the Evangelicals of his day, dogma had come to mean the product of the reflective life of the church in successive generations. But with him dogma was the apostolic deposit of truth, passed on to following generations and forever fixed. It was not the product of church reflection upon the truths and facts of Christianity, but something given from the first by tradition. And it was largely through the influence of writings put into his hands at Oxford by those, some of them Evangelicals, who wished to lay new emphasis upon the apostolicity of the Anglican church, but whose purpose was far remote from the ultimate result, that he was led to incorporate the notion of apostolic tradition in his conception of dogma. Having accepted the apostolic authority of tradition, he of course came to accept as final authority the dogmas of tradition. Whatever the intent of his teachers, they seem always fatuitously to be furnishing fuel to his fanatical zeal for tradition; and there is a certain grim humor in his references in the " Apologia " to the influence of books that were put into his hands by men who would have led him away from Rome, but who were in fact instrumental in furnishing incentive toward it.

His earliest and lifelong conception of the world as the kingdom of evil, set off in contrast with the kingdom of God, came from Calvinistic and Puritan Evangelicalism. The sharp distinction between the sacred and the secular, the saint and the sinner, heaven and hell, mercy and wrath, is essentially Calvinistic; and these conceptions are closely allied with conceptions that prevail in the Roman church. He himself notes the points of likeness, and intimates that this phase of Calvinistic Evangelicalism had precommitted him to the Romish conception of the world. Even Law's "Serious Call," which has influenced so many lives in the cause of Evangelical piety, seems to have predisposed him to the Romish conception of the perpetual conflict between God and the world. His personal companionships also had a like effect. The earliest and strongest influence is that of Keble. That of Froude, however, is scarce less decisive, and one may venture to suggest that it must always remain a matter for surprise, not to say of discredit, that a man of Newman's caliber should have been influenced so strongly by so slight and crude and irrational a person as Hurrell Froude.

Thus by the force of surrounding influences he is gradually set toward his goal. The catholicity of the Anglican church is surrendered and all hope of its autonomy, while he still holds to its apostolicity. Then its apostolicity is placed in doubt, and he holds as a last refuge to its note of sanctity. Then at last, when all the notes of a true church seem to have vanished and in 1843 he resigns St. Mary's, he shows that he is already substantially on Romish ground. Thence onward we hear only of the Catholic church, and in the "Sermons on Subjects of the Day," his church is the regal church, which is itself the kingdom of God. The Christian church is a perpetuation of the Jewish church as a temporal not less than as a spiritual power, representing all the regal functions of Christ. There is but one branch of the Christian church that can rightly claim this, and therefore only one that can be the true church, and that is the church at whose portals he stands. And when during the two remaining years he had written his "Development of Christian Doctrine," which he laid down unfinished, there was but a short step through the open door.

III

NEWMAN THE PREACHER

Newman's loss of position and of prestige in the Anglican church did not result in a loss of personal influence. The English people did not forget him, and he never lost his hold of them. They discredited his theology and lost confidence in his judgment, but they never lost interest in the man. He antagonized their opinions, he cut across their most cherished convictions, he rebuked them for their worldliness, he exposed their inconsistencies and satirized their frivolities, but he always retained a certain ascendency over their imaginations and their hearts. Few modern Englishmen have won a securer place in the interest of their countrymen. It is not altogether easy to explain. Doubtless they always found the Englishman in him still, and he attracted them by the magic of his English style. But there is something behind all this. It is an interesting tribute to the force and grace of his personality. That personality has an irresistible fascination. Its energies disclose themselves in all his writings, but most of all, perhaps, in his sermons. Behind the sermon is the man, and in the reading there is always an indefinable impression of something more, which the product only intimates. What is said is the product of a well-stored mind and of a richly nurtured and severely trained character. It is a keen, subtle, incisive, capacious mind, with stores of theological learning and vast emotional susceptibilities and passions, and the ease, the fulness, the acuteness, and the suggestiveness of the treatment intimate that but a small part is said of what might be said. The thought of the sermons is thrown out in a free and affluent manner, and, if we except the university and the occasional sermons, there is no very elaborate discussion. Newman's career illustrates, not only the influence of a powerful institution upon a richly

endowed nature, but the influence of that nature itself
upon the entire personality, upon its products, and
upon its activities in the leadership of men. One may
get a fair impression of some men's preaching without
knowing much about the men. This is the case with
preachers like Spurgeon and Guthrie, whose homiletic
qualities are somewhat obtrusive. But in the case of
Newman, as in that of Augustine and that of most
dogmatic and apologetic preachers, we must know the
man. And one of the points of interest in Newman's
preaching is the interest it excites to know more about
the preacher. The " Parochial and Plain Sermons,"
preached during the fifteen years of his incumbency of
St. Mary's, the sermons of his young manhood, including some of the very earliest, have perhaps been most
widely read by the English people. Their interest lies
largely in their disclosure of the struggles of his own
inner life. The " Sermons on Subjects of the Day "
disclose more care in the preparation and are of special
interest as disclosing his nearness to the church of
Rome. The " Occasional Sermons " are more thoughtful and elaborate, and the " University Sermons " are
characterized by great subtlety of thought and thoroughness and fulness of discussion. But the " Discourses to
Mixed Congregations " disclose a spontaneity and freedom of movement and a power of eloquence that are
not found in any of his earlier sermons. They were
delivered soon after entering the Roman church and,
as Mr. Gladstone suggested, indicate that he felt himself " unmuzzled." There is a passionate intensity of
emotion and a rushing movement of style in these discourses that are not found to so large an extent in other

U

sermons, and they disclose the fact that he is beginning to cultivate his style more carefully than it was possible for him during the days of controversy. And yet there are but few discourses, if any, that stand out in such solitary greatness as some of the sermons of Robertson, or of Bushnell, or of Brooks. We really do not know much about Newman's preaching by reading here and there a sermon, we must read them widely and in the light of his career. These sermons are still read by all classes of Englishmen and in all parts of Great Britain. And by Romanists, high Anglicans, Broad churchmen, Evangelicals, and Dissenters alike they are regarded almost as classics. There is hardly any exaggeration, from the cultivated Englishman's point of view, in a remark of Mr. Hutton, I think it was, of the *London Spectator*, in the *Contemporary Review* a few years ago, to the effect that if he were condemned to solitude in some remote part of the earth and had choice of the authors that might beguile him in his isolation, he would select Shakespeare's plays and Newman's sermons. But it is not the technique of the sermon that commands men's attention and interest. It is the man and the intensity of his message. This is why in the reading the first impression is inadequate, and why the sermons increase in interest by frequent reading. It was in part perhaps, because Newman recognized the offhand, unconventional, unartistic character of his early sermons, and because he had no time to perfect their literary form, that for a long time he refused to have them published. But the fact that they were prepared with distinct reference to the spiritual needs of his congregation was a still more weighty consideration. It seemed like parading before the public the secrets of domestic life.

But let us see if we can discover some of the chief points of value in Newman's preaching.

Perhaps its most striking quality is its elevated and intense religious tone. Newman was intensely hostile to the worldliness of his time. There is therefore a certain unearthly note about his preaching. He was a most skilful and powerful advocate of religion as belonging to the realm of the invisible and eternal. As we have seen, a most vivid sense of invisible realities was the mark of his religious genius, and he set forth their glories with all the vividness of his imagination, all the passion of his emotion, and all the skill of his dialectic. The reality, the priority, the commanding and compelling authority, and the unchanging glory of the invisible and eternal may almost be called the stock of his message. And perhaps no modern preacher has equalled him in the cogency with which these realities are presented to men. To be their advocate was his conscious calling. In "The Parting of Friends,"[1] which contains his last words to the Anglican church, when he left St. Mary's, he discloses the conscious recognition of the worth of his message. The sermon closes as follows: "And O my brethren, O kind and affectionate hearts, O loving friends, should you know any one whose lot it has been, by writing or by word of mouth, in some degree to help you thus to act; if he has ever told you what you knew about yourselves, or what you did not know; has read to you your wants or feelings, and comforted you by the very reading; has made you feel that

[1] "Sermons on Subjects of the Day," XXVI.

there was a higher life than this daily one, and a brighter
world than that you see ; or encouraged you, or sobered
you, or opened a way to the inquiring, or soothed the
perplexed ; if what he has said or done has ever made
you take interest in him, and feel well inclined toward
him ; remember such a one in time to come, though you
hear him not, and pray for him that in all things he may
know God's will and at all times he may be ready to fulfil it." The pathos and delicacy of these words are not
more impressive than the ardent affectionateness of the
man that is disclosed by them, and they give us an insight into the secret of his personal influence. They
reveal, too, the consciousness that he knew the souls of
men, that he could interpret them to themselves, making
clearer what is already known, bringing to light what is
not known, encouraging the faint-hearted, sobering the
frivolous, opening a path to the hesitating, and comforting the perplexed. And what he thought himself to be,
he was, and such was his work. But the specific point
in hand just here is his delicately expressed conviction
that he had made men see and feel "that there is a
higher life than the earthly one, and a brighter world
than the one men see." And it was because they are
native to the human soul that he found men.

To the method of this message of "a higher life" and
"a brighter world" we may object; it is the extreme
method of the ecclesiastic and the dogmatist. It is in
some respects a gloomy message. Its picture of human
life outside the church is exaggerated and distorted.
Religion, as representing the realm of the invisible and
eternal and as the supreme interest, must be isolated
from life. It must also be embodied in a visible catholic

church, and it must be brought to men by that church with the notes of divine authority. It is the calling of the church to represent the invisible realm of redemptive grace in outward, visible form. God is in the church, and in the church alone, as the invisible, ever abiding, redemptive presence, and that church is the holy, apostolic catholic church, which is identical with the kingdom of God. Protestantism belongs to the uncovenanted and unconsecrated kingdom of this world, that stands over against the holy catholic church. What Protestantism, and what the philanthropic agencies of the world are doing for the advancement of the kingdom of God, which is wider than any church or all churches combined, he does not see. It is a lost and depraved world, under the curse of God as the kingdom of evil, a " vain, unprofitable, overbearing world." Worldliness is living for the life that now is, and religion is living for the life to come, which is the life invisible and eternal. The world exists for visible and temporal ends, the church for invisible and eternal ends. But the contrast between the church and the world is not merely the contrast between the invisible and eternal and the visible and perishable, which is in fact a false contrast, but it is a contrast between the holy and the unholy. Sanctity belongs to the church alone. Unsanctity belongs to the world. The worldling has not only lost all good, but all vision of the good, all vision of the invisible and eternal. He cannot see or know the things of God. Things of temporal interest he may know. He may know justice, but faith, hope, love, he cannot know. If he comes to know them, it is not simply by the awakening of what is already within him and native to him, but by the infusion of supernatural grace from without. Hence all right of private judgment in matters of religion is lost. The church must be separated from the world and set over against it. It must win the world by conquest.

This form of representation doubtless holds very important truth, and its presentation by Newman is singularly effective. This conception of a mighty, conquering church, that has put the nations under its feet and is subduing the world to God, produces a certain sense of awe, and this message from Newman's lips was a mighty message. It is the specific message of the later years, but it is substantially the message of his life. But it is a gloomy and disheartening picture which the world presents. It is a world without God, save as it is the dwelling-place of a holy catholic church.

But with all its limitations of conception and representation, it was still a great message, and it reached the souls of men. Newman had a false conception of saintliness and of separation from the world. Robertson, as unworldly a man as Newman, had a much more rational and healthy conception of the unworldly life. And yet Newman was a genuine saint. He was a man of profound religious convictions, of powerful religious emotions, of quick sense of spiritual realities, and of a consecrated spirit. Submission to the will of God in the crucifixion of earthly affections is a theme on which he likes to dwell. Such a man must speak with power, if he has any vocation to speak at all. He took no secular or semi-secular subjects into the pulpit, but dealt wholly with spiritual themes. He was not a ghostly man. He had a genuine interest in human life and dealt with things that are real. But the tone is unearthly. In an age when men are so almost wholly absorbed in things that are visible and temporal, when the lusts of the flesh and the lusts of the eye and the vainglory of life are dominating their souls, it is a great blessing to the church and to the world that so great a voice should be heard, telling them of better things. The church needs to be reminded that there is a difference between the kingdom of God and the kingdom of this world, between the saint and the sinner, between the church and the world, between him who serves God and him who serves Him not, between grace and nature, between the regenerate and the unregenerate man, between the sacred and the secular, between the good and the bad, and between heaven and hell. It should indeed be a discriminating message, but better the exaggerated form than no message at all. Newman's unearthly voice has been heard in the Anglican church, and but for him its preaching would be far less effective. As we read Newman, we think of Robertson, and hear an echo in new form of the same unworldly spirit. Remote as their points of view are, Newman reminds us not a little of Schleiermacher, in the emphasis that is laid upon the invisible and eternal realities of religion, and upon the sharp distinction between the religious and the worldly spirit. It was Schleiermacher's voice that rallied the church to the recognition of the inner realities of religion. It is Newman's voice that holds our attention to the consciousness of the church as the organ of the invisible and eternal.

The ethical significance of faith for the Christian life is another point of value in Newman's preaching, closely allied with the preceding. To show that it is natural to

believe, that it is better to be credulous even than to
be doubtful, that it is a wrong done our manhood not
to believe, to vindicate the reasonableness of faith, to
justify its claims, and to magnify its power, was one
of his leading aims. He was doubtless mistaken in his
conception of the object of faith, but this did not fatally
vitiate his conception of the reality and power of faith.
Substitute for the church the proper object of faith, and
Newman's teaching is what we need to-day. He lays
much stress upon the naturalness of faith. We are constitutionally predisposed to believe. It is the normal
habit of mind, and the sceptical habit is abnormal.
Better believe too much than too little. Doubt is not
only a weakness, but a sin, for in doubt one refuses to
follow the higher impulses of his nature. It is a refreshing thing to come into contact with a man who
discredits the sceptical attitude of mind in an age that
inclines to glory in it as if it were the mark of a superior order of intelligence. Newman constantly presses
upon our attention the fact that the truths of religion
are not revealed primarily to the reason of man, but to
faith. Faith is truly natural, as being an inclination to
commit ourselves to what is external to ourselves, as
object of trust, and yet in its religious aspect it is the
gift of God. For without divine help the soul does not
commit itself to invisible spiritual realities. " The arguments for religion do not compel any one to believe,
just as arguments for good conduct do not compel any
one to obey. Obedience is a consequence of willing to
obey, and faith is the consequence of willing to believe.
We may see what is right, whether in matters of faith
or obedience, of ourselves, but we cannot will what is

right without the grace of God." [1] This is Newman's
contribution to the doctrine of faith. Faith is an ethical
act. It is willing to believe. It is the soul's self-sur-
render to what has the right to claim its allegiance.
It requires no act of will to accept mathematical demonstrations. But to accept the august claims of religion
does require an act of will. This surely has a modern
note. That Newman swung away from the rationalism that assumes the competency of the speculative
intellect, to deal successfully with the problems of religion, indicates that he was in line with a better and
a more Christian type of thinking than had been current. That he vindicates the self-committal of the soul
to its higher intuitions and convictions and impulses
and instincts and longings and strivings shows that, so
far forth, he was in line with the modern experimental
school, the school that believes in the validating power
of Christian experience in vindicating the claims of religion. It is this validating power that he claims for
religious experience. [2] But this for him is not enough.
He adds the objective authority of the church. Neither
rational nor religious experience alone is sufficient for
faith. It must have a dogmatic basis. It must rest
upon the divine authority of the church. But, after all,
this dogmatic note of faith does not fatally vitiate the
main point of his teaching with respect to the ethical
significance of faith. For faith is still the soul's willingness to commit itself to its higher spiritual experiences,
which are evoked by the church, and to which the
church, as the voice of God, summons it.

1 " Discourses to Mixed Congregations," IX, X, XI.
2 " Sermons on Subjects of the Day," XXIII.

The intensity of its emotional and spiritual fervor is an element of great interest and impressiveness in Newman's preaching. All of his writings, particularly those of a popular and controversial character, and above all his sermons, leave the impression that there is behind them a man not only of strong convictions and of resolute moral purpose, but of ardent affectionateness and of tender sympathies. The " Apologia," with all its polemic severity and biting sarcasm, supports this impression. Whatever he holds to be true he holds with constitutional energy and advocates with passionate eagerness. Traditionalist and dogmatist of an extreme type though he was, he stoutly maintained the necessity of an ethical and spiritual appropriation of the truth. " He who has the truth within him, though he cannot evolve it out of his heart in shape and proportion for another's inspection, is blessed beyond all comparison above him who has much to say and says what is true, but says it not from himself, but by rote, and could say quite as well just the reverse, did it so happen that he mistook it for truth."[1] The sermons furnish abundant evidence that he proclaimed the truth "from himself" and not "by rote." The preaching of the period in which he was connected with the Anglican church bears witness to the passionate earnestness with which he tried to make the truth of his position perfectly real to himself, although he might not be perfectly sure of his ground. And his subsequent career indicates the sincerity of his convictions and a certain apostolic earnestness to convince others of the truth that has evidently become a great power in his own soul. With all his in-

[1] " Sermons on Subjects of the Day," XXIII, p. 345.

tellectual subtlety and reserve and caution, he was a man
of intense and tender feelings.   His brother, it is true,
regarded him as "lacking in humility and tenderness,"
and even as "contemptuous and self-conceited."   It is
a singularly unfraternal judgment, but the basis of it
is perhaps not difficult to discover.   Newman was a
dogmatician, and such a man, as already suggested, may
be harsh and severe and seemingly arrogant in his
enforcement of what he holds for truth.   We find something of this in his sermons.   But this is not the prevailing note.   He loved what he held for truth, but he
did not cease to love men.   There was the heart of a
man behind the conscience and the will of the ecclesiastical dogmatist, and at times it burst forth as in a sort of
wail of passionate human sympathy.   This quality in
him largely accounts for the interest the English people
have continued to take in him.   His appeal to Anglican
friends to remember him in time to come, if anything
he had said or done had ever made them take an interest
in him, was not in vain.   No one can read his strong
exclamatory utterances, full of pathos and fiery zeal,
full of apostrophe and appeal, without recognizing the
intensity of his nature, his attachment to his friends,
and his love for his church.   There is something particularly interesting and impressive in his utterances of
passionate adoration, not only for our Lord, but for His
Mother.   They suggest, what Robertson felt and recognized, the power of the humanly sympathetic element
in the religion of the Roman church.   It is a human
heart that brings the heart of God near to us, and what
wonder that the Mother of our Lord has mightily moved
the imaginations and feelings of men, especially of men

who, like Newman, have found themselves in reaction
against the technicalities of an abstract religion, and
who have felt the "all-corroding power of intellectual
scepticism." Such a recoil is not unnatural. It was this
early recoil of the emotional, sympathetic, and imaginative element in Newman's nature from the coldness of
Protestantism that accounts for his early inclination to
adore the "holy Mother," and for the attractiveness
which the humanity of the religion of the Roman church
had for him.

Newman's preaching has interest and value in the
evidence it furnishes of his insight into the human soul.
It is said of him that he did not know men. This is the
testimony of his brother-in-law in the "Oxford Reminiscences." The meaning of this is evident. He did not
know men on the lower side of their nature, had no
handling of practical affairs, could not adjust himself
to men's weaknesses and perversities, had no tact for
practical leadership and no skill in organizing the political elements of the Oxford movement. But this involves no lack of insight into the hearts of men. It
suggests, perhaps, the deeper insight. In this gift of
insight he surpasses all the men of his time. In a
church whose leaders are obliged to study and to know
the human heart, whose casuistic subtleties are often
our admiration, a church that is in many respects matchless in its guidance of men, Newman was at once at
home, and stood at the front as a shepherd of souls.
He was a matchless priest. His intellectual subtlety,
his skill in psychological analysis, his insight into
human motives, his vivid imagination, his sympathetic
earnestness, his study of himself in the broodings of an

introverted life, his isolation and loneliness, his study of
the records of human passion and conflict in the history
of the church, his knowledge of dramatic literature, all
fitted him to interpret the human soul, and to become
its shepherd.   To tell men what they knew about themselves, but to make the knowledge clearer and more
significant; to tell them what they did not know and did
not imagine, and to surprise and confound them in the
telling; to read their wants and feelings, and to comfort
them in the very reading — this was his choice gift, and
he knew it when he made, and not in vain, his final appeal for remembrance by his honest, true-hearted English countrymen.   It was precisely this knowledge of
the hearts of men that made him the attractive teacher
that he was, and brought the young men of Oxford, as
well as the commonest of the common people, to St.
Mary's, and has left its traces in those sermons that he
poured out with such wealth of thought and feeling for
fifteen years and that will remain a literary attraction
for other generations.

If we look at Newman's preaching from the point of
view of its subject-matter, tone, and method, we shall
find much that is of interest and value.   He may be
classed as an apologetic preacher.   All of his sermons
bear the mark of the apologist.   We are never left in
doubt about his doctrinal opinions.   They are constantly
emerging, although never in technical form, and they are
never defended by elaborate argument.   Even the sermons that have a definitely ethical and evangelistic character have a doctrinal basis and an apologetic interest.
The doctrinal and the practical are in his view identical,
for there can be no sound practical Christian life that

is not grounded in the truths of Christianity as interpreted by the church.   It is with considerable effort
that we get at the theology of some preachers.   In
our day there is but little to get at.   But we have no
such difficulty with Newman's preaching.   We readily
gather all the essential features of his theology, as we
do of Schleiermacher's, from his sermons.   He is content
with no vague statements of truth that is held in solution as mystical sentiment and feeling.   He will have
the right conception, and he proposes to lodge it in the
mind of the hearer.   Sometimes the doctrinal references
are incidental.   A few passages stricken out would leave
a sermon that would prove edifying to any congregation.
The depth and compass of his religious life rendered it
impossible that he should fail to deal largely with truth
that is common to the entire Christian church.   But we
readily discover not only the doctrinal but the ecclesiastical interest.   There is consequently considerable range
and variety in the subject-matter of the discourses, and
they are applied to a great variety of religious interests.
They are not commonplace themes.   If they are familiar, they are discussed with such freshness and individuality of method that they have the interest of novelty.
Each subject is discussed in a free and unconventional
manner, and in a way appropriate to the end he would
realize.   There is therefore nothing stereotyped or repetitious, no traversing of ground previously gone over in
some other form.   Each sermon has a fresh interest of
its own, and we find the old freshness lingering about it
still, whenever we go back to it.   He is faithful to his
own teaching that the preacher should always have a
proposition before his mind, and that he should speak

definitely to the proposition, although it may not be
thrown into definite form, nor be defended by elaborate formal argument. He is quite sure to find the
difficulties of the subject and to answer objections.
He will secure the greater cogency for his argument
by giving his assumed antagonist every possible advantage by a careful statement of his position. Having
given him this advantage by putting his position in its
most favorable light, he proceeds with his undermining
process. His reasoning is acute, but often fanciful and
inconclusive. It is after the dogmatic method. He has
his premise already in hand, and his conclusion is contained in it. It is the deductive process. Give him his
premise, and it will be difficult to meet his argument.
The reasoning process is free and facile and in the
popular manner of a man of prevailingly rhetorical
instincts. His Scriptural citations are copious, and are
a prominent feature in his development. Citations from
secular sources are excluded. Ecclesiastical citations
are often colored by his prepossessions, and Scriptural citations are not, and are not intended to be,
exegetically exact. From the critical point of view,
they are sometimes grotesque. But in their rhetorical
or poetic, as distinguished from their didactic, quality
they are highly interesting and impressive. He was
apparently entirely ignorant of the modern science of
exegesis, and would probably have regarded it as a
hindrance. Doubtless he regards his citations as throwing light upon his discussion, but they do it, if at all,
suggestively and by an allegorizing accommodation. The
freedom, not to say abandon, with which he uses his
texts, the unexpected themes he deduces from them,

are rather shocking to the critical homiletic mind, and
the whole discussion hangs as loosely about the theme
as the theme about the text.   But the rhetorical impression is always vivid.   The preaching of the Roman
church is strong in its imaginative elements.   It is
stirring preaching, and has, according to its kind, an
evangelistic note.   In this, as in other respects, Newman was from the first a Romanist in his homiletic
genius.   His sermons are shaped with reference to
impression.   Their very dogmatism has an element
of power.   Preaching with a strong, positive dogmatic
basis, if handled with rhetorical skill, is always forceful.   The most powerful preaching of the church has
been of this sort.   Witness Chrysostom, Augustine,
the Cappadocians, and the classical French preachers.
It is not in harmony with the tastes of our time.   But
it is pertinent to suggest, that, although the dogmatic
method will not avail, it would not injure the preaching of our day if it had under it a more consistent and
a better-defined theology.   Preaching that holds its theology in solution, that never pushes it into definite conception and formal statement, will lack grip and force.

The structural quality of Newman's preaching bears
the same general mark of freedom.   He does not respect the standard methods of homiletic order.   The
rhetorical rather than the logical interest dominates him
in the ordering of his thought.   He early chose the unconventional style and never changed it materially.   He
preached, moreover, to congregations composed largely
of educated people, who exacted but little upon his
method.   His mental productiveness, the fulness of
his material, the energetic grip of the subject upon his

mind, the intensity with which it moved his feelings, and the rush of his style naturally resulted in riding down all questions of architectural outline as a sort of hindrance to the onflow of the sermon, and he satisfied himself with a progressive movement that had no definitely marked outline as best serving his purpose.

Three things impress us. First, the directness of the address. He gets to work promptly, drives straight at his mark, and closes with direct appeal. From beginning to end a definite apologetic and ethical interest is manifest. The fulness and the free flow of the thought is another feature. No loose verbiage, no padding, no hard pressure upon the homiletic pump. All is free and affluent, — keen thinking and straight but facile speaking. And then there is the progressive movement of the thought. It is not closely articulated, nor definitely outlined, but it moves rapidly onward to its goal. He has mastered his thought and he holds it freely in its relations. In the university sermons, which of all his discourses are the most elaborate, he marks the progress of his thought by numbered divisions. They are not homiletic divisions, marking the main steps of the development, but numbered paragraphs, marking transitions of thought. Within these numbered paragraphs we may sometimes, but not always, easily trace the outline of the sermon from introduction to conclusion. In most of his discourses there is no careful paragraphing and but little formal division. The " Discourses to Mixed Congregations " are without texts, and they show that without texts the preacher is likely to allow himself the wider freedom in the movement of his thought. The sermon entitled " God's Will

x

the End of Life," impressive in the quality of its thought, also furnishes a good illustration of his free structural method and of his affluent rhetorical style. The closing appeal to Christ is impressive in its pathos and in its emotional fervor. The delineation of the worldly life and especially the passage relating to the damnation of Catholics is vividly graphic. The title is only indirectly the subject of the sermon, but suggests the background of the entire discussion.

Newman is best known to the general public as a master of English style, and the attractiveness of his preaching is largely conditioned by its diction. It is a simple style, sometimes even colloquially direct and familiar, bringing high things down into the experiences of common life. Yet it is elevated and dignified, and never descends below the proprieties of the august subjects discussed. It is clear and exact, speaking directly to the mind and conveying thought with discrimination. This discriminating quality, indeed, is very notable, and secures for us most delicate shadings of thought and results in a free expansion of style. The emotional and affectional quality of his utterance secures for it a certain pathos that is a marked quality in his style. We are never offended when he addresses us as his "dearest children," but are rather attracted by it. His apostrophe to Christ at the close of the sermon entitled "The Mental Sufferings of Our Lord in His Passion" is characterized by great delicacy of feeling, and illustrates the passionate intensity of his nature. Note the pathos and delicacy of his last utterance from the pulpit of St. Mary's to his Anglican friends. Note the not infrequent appeals to the Mother of our Lord.

The gracefulness of his style is generally regarded as its most characteristic quality. Matching the purity of sentiment and feeling and the refined taste that mark the whole tone of the sermon, is the elegance of his vocabulary, the skilful placing of words and marshalling of clauses, securing for his sentences a rhythmic flow. His skilful delineations, whether of the external experiences of life or of mental or psychical states, are always an element of grace in his diction. But the energy, what we may call the momentum, the rushing movement of his style, is still more notable. This momentum is a quality of great intensity. Note the rapid, sketchy description of the gay and active scenes of human life in the sermon to which I have already referred, "God's Will the End of Life." "The ways are thronged, carriage-way and pavement; multitudes are hurrying to and fro, each on his own errand,"[1] etc. Note his description of Christ's earthly life.[2] Read his description of Dives.[3] Recall his description of the Catholic who would imitate the worldling, and read the pathetic appeal in the conclusion of the sermon. The intensity of the style is its impressive feature. The rush of the sentences is also an element of grace.

For his effectiveness as a preacher Newman was not at all dependent upon the appointments of the orator. There was a slight stoop in his shoulders as he stood in the pulpit, and he never disclosed his full height. He read his sermon without action in the reading, but it was not without the animation of earnestness. His eye was clear and penetrating, and his voice was

[1] "Discourse to Mixed Congregations," pp. 105–106.
[2] *Ibid.*, pp. 109–110.   [3] *Ibid.*, pp. 112–114.

musical, and this compensated for other defects. His dress was that of the Oxford clergyman of his day, which was sufficiently distinctive but not extreme. He read the ordinary service rapidly, but in the Sunday worship he was more deliberate; and his brother charges that the service of worship was of so much importance in his estimate that he undervalued the sermon. If the sermons left us are a proof of this, it was an undervaluation for which the world will never seriously reproach him.

Mr. Gladstone has left on record his impression of Newman as a preacher in the following words: "There was not very much change in the inflection of the voice; action there was none. His sermons were read, and his eyes were always bent on his book; and all that, you will say, is against efficacy in preaching. Yes, but you must take the man as a whole, and there was a stamp and a seal upon him; there was a solemn sweetness and music in the tone; there was a completeness in the figure, taken together with the tone and with the manner, which made even his delivery, such as I have described it, and though exclusively from written sermons, singularly attractive." [1]

In brief summation, then, let it be said that for subtlety and delicacy of thought, for skilful dialectic, for expository grace, for seriousness of tone, for such persuasiveness of inculcation as is conditioned by strong conviction and intense feeling, and for all the elements of an effective style of public address, but especially for freedom, flexibility, and momentum, Newman's sermons are a valuable study for serious-minded men of any sect or of any age.

[1] See Hutton's "Cardinal Newman," p. 87.

CHAPTER VII

JAMES BOWLING MOZLEY

I

THE MAN AND THE THEOLOGIAN

AMONG the Oxford men who were brought into connection with Newman, and who participated in the theological and ecclesiastical discussions of the Oxford controversy, there was no abler nor more independent, honest, or judicious thinker than Canon Mozley. In his own day he was more widely known as a theologian than as a preacher. With all his intellectual suggestiveness and extraordinary moral impressiveness, he was not a particularly acceptable preacher, even to an Oxford audience, by which the gifts of oratory were not and are not held in very high esteem. Yet there are elements of intellectual and moral power in his published sermons, elements that seem almost to be more effective in the printed than they were in the oral form, that, after their kind, have not been surpassed by anything in homiletic literature that has been given to the public during the last half-century. They lack the intensity and literary grace of Newman's sermons, and are somewhat heavy and slow in movement; but they are intellectually stronger and, from the ethical point of view, more impressive than any that ever came from Newman's pen. Of these sermons, the *London Spectator* has said that "the reading of them would be enough to change the whole character and life of a man." It is certainly an extraordinary experience for a preacher, and an extraordinary test of him, that his sermons must be known through the press before his value as a preacher can be adequately estimated. This is the test to which Mozley has been subjected, and it suggests somewhat significantly the possibilities of loss to the world if the manuscript were to be banished from the pulpit. Unlike Newman, whose intellectual vivacity and emotional fervor and force and grace of literary style fitted him after his fashion for the mastery of assemblies, Mozley reached only a limited circle of hearers. But, like Newman, he has reached and influenced a wide circle of readers. No intelligent and cultivated man who becomes familiar with these virile discourses will, I venture to say, fail to receive a strong moral and mental impression from them ; and no preacher, especially, who would acquaint himself with the best that has been spoken in the modern pulpit, or who would study intelligently the elements of moral power in modern preaching and would avail himself of the strongest moral incentive, will willingly fail to acquaint himself with them.

Mozley was born in 1813 and was Newman's junior by twelve years. We are told that as a boy he disclosed, in a marked degree, just those qualities for which he was subsequently distinguished. He was strongly individualistic, high-spirited, and, according to his brother of the "Oxford Reminiscences," who might well have told us more about him and less about himself, quick-tempered. This strong individuality and high spirit he disclosed during the Oxford controversy in his resistance of Newman's influence and in the gradual formation of his own independent opinions, but he curbed his temper and secured the mastery of himself, accounting as a dishonor in himself and disliking in others any loss of it. Like Newman, he was of a reflective turn, taking no interest in the games of his school, finding "thinking his diversion." He was shy and sensitive and easily impressed. Anything that was striking or characteristic always arrested his attention and became a basis for reflection, and, as we shall see later on, the disclosure of this impressibility became one of his most interesting homiletic peculiarities. It is this impressibility of the man that accounts in large measure for Newman's strong early influence over him, an influence, indeed, which it could not have been easy for any one, even the most independent, to resist. In his maturer years he speaks somewhat depreciatingly of this influence of Newman upon his literary style. Whatever may have been Newman's influence upon his opinions, there is no evidence that he recognized it as an important or permanent factor in his life; and whatever may have been true of his style, it is perfectly evident that it was but a transient influence, and it is equally evident that he formed his opinions independently of Newman's domination. It is not difficult to see how a man so slow in his development and who struggled as he did with the barriers of language should have been by contrast strongly impressed by Newman's facility and brilliancy of literary expression, and the very recognition of the influence discloses his exacting independence of pur-

pose.   In one of his sermons, entitled "The Educating
Power of Strong Impressions,"[1] there is a very interesting discussion of the educative influence of one mind
over another.   It is not impossible that he may have
had in mind Newman's influence over others, himself
included.   At any rate, in reading his words, one naturally thinks of his own experiences in connection with
Newman.   The point he makes is that although subjection to such an influence makes a child of a man, yet it
is necessary to the development of his manhood.   One
"may be so much under the influence of an extraordinary and superior being, that it may prevent him, for
the time, from finding out his own power."   Yet all this
may be necessary to one's personal development.   "It
is only the common truth, and a very familiar truth, of
education."   Such an one is all the while "collecting
the maturity and vigor of a man."   This was eminently
true of Mozley.   It was a wonderfully stimulating atmosphere in which he was placed, and the large and
long result was seen in the virility of his intellectual and
moral manhood.   He was of a controversial turn of
mind, and very early disclosed his readiness for discussion or debate.   It was the product, not only of a combative temperament, but of his intellectual inquisitiveness,
his positiveness of conviction, and interest in and devotion to the truth.   One can easily conceive of him as
exhibiting in private discussion the mental pugnacity
and tenacity of the typical Englishman, but it is interesting to observe that, although, like Canon Liddon, he
seems to have an antagonist in mind and is always defending some cherished interest, there is yet in his public

[1] "Occasional and Parochial Sermons," XXI.

discussions and in many of his theological essays an almost entire absence of the polemic temper and method. He gripped his subjects by the roots and his mental movement was strong. It was necessary for him to get at the bottom of things. He always struck for the centre. He must master his subject. This was his life habit. He was, therefore, relatively slow in his movement and developed somewhat late into the maturity of his powers. One can easily imagine the powerful influence Dr. Arnold would have had for so slow but responsive a nature. It is certain that Mozley always had the highest admiration for Arnold, Broad churchman though Arnold was. But he failed to enter Rugby as a student because Arnold had fixed the age limit for entrance at fifteen, which young Mozley had already passed. It is interesting to conjecture what Arnold at that time of intense intellectual activity might have done with such strong timber. It is conceivable that Newman might have found him a formidable antagonist. But as for Mozley, he seems always to have regarded his rejection at Rugby as special good fortune, since he made better head in his studies alone and thus developed his own individuality to better advantage. His brother expresses the opinion that Arnold's exacting standard might have embarrassed one of his slow habit of mind, and that the two men were too much alike in their intellectual independence and fiery and pugnacious temper to get on together. Whatever may be the truth of this, it is clear enough that the two following years of private study were fruitful years.

In 1830, three years before Newman began the Anglican agitation, and three years after he had taken St.

Mary's, at the age of seventeen, Mozley entered Oriel College, where Newman had a tutorship and his brother a fellowship, and where the Anglican movement found its centre. His brother's influence, his own thoughtfulness and modesty, the delicacy, the deference, and eager inquisitiveness with which he listened to the vigorous discussions that were going on about him, and at the same time the independence and positiveness of his own opinions, secured for him at once a favorable introduction to the society and friendship of the older Oriel magnates. He was cordially welcomed by Newman, Pusey, and Keble, the latter having associations with Oriel, and he soon entered into the discussion of questions that were already stirring Oxford students. Some of the then important questions were the apostolicity and catholicity of the Anglican church, the claims of the Roman church, baptismal regeneration, the real presence, and the relation of the church and state, questions all of which were subsequently discussed in "Tracts for the Times." On account of Mozley's interest in these questions he did not reach so high a rank in his college studies proper as he otherwise might have done. He graduated in 1834, the year following the formal opening of the Oxford controversy. It was a year of immense intellectual activity and of intense feeling. The new apostles vied with each other in the voluminousness of their publications in the form of tracts, sermons, and essays, and in the enthusiasm of their active propagandism. Although but twenty-one years of age, Mozley was already a participant in these agitations. At that time there was no proper provision at Oxford for the training of men for the ministry. It was the Oxford method, and always has been too largely, to train individual men under tutors without the stimulus of associate life. The patrons of the new movement saw the need of a theological school. Accordingly Newman and Pusey rented a house near Christ Church and fitted it up as a sort of family school, where graduates might board and associate themselves in theological study. Mozley became one of the student inmates of this school and remained there two years under the tutorship of these two men, Pusey, however, bearing the chief burden of the teaching; and when, at the end of the two years, the school was given up, Pusey took the students to his own home. Mozley remained with Pusey till 1840, when he was appointed to a fellowship in Magdalen College. For six years he had been associated with Oriel men, who were the prime movers in the controversy. He had been in the very storm centre of the movement, in a way allied with it through his High Church sympathies, although apparently not closely allied with it or in complete sympathy with it. His election to Magdalen terminated his immediate relation with the agitators. During all these years he had been developing an independent position, and he at last dropped away from them, his writings disclosing at the end a break with them. During those student days, a year after his graduation from Oriel, he secured the prize for an essay on "The Influence of the Ancient Oracles on Public Morals and Life," which is pronounced by his brother a remarkable production for a man of his age. He held the Magdalen fellowship for sixteen years, or until the year 1856. In the year 1838, at the age of twenty-five, he was ordained as deacon and six years later was ordained as priest. During all these years, from the time of his entrance upon his theological studies, he was not only associated with the representatives of the High Church branch of the Anglican communion, but was a contributor to the *British Critic*, which Newman had edited for two years, and which was, in a sort, the organ of the Oxford movement.

When in 1845 the break came and Newman went over to the Roman church, Mozley stood by Anglicanism and was in a sort associated with the men who initiated the ritualistic movement which followed the break-up under Newman. But while affiliated with them, he was recognized as occupying an independent position. He gradually became alienated from this party and ultimately occupied almost as independent a position, as a theological thinker, as Robertson, although of course a very different position. At the time of the disruption, the *British Critic* ceased to exist, and Mozley started the *Christian Remembrancer*, to which he was one of the most weighty contributors for the next ten years, or until 1856, when he left Oxford. In this periodical appeared some of his most interesting and able essays, notably the article in which he made a vigorous onset upon Martin Luther, and his exceedingly able essay on the Book of Job.

On leaving Oxford he took charge of the parish of Old Shoreham, in Sussex County, near Brighton. It is interesting to think of Mozley as so near the scene of Robertson's brilliant ministry, and to recall that while Robertson, who had died three years before the entrance upon this Old Shoreham ministry, was becoming widely known through the English press as the greatest of

English preachers, this quiet man was discharging the duties of a parish minister near at hand and was continuing those studies which should become tributary to his reputation as the ablest theological thinker in the Anglican church.   Here at Old Shoreham most of the sermons contained in the volume entitled " Occasional and Parochial Sermons " were preached.   The volume was published in 1879, the year after his death, and without the revising touches of his own hand, which, in the case of some of them, may account for a certain lack of literary finish.   Most of them bear evidence of having been prepared in the course of ordinary parish work and are of a practical and helpful character.

By Mr. Gladstone's recommendation he was, in 1869, appointed Canon of Worcester, and in 1871 was made " Regius Professor of Divinity " at Oxford, the position that had been filled by Dr. Hampden, whose appointment had been so strenuously opposed by Newman and his party.   At the same time he was appointed Canon of Christ Church and select preacher to the university, holding still his living at Old Shoreham.   The publication, in 1858, not long after going to Old Shoreham, of his essay on the " Augustinian Doctrine of Predestination," in which he disclosed the increasing independence of his theological position, widened the breach between him and the high Anglicans.   His article, subsequently, on the baptismal controversy had a like result. In 1865 he gave the Bampton Lectures on " Miracles," in which he commits himself to the position that Christianity cannot be successfully defended and vindicated apart from the external evidence of miracles.   It is an able presentation of the old argument, but contains noth-

ing that is new and is not by any means conclusive.
The published result of his work as professor of divinity
from 1871 to 1876 appears only in his university sermons,
issued in 1876, the last sermon in the volume being the
last he ever preached, and in the volume entitled " Ruling Ideas in Early Ages," compiled from his lectures
to students in divinity, mostly Oxford tutors, a work
which, although superseded by a more advanced stage of
thought, is still of great value for the breadth and originality and clearness and force of its treatment of some
of the difficult problems of Old Testament ethics.

Canon Mozley was one of the ablest and best-trained
theologians in the Anglican church.   As an original
and forceful thinker, it is doubtful if any man of his day
was his superior.   All of his theological writings, and
his sermons not the less, bear the mark of a man who is
accustomed to get at the roots of things, and who by
years of patient, manly effort has attained to master-
ship in his thinking.   We may not accept altogether
the point of view from which he looks at Christianity.
We may not accept all of his estimates of its proper
defences.   We may not agree with all of his fundamental
positions, or with all of his methods and conclusions.
But of the virility of his thinking, and in general of its
sanity and of his power of lucid and cogent statement,
there can be no question.   He has been compared with
Bishop Butler, with whom in his equipment he has
much in common, of whom he was a thorough student,
mastering, as Newman did, Butler's doctrine of probability, and using it in his discussions in a very effective way, although in a way quite different from
Newman.   In the strength, thoroughness, and steadiness

of his mental grasp he is like Butler, but in literary
accomplishments he bears the mark of the better modern
culture, and is greatly Butler's superior.   In the early
years of his student life, when under Newman's influence, especially his literary influence, his style was
much more rhetorical than in later years.   But as
Newman's influence in this and other respects declined,
his style acquired that mental sobriety and solidity, and
that increasing lucidity and forcefulness, which so strongly
characterize it as an expository style.   He had nothing of Newman's brilliancy, productiveness, and facility
in turning off work.   He was slow, but he was strong
in the movement of his thought.   He felt his way
into the interior of his subject, and he needed time.
He went at his work deliberately and with mental poise,
and with the tenacity of a true Englishman.   He felt
within him the movings of power, and with self-reliant,
steadfast purpose to make it felt he bided his time.
He was not anxious for intellectual domination, as Newman apparently was.   He had less of the passion of the
advocate.   He was willing to let the truth do its own
work, when once he had interpreted it and laid bare its
moral demands.   But he had a passion for mastering
intellectual obstacles.   He liked to clear away difficulties
that gather about an important problem.   He loved the
truth because it is truth.   He liked indeed the agitation
of conflict and liked to carry his point.   But he coveted
still more the joy of communication and the feeling of
strength that comes from conscious mental and moral
alliance with the truth.   Difficulties only stimulated his
purpose.   It is said of him that in his early student days
he struggled with defective power of expression.   He

had a hesitating manner of speaking. There was a
struggle of mind with the intractable barrier of language ;
and he himself expressed gratification that he had failed
to enter Rugby, where Dr. Arnold's exacting standard
of classical expression would have kept him at a dis-
advantage. His thought was larger than his vocabulary.
His mental activity was ahead of his linguistic. It is
said of him that "no man ever started with a less prom-
ising outfit of fluency and facility of language, or of
the power of readily disentangling and ordering his
thought." The issue left no trace of this behind. No
one would imagine such a struggle. His speech bears
no such scars of battle. He was bent upon the realization of clear, comprehensive, orderly thought, and he
was exacting with himself. He was intent upon getting
at the heart of all subjects investigated, and this slow-
ness in clearing up a subject and his deliberation and
fastidiousness with respect to his diction embarrassed
him. But it also rallied him, and it evoked all that was
in him. The result was a mastery of thought and an
exactness and clearness and strength of speech that are
more than an offset for the difficulties he encountered ;
and one can hardly fail to see that this patient, self-
poised mental habit saved him from one-sidedness and
kept the balance of his judgment and made him the
safer guide. We see here the immense value of thorough
mental training. If Mozley had produced with greater
facility, it might have proved, as in the case of Newman
it did prove, not a "fatal," but an unfriendly facility.
It was here upon this inner battle-ground that he won
his mental and moral victories, and the rest followed in
due order. Perhaps no preacher of his day showed what

would seem to the ordinary hearer or reader an easier handling of the main thought of the discourse.

II

THE APOLOGETIC AND ETHICAL PREACHER

What can a man like Canon Mozley, a lifelong student, a trained theologian, associating chiefly with scholars, a university teacher and preacher and an Oxford man at that, living largely in the realm of abstract thought, and during most of his life remote from the people, — what can such a man do for the untrained hearer or reader? What especially can he do for men who must preach to the uninstructed and untrained so-called common people? Let us see. In discussing some of the salient qualities of Mozley's preaching its helpfulness will perhaps appear.

1. The apologetic note will be recognized at once, even by the most uninstructed reader. It is true that the interest of the advocate is not particularly apparent. It is the ethical rather than the apologetic interest that seems to predominate. But in the background there always lurks the defender of the truth. To him Christianity is truth that has been placed as a sacred deposit in the hands of the church, and it is the preacher's vocation to defend it against attack and to combat the opposing error. His attitude was therefore the necessity of his conception of Christianity and of the church, and this must always be the High churchman's position. Mozley's writings are in general of the apologetic sort. His bent was in that line, his training followed his bent,

Y

his circumstances largely conditioned his training, and his interest in the work of defence shows how strong was the incentive. But his method somewhat obscured the apologetic aim of the sermon, and this is precisely the stress-point of value in it. He always selects some important truth or principle for interpretation, defence, and application. To interpret it to the intelligence of his hearers and to carry it home to their moral sense is his aim. But his method is his own, and it is an interesting study.

This method is in general the non-dogmatic method. It would not be correct to classify him as a dogmatic preacher in the full formal sense of that term. He is not a defender of the teachings of the church, as in a former period Tillotson, South, and Barrow were. He had not the aggressive dogmatic impulse that Newman had, nor does he illustrate the dogmatic temper or method as Liddon does. He has no dogmatic or even doctrinal sermons in the formal technical sense. It is his custom rather to take an important truth, — and he has no interest in truths that are not of fundamental importance, — it may be a truth of natural religion, but more commonly a distinctively Christian truth, without any reference to its definition or formulation by church authority, and without reference to its relation to any other formulated truth ; and he proceeds to expound it by itself, looking into its inner elements, and especially its psychical and ethical elements. It is evident that to him as a preacher the moral evidences for the truth were practically supreme, and that the moral value of the truth was its supreme value. This is an interesting fact, especially when we recall his essentially High Church dogmatic attitude with respect to the truth. For a High churchman must be a believer in the dogmatic principle, and must react against the liberalism that denies this principle and lays supreme stress upon the subjective principle. As a theologian, trained in the dogmatic school, he held to the importance for the church of the objective evidences, and of church authority in the defence of Christianity. He is a stalwart defender of the evidential value of prophecy and miracle in Christian apologetics. He held, as a High churchman, positive opinions with respect to the apostolic authority of the church in fixing dogma. But the notable thing is that we find almost nothing of all this in his sermons. It is not at all the dogmatic method of Newman or even of Liddon. Holding stoutly to the objective defences of truth, he still in his preaching dealt mostly with the subjective, and the moral evidences, as already intimated, most deeply interested him. In this he carried beyond Butler himself his defence of religion, as belonging to the moral constitution of man, and it is not the authority of the church that validates the truth, but the witness of the human soul and especially of the moral nature to its reality and power. This shows that Mozley, with his largeness of vision, his responsiveness to strong impressions, and especially with his strong ethical sense, was more completely under modern influences than he may have realized, and that, as a religious teacher, he had a clear conception of the needs of the men of his time. The significance of this will become the more apparent if we look somewhat into his method of treatment in the two volumes of sermons. We might assume at the outset that in the parochial sermons,

which were preached to an ordinary worshipping congregation, he would follow the non-dogmatic method,
and make but little appeal to the authority of the church,
but would try to adapt his teachings to the simple, practical needs of his hearers. And such we find to be
the case. But if we examine the university sermons,
preached to audiences of the highest intelligence and
culture, whose allegiance to the authority of the church
it would be of supreme importance to hold, as Newman
plainly saw, we find the same non-dogmatic method.
These sermons deal with truths of primal importance,
and the discussion is always strong and convincing. A
casual glance at the titles will disclose the fact that they
are mostly ethical sermons, but in every case we have
an ethical defence of some strong truth.

In his discussion of the Roman Council of 1870, that
confirmed the papal syllabus of the previous year, we
might expect a doctrinal sermon, exposing the errors of
Romanism as contained in the action of the council.
But instead we have a strongly moral argument against
the right of the church, as a spiritual body, to coerce
the conscience. It is a defence from the moral point
of view of the Protestant doctrine of the right of private
judgment against which Newman and his associates so
vigorously contended. In his sermon on the " Pharisees,"
we have not so much a presentation of the Scripture
representations concerning them, as we are led to expect,
or a doctrinal argument against their errors, as a psychological and ethical analysis of the Pharisaic type of
character.

In the sermon on " Eternal Life " we have, on the
one hand, a criticism of the ethics of Compte, and on

the other, a discussion of the value of probable evidence, as related to the problems of religion, and not an argument for immortality at all, save in an indirect and incidental way. In his "Reversal of Human Judgment," the most masterful of all his discourses, we have no discussion of the doctrine of the final judgment, but rather an analysis of the various sources of error in the moral judgments of men which may well furnish ground for ultimate reversal. In his discussion of the "Work of the Spirit" he deals not with the church doctrine, nor even with the Biblical doctrine, but wholly with subjective considerations, in which he shows that a spiritual religion must have its seat in the affections, rather than in the conscience, because it has its source in the Spirit of God. In his discourse on the "Atonement" we have no doctrinal discussion, but a single ethical phase of the atonement which he regards as central and characteristic ; and having discussed this, he leaves the subject to make its own moral impression. In the "Ascension," instead of discussing the fact or its doctrinal import, he presents but a single inferential suggestion from it, viz. the influence of the thought of the enthroning of the divine Man upon the soul's reverence and upon the conduct of life. All this indicates that it was his chosen method to present the practical applicatory aspects of the subjects discussed. As by native bent and by fixed habit, he always looked upon the ethical aspects of doctrine. And in this we have a great advance upon the apologetic preaching of the Anglican church.

Another distinctive mark of value is the affirmative or declarative method of presentation. Of elaborate formal argument there is none. For the negative method of fighting up truth by fighting down error, he had no inclination. From a man of his pugnacious temper, we might expect the theological polemic and occasionally the philippic. But the method is not only non-dogmatic, but non-polemical. The nearest approach to a polemical sermon in the university discourses is the one on the Roman council. It combats the Vatican's claim to the right to use force in matters of conscience. The opportunity might seem a tempting one to a man of Mozley's dialectical ability to enter upon an elaborate and crushing argument in refutation of that claim. The time was favorable. There was a great stir in the ecclesiastical and political world over the publication of the syllabus and the subsequent decree of the council. In Great Britain there was special interest in the bearing of the decree upon the problem of civil allegiance, which stirred Mr. Gladstone to enter the lists against the Vatican. It would seem to have been the favorable moment to strike an effective blow against the Roman church in defence of the rights of conscience, and Mozley was the man to do it. But we have nothing of this sort. Throughout the sermon he shows more interest in establishing the positive principle suggested by his text, John xviii. 36, " My kingdom is not of this world," than in combating the error that had been enunciated by the Roman council. Mozley had learned the wiser method. One thinks of Robertson's positive method of dealing with contested questions. There may be no ground for surmising that Mozley may have felt Robertson's influence in this regard, and yet it is possible. It is at all events not improbable that both men may have learned the lesson of method from the same sources. One surmises that they both brought a salutary lesson from the Anglican controversy of other years. At any rate one finds a modern note of great value in this straightforward, positive, clear, and cogent method of stating the truth, and in this appeal to the hearers' moral sense.

There were two qualities in Mozley that would naturally lead him away from the polemical method. One was the tolerance of his spirit, and the non-partisan character of his thinking. It has been the misfortune of the church that its apologetic preaching has been too largely polemical. We have historic illustration of the weakness of the method. The partisan preaching of Robert South is an example. Such men seem to care quite as much to tear down the work of their opponents, whom they come to regard as personal enemies, and to cripple their influence, as to establish the truth and to bring men under its power. This is the curse of the partisan divisions of the church. When doctrinal errors are associated with moral evils, especially public and social evils, the polemic may be necessary, as seems to have been the case in the time of Augustine. In our day such preaching would be impossible. But in an earlier age it seemed necessary to combat moral corruptions that were associated with doctrinal errors. Luther's preaching was largely polemical. But it was not simply false doctrine that awakened his wrath, but the associate corruptions of moral life. In our own day, however, errors of thought are not so closely allied with moral corruption, and the best tendencies of the age are hostile to the polemical spirit and method. Much of our

modern tolerance may indeed be indifference to the
truth.   The agnostic spirit may promote such indifference.   The man who despairs of arriving at positive truth
will dislike polemics for the reason that, in his opinion,
one side of a question may have as much truth in it as
the other.   There is a good deal of this sort of agnostic
tolerance in our day.   It is true that there are always
men who like polemics, for in the average man the partisan spirit, whether ecclesiastical or political, is strong.
But right-minded men in our day see that the partisan
spirit in defending the truth is unprofitable, and they
turn away from it.   It is questionable whether any
man's religious opinions, merely as such, should be the
object of polemical attack in the pulpit.   It was partly
because Mozley would not be a partisan that he rejected
the polemical method and dealt positively and declara-
tively with the truth.

Moreover, he was a fundamental thinker, and for this
reason also he was more intent upon expounding truth
than upon attacking error.   Polemical preaching is likely
to be shallow.   It fails to reach fundamental truth.   In
concentrating attention upon error, it fails to detect the
truth that lies behind it, and that must be known in
order that in the light of it error may be adequately disclosed.   The man who is bent upon making out his case
against an opponent is pretty sure to lose sight of a good
deal that it is important for him to see.   By failing,
therefore, to get at what is fundamental, the polemist
becomes superficial.   But the man who is confident that
he has got down to hard bottom and treads on solid
ground, who knows that he has a steady grip upon what
is fundamental, is less likely to indulge in the polemical

spirit. There is a staying and steadying power in such confidence. We see this in Mozley, as we saw it in Robertson. They were both high-spirited, constitutionally controversial and combative. But with their independence and non-partisanship there were associated supreme devotion to fundamental principles and supreme love for the truth for its own sake. Mozley was a masterly expounder but a poor pleader. He was strong in the teaching impulse, but weak in personal ambition to dominate men's opinions. He is, therefore, supremely intent upon a clear and thorough handling of his subject, and is willing to let it work its own way. Hence the non-rhetorical and non-oratorical quality of his preaching.

The most effective pulpit orator must, of course, be something of an advocate. It is not enough for him to expound the truth, and leave it without moral enforcement to make its own impression. He must persuade as well as convince. He must use the truth as an instrument for strong incentive. The sermon must be shaped with reference to this end. Unity, progress, cumulative force, are necessary for strong impression. The address is more than an essay. Emotional energy and imaginative representation must have free play, and drive the truth home, that it may secure determinate results. The sermon is an instrument for moral impression, not merely a method of expressing opinion. He is the true preacher who recognizes this. He who fails in this can be at best only a pulpit teacher. Mozley was precisely such a teacher. He was defective in the preaching impulse, as Newman was not and as Liddon was not. Hence defect in the structural and rhetorical quality of the sermon. The sermon is notable for its mental fulness. The preacher has mastered his thought from beginning to end. There is almost a surplus of thought. The first words are weighty, the last equally so, and the body is full. The sermon is just a chance for the preacher to say out what in its fulness is in him to say; and he talks straight on, not leaving many boundary marks, running from introduction to theme and from theme to discussion and on to conclusion without a very well-defined trail. It is a steady pull straight through, and when he has said out all he wants to say, he simply stops. In the whole process there is little or no kindling of emotion or excitation of imagination, and no effort at cumulative effects. Nor does he, as he moves on, seem anxious about making application of the truth, much less about gathering applicatory reflections at the end. He lets the sermon apply itself. Whatever there may be in the way of conclusion is of the inferential sort that perpetuates the mental or didactic impression of the sermon. In a word, the sermon is not a rhetorical instrument. For the intellectual hearer or reader there cannot fail to be a tremendous impressiveness in that strong, steady mental movement, in that searching psychological analysis, and that ethical vigor of the man. This is singularly true of that most masterful sermon, "The Reversal of Human Judgment." As preached it must have made a strong impression on thoughtful and serious minds. But in the reading, as one pauses and reflects upon it, one fancies that the impression may be quite as strong. It is not, however, the work of cogent inculcation, but of masterly exposition, of searching psychological and ethical analysis. It is the work of a great pulpit teacher, and in the positive, declarative method of it, Mozley is eminently helpful, and he shows how best to attain success in this method, viz. by cherishing a supreme love for the truth, by getting a thorough grasp of it, and by refusing to use it as a partisan instrument. To any preacher who is feeling his way after an effective apologetic method, the freedom, strength, steadiness, stateliness, and positiveness of Mozley's mental movement will prove to be a valuable study. His sermons let us inside great truths. They enlarge the scope of our vision. They support a high ideal of apologetic preaching. They suggest the importance of grappling with the highest truths of religion and of keeping petty themes out of the pulpit.

2. The ethical quality in Canon Mozley's preaching and its great value in this regard have already been suggested. We are now ready somewhat more fully to consider it. The above-quoted remark from the *London Spectator*, touching the moral impressiveness of his sermons, indicates the ethical character of his preaching by suggesting its strongest possible ethical result. The truth supported is taken into the realm of the moral nature, and is there vindicated. He rallies the consciences of his hearers to its support, and so in turn the truth as discussed becomes the more effective instrument in educating and training the conscience. A glance at the titles of the sermons will suggest the prevailingly ethical character of the subjects discussed, and only a slight investigation of them will disclose their prevailingly ethical aim and method. They are all adapted to the production of a strong moral impression and illustrate the fact that weighty religious truth

is necessary to profound moral conviction. They illustrate the value for impressive ethical preaching of a
habit of going to the roots of things, and of a habit of
thorough reflection. They illustrate especially the value
of a habit of moral analysis. Mozley was always a student of character and a student of institutions. He
studied men while he studied theology. In fact, he
studied theology in studying men. He was a close
observer and a keen analyst of human nature. He
studied the practical workings of principles and motives
in human life. He studied his own soul. He watched
the working of the moral nature. He was a student of
the drama. In all this lies the secret of his power as
an ethical teacher, and it made him exceptionally valuable as an adviser and counsellor and comforter. In
the Roman church he would have become an illustrious
father confessor. A careful analysis of the elements
of moral power in his sermons would be a profitable
task for any student of preaching. It would disclose
how great truths, like the atonement, providence, the
Trinity, the Holy Spirit, the new birth, may be treated
ethically and with most effective practical results, and
how the more ordinary class of ethical subjects may be
made, not only impressive, but interesting, by directing
attention to ethical processes and results that are not at
first obvious, and by holding them in relation with what
is fundamental in the constitution of human nature.
Canon Mozley is on the whole one of the most forcible
ethical pulpit teachers the modern church has furnished.
His power lies largely in his singularly subtle but clear
analysis of the workings of moral forces and principles.
There is something remorselessly searching and, although

not repellent, most formidable in his tranquil handling of the moral forces and processes of the human soul. There are many methods of handling the ethical sermon. The analysis of motives, the tracing of moral processes, the delineation of the effects of truth upon moral character, and the unescapableness of moral consequences are among the most obvious elements in Mozley's ethical preaching. He lays hold of the energies that are bedded in our moral constitution and brings them to light. He shows men the workings of their easily besetting sins. He shows them how they cheat themselves, for example, by using opportunity as an invitation or a permission to sin, rather than as a summons to resistance. He shows us the value of sacred habit, and how it may be formed. He lays stress upon the ethical element in faith. There are but three or four character sketches in the two volumes, but they all deal with the motives and principles of action that are illustrated by the characters presented. The process of moral neglect is described with lucid tranquillity, and the fatal necessity of growing worse by simply letting one's self alone, as illustrated in habits like those of avarice and vindictiveness, is set forth in most masterful manner. His two most powerful sermons are perhaps "Our Duty to Equals" and the "Reversal of Human Judgment." In the first we have a very forcible setting forth of the moral difficulties in treating our equals as we should. He examines the comparative ease with which we exercise kindness toward inferiors, and contrasts it with the difficulty we find in dealing justly with those who are at our own level in life. The compassionate attitude toward our fellow-men involves a protected state of mind, for there is a sort of relief in charity. But justice toward an equal tests severely the moral fibre. This leads to a discussion of the two contrasted conceptions of life, as on the one side that of a mission, and as on the other side that of a probation. I know of nothing more forcible than this discussion. It contains the gist of all that may be said upon the individualistic and altruistic conceptions of life, and the discussion is a wholesome tonic for men who in our day are wildly and irrationally advocating altruism, and are undermining the rights of individual manhood.

But the " Reversal of Human Judgment," which Dr. William M. Taylor has called the greatest sermon of modern times, and which the president of one of our New England colleges has told us he reads once a year for the moral tonic it has for him, illustrates in its highest reach of power Mozley's ethical method. It must have occurred to every thoughtful person that there may come sometime a great change in our estimate of men. The Scriptures encourage this suspicion. They speak of a great deception, of great errors in human judgment. The reason for this deception is the working of a pure religion upon a corrupt nature. A great show is the result, a counterfeit religion. There are manifold sources of error in our estimates of men, that account for our mistakes of judgment, and these mistakes must some day be rectified. This is the introduction to the discourse. Then follows a discussion of the sources of these misjudgments in a very acute analysis of the workings of selfish motive, *e.g.* in the political leader, in the theological partisan, in the philanthropist even, in the gifted man of genius, in the favorite of earthly fortune. Christianity calls for the exercise of the primary motives of action, and accepts no substitute. But in all these spheres of life we find men substituting the secondary for the primary motives, and deluding themselves with the notion that Christianity may accept this as a proper basis for estimating men. All this must ultimately be rectified. This discussion is the most cogent setting forth of the delusive workings of the human imagination and heart that has been given in sermon form to the public in our age. The minister or the politician who needs a salutary admonition against the delusive snare of theological or political partisanship will find his corrective here. The discussion of the selfish use of gifts of the imagination and of the selfishly exaggerated conceptions of a mission in the world, that fail to recognize the solemn fact of personal moral probation, is particularly impressive and profitable. Lest the picture of life here presented should seem too dark, the conclusion directs attention to the blending of the sagacious and hopeful view of life as presented by Christianity, and is a most just and helpful conclusion. In all this, as elsewhere, he lets the truth do its own work. He is not urgent to enforce it, and he need not be. He lays bare the workings of the human soul, and especially of the moral nature, and lets us make our own application. There are three phases of the discussion: first, it takes note of the severe judgment power of Christianity and the deceptiveness of the human heart, as related to it; secondly, we have an analysis of the way in which Christianity operates upon the selfish heart in general; and thirdly, illustrations of this selfishness in different spheres, with a conclusion that touches upon the blending of realism and idealism in Christianity. And we find here three important elements in ethical preaching. We have first a Biblical element. There is need of a Biblical conception in connection with an ethical subject of such importance as this, for it deals with the future, which, if known at all, must be known through Biblical revelation only. It is just this Biblical revelation, however, that confirms our own suspicions with respect to the future. The psychological analysis of the effect on selfish human nature of the claims of a pure religion is the second important element; and finally, we have an illustrative element, showing in different realms of human experience the workings of the soul in relation to the claims of Christianity. The sermon is an example especially of the analytical and illustrative method of dealing with ethical subjects. There is demand for more of this searching, morally impressive preaching, that lays bare the effects of Christianity as a holy religion in furnishing occasion for the development of the deceitfulness of the human heart in the substitution of secondary for primary motives, thus exposing the delusions of sin, that warns of moral danger, and that lays upon men a burdening sense of moral obligation which will permit no rest till they find it in the obedience of righteousness. In such preaching Canon Mozley may be of great service as exemplar and guide.

Mozley's view of the world and of life has an important bearing upon the tone and character of his ethical preaching, and demands a moment's attention. He took life seriously. A mind so reflective and so impressible could not fail to do so. Existence is a solemn reality. Life has for him a tragic aspect, and he makes the pathos of it felt by the force of his represen-tation. He finds himself in a world of conflict. He has been taught to fear and distrust it. There is a great conflict between the church and the world, and perpet-ual dread of hostile aggressions, that cripple the life of the church and stain its purity, is perhaps an inheritance from the Anglican controversy and very likely bears the mark of Newman's influence. That the world, as we know it, is hostile to the religious life was one of the cardinal teachings of the Anglican revival. Mozley, therefore, did not share the optimistic view of the world and of life which so strongly characterizes the religion of our day. Sin is the dark reality that hovers ever in the background of life and thrusts itself out at every turn. He has, indeed, no extreme views of human de-pravity, and he is kindly and tolerant in his personal judgments. His conception of the world as a lost world is not so gloomy, and often seemingly contemptuous, as Newman's. He never deals in eschatological terrors. But his world is a sinful and lost world. It is a world of temptations. It is full of delusions and snares, and men should be on guard. We are not to assume that what the world presents to our inclinations is innocent, just because it is in harmony with our inclinations. That we belong to the world does not mean that we are so wholly a normal part of it that it may be regarded by us as a legitimate sphere for self-indulgence. The solicitations of the world may be temptations to be re-sisted rather than opportunities to be embraced. We are here to resist the world and put it under our feet. Life is a moral conflict, and the drifting life is not a

z

moral life. For the man who treats his soul as if it were not held in the grasp of inexorable law ; for the man who is all the while growing worse and does not know it, simply because he lets himself alone; for the fatalist who undertakes to eliminate the guilt of sin by calling it the necessary product of the forces of his own nature ; for the "midway man," who dallies with temptation, neither on the one hand yielding completely to it, nor on the other wholly resisting its solicitations; for the man who lives in the delusions of sin, and perverts an august and solemn existence into a scene of folly ; for any man who in any way treats sin lightly, — Canon Mozley has a most serious message. Life confessedly, as it comes to us through his representation, is not so great an inspiration and joy as it might be. We miss the note of triumph. It is a scene of danger. It cannot be a world of surpassing joy to any man who does not know the remedial grace of God. The choicer joys of life are the joys of grace. And all this is to him the Biblical view of life. Doubtless it is the earlier Biblical view, and it is a view that is true to many of the facts of the life of the present age, and the men of our time are in sore need of the faithful presentation of this truth. The church cannot afford to be deluded with the semblance of godliness. Christianity comes with a tone of distrust. It looks upon the world with a certain air of suspicion. The Bible is a sagacious book, and does not too freely trust the world. It is not easily deceived, and it is a matter of great value that we have a vast repository of truth that is not subject to illusions. It challenges the world. It questions its right to rule. It sets it at naught. In the last conflict it sets it at

complete defiance and puts it beneath its feet. The
Bible is not hostile to God's world, but to man's, to the
world as it finds it in its sins and delusions. And this,
he thinks, is our Lord's view of the world. His pure
religion comes into contact with the corrupt, deceitful
heart of man, with its hidden selfishness and pride, and
a great process of deception begins. The semblance of
religion takes the place of its reality. Christ foresaw
all this, and warned His disciples against it, and it was
this that saddened His life. Of worldly success He would
have none. It was to Him a delusion and a snare. He
resisted its solicitations as a Satanic temptation. He
lived in the shadow of His cross. Every hour of prom-
ised worldly success was but a preintimation of His
last hour of mortal suffering and of earthly defeat. As
He was here to fight this world, so are we. It is a heroic
life, yet solemn and tragic in its processes and results.

In all this we may miss the note of triumph. It is
rather too gloomy a world for our bright day, and men
are likely to turn away from it. Our preacher does not
seem to live, as the modern preacher wishes to live, in
the kingdom of redemption, and does not seem to behold the world as evermore God's world, struggling onward to the goal of sinlessness and completeness. The
victorious Christ is not put into the forefront of the representation, as we might wish. The positive and productive energies of redemption, as they centre in the
ever abiding presence of the Spirit of the Eternal, are
not brought to our attention as they well might be.
The point of view of natural religion, as distinguished
from the Christian point of view, is too often apparent.
It is the philosophical view of life, such as we find in

Bishop Butler, and with both the evangelical note of redemption and the note of personal conquest in Christ, although everywhere presupposed, are less conspicuous in their representation than might be wished. But for the man who needs to be warned, to know himself, to distrust himself, to stand on guard, or to walk warily, or to fight valiantly, Mozley is a messenger from God. The very reading of his searching words should, indeed, with ministries of grace, be "enough to change the whole life of a man."

But his world is more than a sinful world. It is an inadequate world. The life that now is, as such and in and for itself alone, has for him but little significance and value. It finds its worth in its relation to the life beyond. His point of view is not the eternal life with its present and future as two phases bound indissolubly together, each with its own essential and relatively independent value. The present and the future stand in too strong contrast. Only from its relation to the future does the present life find value. The present, indeed, may have a relative value. But it is the future alone that has absolute worth. Hence he dwells upon the transitoriness of life, upon its inequalities, its inadequacies, its delusions and follies. The future life alone is the real life, and the present life is preparation for it. With all of Robertson's strength of conviction, but not with his intensity of emotion or poetic stateliness of diction, does Mozley set forth the transitoriness of an earthly life, its emptiness and unreality, when it is cut from its connection with the life eternal. The hectic flush of the passing glory of the world we do not see. The pathos of a pageant scene that passes before our

eyes we have not. But with solemn step he treads amid
life's inadequacies, and with steady hand he points us
to a higher world. His prevailing conception of life is
that of a probation. It is set over against the conception of life as a mission. He would not minimize the
value of life as opportunity for noble philanthropic
achievement. But he is distrustful of some phases of
modern altruism, as involving an inadequate representation of life, for it too often loses sight of that conception
of life that regards it as a sphere for the training of
personal character, and for this reason he sets the probation over in contrast with the mission of life. It is
easy to make a great show of life. Men magnify success and minimize the discipline of life. Life becomes
a stage and they lose a sense of reality. They act a
part and imagine themselves as still living in the realm
of reality. Here, then, we find in a strongly socialistic
age a sturdy individualist. An institutional religion,
High churchman though he is, has for him no permanent value, and just as little a secularistic religion that
knows of a mission but of no probation. Personal character is the supreme interest. Without it the world is not
saved. According to Froebel what is individual in man
is the divine element within him. Mozley advances
upon this and makes individuality the product of God's
grace. To develop unto perfection what is most individual and distinctive in man is the work of God's Spirit,
and this, not less than the unification of men in the body
of Christ, is the end of existence. No man knows himself, no man comes to himself, no man is himself, till he
is born again. It is the highest mark of the divine in
man, that he should be himself, and no man is him-

self who is not his higher, his ideal, his religious self.
Such being Mozley's conception of life, it is natural
that, with his moral sensitiveness, he should stand in a
sort of awe of it.   It is natural, too, that the sentiment
of awe, or that the quality of reverence, should be a
more marked quality in his religious character than
affectionateness or delicacy of religious emotion.   He
had not the genius for ardent religious devotion.   He
was critical rather than enthusiastic.   He was, in fact,
suspicious of enthusiasm, as he was of all forms of sec-
tarian religion, as involving unlimited possibilities of
delusion and of delusive selfishness.   The attitude of
fear is for him the normal Christian attitude.   Dread
of the august realities of the moral universe is more
Christian than that overweening confidence that may be
the product of high-mindedness and pride.

But it would be a great mistake not to recognize the
more hopeful view of life that modifies what in our day
would be called, and has been called, Canon Mozley's
pessimism.   He fully recognizes the optimistic element
in Christianity, and finds a place for it in his own view of
the world.   He was a Christian realist, but he was also
a Christian idealist.   He held the ecclesiastical point of
view in his outlook upon life, but he was also humanistic
in his tendencies.   He knew the world as under the
dominion of sin, but he knew it as a world redeemed.
Between the spirit of the world and the spirit of true
religion, and between the world as under the dominion
of sin and the church as the organ of God's kingdom,
there is an irreconcilable antagonism.   But there is no
principle of dualism in his conception of the world.
Nature is from God's hand and nature is good.   Man

has never lost the divine image nor the world its sacredness. All forms of natural life have a good of their own, and outside the church there is an independent moral life. A man is not a sinner merely as being subject to the impulses of nature, he is such rather because he fails to rise to the realm of the spirit. Sin is the missing of the mark of the higher spiritual manhood. Sin is not natural, but is the misuse of nature. The problem of religion is not to crush nature, but to regulate it. Moderation contains the principle of virtue. "Virtue turns vice being misapplied." Worldly occupations are God's ordinances, and fidelity to the little duties of life is better than aspiration for showy gifts. There are people who are in some proper sense born religious. So fully and so early are they under the guidance of the Spirit of God, that the boundary line between the natural and the spiritual man is obliterated. In a nobly eloquent passage in "The Reversal of Human Judgment," he recognizes the possibility of stored treasures of good, even in those in whom we might not expect it, that may be disclosed at the last day. There are great surprises even here and now. The last are often found to be first in latent good, and the first prove to be last. The thief on the cross is a surprise. Remember the discipline of life among the poor and the sorrowing. Think of the agencies in a soldier's life that lift the soul beyond itself. A foundation of goodness is laid in lowly places, and the world sees it not. Some rich fruit of all this will emerge in the future life. Single acts of virtue often "spring from minds in which there is not the habit of virtue." "Sudden leaps in virtue show an unseen spring in a man, which are able to compass in a moment the growth of years."[1]   The nation as such has a moral life of its own.   War is one of a nation's rights, and Christianity, in recognizing the state as one of the divine polities, whose essential sacredness has not been lost by sin, recognizes also as one of its rights the right of war.   In a sermon on "War," which is on the whole rather unsatisfactory, he criticises the ecclesiastical view of the nation in accordance with which patriotism is regarded as one of the "sentiments of nature which grace has obliterated."   Christianity adopts nature in all its phases, poetry, art, philosophy, and will not crush it. Nature furnishes "the material which religion is to penetrate."   He is severe upon the attitude of suspicion and of passionate hostility toward the unconsecrated kingdom of this world, as if all good had vanished from it, which is manifested by the representatives of the Roman church.[2]   In all this it is evident that Newman had left no unhealthy influence upon his thinking, and that his high Anglicanism had not left him the victim of a ghostly and unnatural type of religiousness.   With all his high ecclesiasticism he was simple and real in his conception of religion.

3.   With respect to the formal or artistic aspects of Canon Mozley's preaching there is nothing that demands special consideration, and there is but very little here that is of value.   The artistic sense was not a prominent gift; and he attached but little value to homiletic form. It is the substance of his thought that deeply interests us, the fibre of the sermon rather than its form.   The thought is thrown out in a seemingly easy, natural way,

[1] "The Reversal of Human Judgment," "University Sermons," p. 95.
[2] "Roman Council," "University Sermons," pp. 14–15.

suggesting no conscious effort, although the seeming spontaneity is doubtless the conquest of years of hard work. So full is he of the subject in its largeness and productiveness that he launches at the outset into a group of interesting preliminary thoughts that set us at once in relation with his discussion, and when he comes to the close he leaves the impression that there is enough more to say, and that he has not half exhausted the resources of the subject. The thought of the conclusion, too, is as large and full and as suggestive of intellectual resource as the rest of the sermon. The discriminating quality of thought is notable. It is the work of a trained thinker. There are no crude statements here. All is well-considered, well-related thought. In subtleties he is not over nice. There is no elaborate following out of distinctions into regions too remote, but the thought is presented in its larger and more salient outlines. This closely observing and discriminating quality is associated with a characteristic that is quite distinctive and of which I have already spoken, viz. his intellectual impressibility. Anything that is striking, anything that is unique or distinctive in the thought of a text or in any phase of the subject in hand, readily impresses him, and he is sure to direct attention to it. This is done especially in the introduction to the sermon, and there are, in fact, but few sermons in the two volumes that fail to arrest our attention to these surprises of thought. Some perplexing question is introduced, and the sermon proceeds to clear it up. We start with some impressive scene like a kneeling, silent congregation in the presence of an invisible object, and, of course, the whole sermon has from the outset the

advantage of this first impression. Something surprising in the relation of Christianity to human life is
brought to our attention, and he makes it his task to
clear up the perplexity. For example, the strange and
startling fact that Christianity recognizes the right of
war. In order to make the strangeness of this recognition as impressive as possible, he presents a somewhat
extreme statement of what it involves, and then he proceeds to discuss the basis of the recognition. He
pitches upon what is perplexing or searching or repul-
sive in his text, proceeds to expound it, and makes it
the key-note of the entire sermon, or rests the entire discussion upon it. The text he chooses is a searching
text; it is an eye that has through all the Christian
generations been looking out calmly and reproachfully
upon the church and held it in judgment! The thought
of the text causes us to shrink back as in a sort of
dread, and we are told why this is so. It is surprising
that a being so unworldly as Christ, so apparently absorbed in the visions of heavenly reality, should have
exhibited an habitual, cheerful love of nature. The
highest spiritual life, therefore, is not ghostly and unnatural. If he quotes as his text the resolve of " The
Preacher " to test folly as well as wisdom by experiment,
he cannot withhold surprise that any sane man should
give himself to folly as well as to wisdom, as if any
experiment were needed to determine that folly cannot
be matched against wisdom as an object of investigation
and experiment. It is this peculiarity in Canon Mozley
that contributes to his preaching the element of suggestiveness. There is always something new and fresh.
The thought-grip of the subject appears in the main

body of the sermon in his free method of handling. The movement knows but little homiletic restraint. The path is clear to him, and the journey is onward, but he leaves but few mile-stones to mark progress. He has a large, interesting, impressive thought in his mind, and it has been thoroughly and discriminatingly excogitated; but he plunges rapidly into the midst of his discussion and runs easily across the boundary line of introduction and discussion without marking the transition. The very fulness and freedom of his handling seem to mislead him into a lack of distinctness and definiteness of outline, and sometimes into lack of discrimination in the conception of his theme. The thought is large and full and does not rigidly define itself. The great sermon to which reference has so frequently been made fails in a certain definiteness of outline, and in a close previous analysis of the theme. The general subject is doubtless suggested by the title. There is to be a final reversal of human judgment. But, as is not infrequently the case, the general subject is not the exact theme. The main thought discussed is the perversion to which Christianity is subjected by the exercise of wrong motive, particularly by the substitution of the lower for the higher motives in the lives of men. Christianity demands the highest and purest motives, and condemns men for displacing them. The sequel of this displacement of what is primary by what is secondary will be an ultimate reversal of the judgments of men. Men accept the lower standard, but Christianity will accept only the highest, and will judge men accordingly. There can be no doubt as to the main thought of the sermon. But the theme and the discussion are not identical and are practically at cross-purposes. The discussion turns upon the grounds of perverted Christianity, the substitution of lower for higher motives. The theme covers the single thought of the issue of such perversion in a divine reversal.

In the formal or technical aspect, his preaching would have been better if his introductions had run less undistinguishably into the discussion, if the theme had been more closely defined, if the parts of the discussion had been more carefully differentiated, and if the conclusion had been more distinct. The sermon does not lack unity of thought, but it lacks proportion and order in discussion, and, as with Newman's sermons, there is often lack of cumulative force. But his preaching has great expository power. In his handling of effective methods of clear and forcible thought-interpretation he is masterly. He lacked, however, the training of the rhetorician and the orator. For a high Anglican, whose vocation it was to preach to an Oxford audience, this will do. But any preacher, even though he preach to audiences that care more for substance than for form, would be more effective if he were to throw his material into the form appropriate to an oratorical address. The reflective, discriminating, and at the same time affluent quality of the thought of the sermon discloses itself in the quality of the style. As in the preaching of Robertson, the style is entirely subordinate to the thought. It changed in the process of his development. It became more simple and clear and exact. He aimed to state what he had to say in a direct and straightforward manner, to crowd back all exuberance of imagination, and all surplus feeling, so that they should have no undue influence upon his utterance. If these rhetorical qualities had found freer expression, he might have become a more effective preacher; but his diction as a teacher could hardly have been stronger or clearer or more readily apprehensible. It is a style that speaks prevailingly to the mind by its strength and transparency, and becomes a fit instrument for impressing the moral nature. And it must be acknowledged that no homiletic or rhetorical defect seems to limit the power of these sermons for the reader, and, after all, this must be the basis of our estimate. In the clearness of his expository method, in the convincingness with which he sets forth the great truths of religion, and in the ethical cogency of his inculcation, he is one of the most princely pulpit teachers of his day.

CHAPTER VIII

THOMAS GUTHRIE

FROM the intellectual point of view, Guthrie can hardly be called a typical Scottish preacher. He lacked the theological learning and training and the intellectual strength and discrimination that we usually associate with the Scottish pulpit. He belongs to the school of Chalmers, but he represents it on the artistic and practical rather than on the intellectual side. And it is as representing the Scottish pulpit in its modified Calvinism, its abandonment of the doctrinal and argumentative method of presenting Christianity, its evangelical devotion, its adaptation to the practical needs of men, especially its evangelical spirit and philanthropic enterprise, and above all its popular effectiveness, that he has been chosen for our consideration. For in his popular rhetorical qualities he far surpassed all the Scottish preachers of his day.

I

GUTHRIE'S CHARACTER AND CAREER

Thomas Guthrie belonged to an old Scottish family, whose ancestors were numbered among the Covenanters. It was always with him a matter of honest pride, which was highly commendable, that he could trace his lineage

to men of such heroic faith, and particularly that one of
them had given his life as a martyr to the cause of the
Covenanters. It is likely that his own brave and manly
life of devotion to the rights of conscience and to the
relief and elevation of the poor and ignorant, and of
struggle against physical disease, found abundant inspiration in the consciousness that he was in some sort the
heir to such Christian heroism. Unlike many distinguished Scottish preachers, he was not, as he says of
himself, "a child of the manse." The Scottish preachers
have for the most part come from humble homes, and in
early years have known the struggles of adversity.
Guthrie knew but little of such early struggles, and his
entire career, although one of hard work, bore the marks
of a well-used prosperity. His father was a well-to-do
merchant-magistrate, and loyal son of the kirk, in the
little town of Brechin, on the eastern border of Scotland,
near Montrose, where, in 1803, the son was born, one of a
family of twelve children. His mother was a woman
who evidently had in an eminent degree the characteristic Scottish virtue of independence and tenacity of
purpose, which she disclosed in regulation fashion by
withdrawing from the Established church, and by join-
ing one of the Secession communities, because, as she
claimed, the spiritual pabulum she received in the kirk
did not further "the welfare of her soul," thus leaving
her husband behind and taking with her the eldest son
and a daughter. This lack of spiritual pabulum, of
which the mother complains, suggests the dominance,
in the Established church at that time, of the "Moderate" party, with its unfruitful moralizings and literary
respectabilities, and it indicates at the same time her

own dominating evangelical sympathies. This independence of character and evangelical zeal, that put
such supreme emphasis upon the interests of the soul
as led the mother to break with her church, reappeared
in the son, who, while loyal to the kirk and unwilling to
break with it, was more loyal still to the rights of the
individual soul and to "the crown rights of Christ,"
which in subsequent years he disclosed in his antagonism to the aggressions of the state authorities in the
sphere of church life.

This quiet country town was his home for twenty-one
years, including the years of his university life. In the
household life Old Testament stories and Bunyan's
"Pilgrim's Progress" early stimulated his imagination,
and fostered those realistic qualities of mind and those
gifts for concrete representation that were so characteristic of his preaching. He himself refers to the early
influence of the Book of Proverbs upon the thrift of
Scottish character. Brechin was not far from the shore
of the German Ocean, and the sights and sounds of the
sea must have impressed his youthful imagination, for
they appear largely as illustrative material in his preaching. He became very familiar, too, with the natural
scenery of the country, and with those objects of human
interest and enterprise and industry that left their impress upon his enthusiastic and practical Scottish mind.
At what the Memoir characterizes "the preposterously
early age of twelve years" he entered the University of
Edinburgh, and graduated at the age of sixteen. His
physical personality was charged like a battery with
vitality. He was intense in his enthusiasm, cheerful
and kindly in disposition, and his rollicking joviality lin-

gered with him through all the storms of life, and alleviated such hardness of lot as he was called to endure, as was the case with his larger-moulded friend and contemporary, Norman McLeod. This limitless exuberance, which suggests the Frenchman rather than the Scotchman, was one of the elements of his effectiveness as a pulpit orator. Even when at last the pitcher was broken at the fountain, this fulness of life was never wholly exhausted. At the university he made but little head in any one branch of learning. It is said, however, that his reading was wide and that it was tributary to his general culture. It is certain that the literature with which he familiarized himself, beginning with the robust and healthy Sir Walter Scott, was of a high order, and that it was a determinative influence for his whole life. But scholarship in the academic sense of the term he had not. The movements of modern life had begun to influence the prominent Scottish preachers of the Evangelical school. Indeed, it was one of the peculiarities of this school that, in reacting against the benumbing influence of Moderatism, they not only sought to quicken the spiritual life of the churches, but to make a more broadly practical application of Christianity. This was the meaning of Chalmers's church extension movement, and while Chalmers was, in his scientific theology, a man of the eighteenth century, in his practical theology, or in his practical conception and application of Christianity, he belonged to the nineteenth. He was a political economist and a practical mathematician, and availed himself of his knowledge of these subjects in his ministerial work; and his commercial and astronomical discourses indicate his interest in

2 A

relating the truths of Christianity to commerce and science. In all these respects we may perhaps see the influence of Chalmers upon Guthrie. But his own native tendencies led him in the same direction. His interest in objective realities and, in general, his non-speculative and practical tendencies gave him a bias toward the physical sciences. He took extra courses in chemistry and natural philosophy when at the university.

The influences that committed him to the work of the ministry are not evident. Very likely the choice was determined largely by the influence of his home. But, however this may be, his entrance upon theological studies, at the close of the academic course, seems to have been a foregone conclusion. He was not distinguished as a theological student at the Divinity Hall of the university, although his gift for facile rhetorical expression and his forcefulness and attractiveness as a speaker, in which gifts he carefully trained himself, must have given promise of his future eminence as a preacher and platform orator. He accepted the modified type of Calvinism that was current among the Evangelicals of his day, of which Chalmers was the representative, and his preaching presupposes it rather than defends it. He never fully appropriated the historical and experimental method of approaching Christianity. For him Christianity is an objective revelation of divine truth which is vindicated by external evidences, which the human reason is incompetent to criticise, although it is competent to defend it, especially in the use of experimental proofs; and of this conception of Christianity he remained to the end an advocate. It is true that he became in his way something of a Biblical student, and illustrated the improvement in Biblical exposition and application that was common in the Evangelical preaching of his day. He expounded the Scriptures with much vivacity and applied them in a suggestive and interesting manner. But his work always lacked a critical basis. As in the academic, so in the divinity courses, he continued to manifest special aptitude for the physical sciences, and it was very likely through these scientific interests in part that he subsequently came into close friendly relations with Hugh Miller. In general literature he continued to read somewhat widely, and its influence upon his literary tastes and style appeared more fully later on. It was not till near the close of the most active period of his life that he became fully conscious of his gift for rhetorical expression. His scientific knowledge and his literary culture, in connection with his habits of close observation of nature, and his familiarity with practical life, served him well in furnishing illustrative material for the pulpit during all the subsequent years. On account of his pronounced Evangelical views and his independent adherence to them, involving a somewhat antagonistic attitude toward the Moderate party that had control of the patronage of the Established church, he was, for five years after his graduation in theology and his licensure, unable to secure a church. But he held conscientiously and tenaciously to his position, and bided his time. It was a very unwise procedure, as the issue proved, for the party in power thus to intensify Guthrie's antagonism. Meantime he pursued a course that was exceedingly profitable to his future ministry; and one may almost felicitate the churches of Scotland that the short-sighted policy of the latitudinarian respectabilities of the Establishment was preparing a more vigorous and effective antagonist of its corrupt system of patronage and of intrusion into the spiritual independence of the church than otherwise might have been possible. He returned for a few months to the university, and continued his studies in chemistry and natural history. The year following, 1826, he spent several months in Paris at the Sorbonne in the same line of study, at the same time attending medical lectures and the medical clinic, and all the while enlarging in a general way by close observation his knowledge of the world of men, in whose affairs he was always chiefly interested. Finding upon his return that his way to the pulpit was still blocked, he entered a banking house, where he continued for three years, holding the responsible position of bank manager. At last, through the friendly intervention of an influential member of the British Parliament, he was appointed to the parish of Arbirlot, not far to the south from his home. He was now twenty-seven years old, a man of multifarious aptitudes, of varied experiences, of increasing maturity and enlarging power. Here at once the results of his manifold interests, his comprehensive training, and his practical aggressiveness began to disclose themselves. He gave himself first of all to the task of refreshing and developing the religious life of his church. He resuscitated the moribund church prayer-meeting and the catechetical class; he established cottage prayer-meetings, which brought the different sections of the parish into closer contact; he started Sabbath-schools and founded a parish library, all of which were kept under his immediate supervision; he threw himself into the general life of the community, carrying his religion beyond the parish into the secular life of the people; he was a vigorous advocate of temperance, and was soon instrumental in clearing the town of the two saloons that had thrived there; and he established a bank for the poor, whose affairs he personally managed. Of his experience in practical life he says, in his autobiography: "In point of fact it was not the least valuable part of my training and education. I became conversant with mercantile and agricultural affairs, and men who both in country and town afterward became my people did not respect me the less when they found their minister was something else than a 'fine bodie' who knew no more about the affairs and hopes and disappointments and trials of men engaged in the business of the world than any old wife or 'the man in the moon.' My people at Arbirlot were all the better for the knowledge of business I had acquired at the bank, as I had not been long there when I established a savings-bank in that country parish, getting two or three of the principal farmers to be trustees along with myself. I was entire manager, giving out money only on Saturday evenings, the regular time for its transactions, and that only on a weekly or fortnightly notice, but receiving it in the shape of a shilling, the lowest deposit, at any time and any day, Sunday of course excepted." The career of Guthrie, as well as that of Chalmers and of Norman McLeod, with their demonstrated ability to manage men and to handle the complex administrative interests of a parish, illustrates the value for the minister of business training. It was during this Arbirlot ministry of seven years that Guthrie laid the foundation for his future success in all lines of ministerial activity, and it demonstrates that the

man who is successful in small things will be called to
greater things. He made careful preparation for the
pulpit. He discharged with scrupulous fidelity the little
duties of a parish pastor, recognizing, as every high-
minded, right-hearted Christian minister should and will,
the great value to his ministry of the " cure of souls,"
thus elevating the religious life of his church, while he
threw himself with undiminished enthusiasm into the
broader spheres of church extension and of ecclesiastical
and moral reform.

The patronage question, in which he was subsequently to have a most prominent part, was already
before the churches, when, in 1830, he took this country parish. The conflict began in earnest, however,
four years later. He had studied it from the outset,
and his position had already been taken with the " High
Flyers," as the Evangelicals were called. The primary
question in this conflict was whether the church as a
spiritual body had an inalienable and indefeasible moral
right to restrict the patron in his legal right to nominate
ministerial candidates to the churches. It subsequently
involved the larger and allied question, whether the
state had the right to obtrude itself upon a church by
forcing an undesirable candidate upon it. The question,
therefore, was whether the state had a right to undertake the management of affairs that belong to the church
as a spiritual body. The Moderate party, then in the
ascendant, in general claimed this right of obtrusion
for the state. The Evangelicals, under the lead of
Chalmers and Guthrie, denied the right and opposed
the claim. Guthrie's position, which he defended with
much skill and force, was that the church as a spiritual

society, whose supreme head is Christ, whose office-
bearer holds his credentials from Christ, and whose
charter is the Bible, had the right to manage its own
affairs so far as they relate to its spiritual interests.
The patron has no right to appoint candidates without
the free and full consent of the church. Guthrie was a
loyal son of the Established church, and was not dis-
posed to break with it. Accordingly, when the question of dissolving the relation between the church and
the state, in the so-called "voluntary" controversy
which preceded the "anti-patronage" controversy, he
espoused the cause of the Establishment. This position he was, of course, subsequently obliged to abandon,
but he always remained a believer theoretically in a
state church. This question of the perpetuation of the
state church, which was involved in the "voluntary"
controversy, had already brought Guthrie during his
early ministry into prominence. Dr. Chalmers had
already entered upon his "church extension" movement.
His object was to make the Established church more
effective. He would abolish the old collegiate system,
in accordance with which the ecclesiastical community
was divided into large parishes, and each parish placed
under the supervision of two associate pastors. Chalmers would multiply the number of parishes and
churches, and thus increase the centres of moral and
spiritual power and make them more effective, placing
each parish in charge of one pastor and holding him
responsible for effective leadership. He would have
the parish work organized with such care that all the
members of the parish, rich and poor alike, should be
brought under the influence of the church. It was an

ecclesiastical movement for the purpose of increasing
the number of churches, and of strengthening the
Evangelical party; it was a philanthropic movement for
the purpose of reaching the unchurched classes; and it
was above all a religious movement for the purpose of
strengthening and enriching the spiritual life of the whole
church.   Guthrie had already arrested the attention of
Dr. Chalmers.   His effectiveness as a pulpit and platform
orator, his pastoral zeal, his executive enterprise, his
evangelistic skill and enthusiasm, his devotion to the
cause of evangelical Christianity, and his interest in the
questions that were in agitation had already brought
him into prominence, and had won the high esteem of
the great leader.   It was natural, therefore, that he
should be wanted in Edinburgh.   A highly successful
country pastor, and sincerely attached to his simple
country parish, he nevertheless had all the appointments, and he cherished a distinct admiration for the
rôle of the popular city pastor.   He had a certain
fondness for the natural scenery of the country, but he
loved the life of the city more, and had no sympathy
with the sentiment of Cowper, that "God made the
country, but man made the town."   His philanthropic
instincts especially inclined him toward the city parish,
where he might reach the unchurched masses.   He
was wanted at Old Gray Friars in Edinburgh, and he
accepted a call there with the understanding that a
church should be built for him as soon as possible, over
which he should be placed in sole charge, and where he
might attempt to put in operation Chalmers's parochial
system, and work out the problem of parish evangeliza-
tion.   The church known as St. John's was accord-

ingly built for him; and after a three years' ministry at
Gray Friars on the collegiate basis, he entered upon his
more distinctively philanthropic career in the poorest
quarter of Edinburgh. The city was well supplied with
able preachers, and it was the home of many illustrious
men who had made a name for themselves in literature,
in science, and in the various professions. Drs. Candlish,
Cunningham, and Charles Brown occupied prominent
positions in the pulpit and in church leadership. Dr.
Chalmers was at the university, at the height of his
popularity and power. Lord Jeffrey, the leader in literature, was there, and Lord Cockburn, the leader at the
bar; and it was no slight task for any man to win the
ear of the cultivated classes, and at the same time to
minister successfully to the poor and degraded people
of the parish. But this was what Guthrie did. His
ministry of twenty-seven years, from 1837 to 1864, was
marked by a popularity that was undiminished and
that surpassed that of any man in Scotland. Under the
most stimulating influences he developed rapidly his
peculiar gifts as a pulpit and platform orator, and as a
philanthropist and ecclesiastical leader. It was during
the first six years of his ministry at St. John's that the
disruption of the Established church took place. In
that movement he was, doubtless, Chalmers of course
excepted, the most popular and effective leader. His
ability as a platform orator brought him into great
prominence in furthering the organization of the Free
churches, and particularly in raising funds to provide
homes for the ministers of these churches. So important was his influence in pastoral, parochial, philanthropic, and educational work, in connection with his

work as a preacher, that reference must be made to it
in another connection.

The demands of his position upon him led him constantly and ever more completely into a type of pulpit
speech of which he was easily the most eminent representative of his day in Great Britain. With ever increasing zeal and devotion he gave himself to his tasks,
and with ever increasing influence, publishing, as he
was able to find time, the results of his work in sermons,
pamphlets, and monographs of a philanthropic sort, like
his "Pleas for the Ragged Schools," which is, perhaps,
his most striking and permanently valuable literary product; and in 1864 he was obliged to lay down his burden,
for the heart could no longer bear the strain. He became editor of the *Sunday Magazine*, to which he himself contributed copiously till his death, nine years later,
in 1873. The published results of his work appear in
sixteen volumes, which for their substance of thought
are of no permanent value, and for their literary qualities might not find response in the tastes of our time,
but have a certain attractiveness in their vivacity of
style, and many of them are worth knowing because
they embody the results of his work as a philanthropist.
It is in this aspect that his claim upon our attention is
preëminent. Guthrie's significance for the modern pulpit is in his popular interpretation of Christianity, and
in his practical application of it to the needs of the poor
and unfortunate.

II

GUTHRIE AS A POPULAR EVANGELISTIC PREACHER

We cannot rely upon Guthrie's published products for an adequate conception of his influence as a preacher. The impressions he made were vivid, but they were not educative and are not suggestive of permanence. His preaching should be considered in connection with his life work.   Let us, therefore, look at the man, the pastor, and the philanthropist, then at the material, structure, and rhetorical form of the sermon, and in the light of the whole we shall perhaps be the better able to estimate his significance as a preacher.

1. The personality of the man was marked. He had the full physical equipment of an impressive pulpit orator.   He was a tall, broad-shouldered Scotchman, with a dark complexion, black hair in early years, touched into an iron-gray as years advanced, deep-set gray eyes, long, prominent nose, and thin, mobile lips. Thus he is described.   So far as impressive oratory is conditioned by physical gifts, these are among the desirable appointments.   It is said of him that he had "an abundance of easy and powerful, because natural, gesture, a quickly and strongly impressive countenance, which age rendered finer, as well as more comely, . . . a powerful, clear, and musical voice, the intonations of which were varied and appropriate, managed with an actor's skill, though there was not the least appearance of art." Lord Cockburn says of him that "he was passionate without vehemence. His language and accent were very Scotch, but nothing can be less vulgar, and his gesture

is the most graceful I have ever seen in any public speaker. Everything he does glows with a frank, gallant warm-heartedness often rendered more delightful by a boyish simplicity of air and style." This boyish frankness, freedom, intensity, and joviality always lingered with him, although he rigidly excluded all unseemly exhibitions of it in the pulpit. But taking this temperament into the pulpit and giving it proper range, he had the greater power as a preacher. No gloomy view of life ever darkened his message or shadowed his influence. He was a man of Scotch sense. He had, indeed, a poetic fancy of a sort, not of the highest order, a little garish, a trifle strained and remote in its uses, but vivid and striking, and doubtless it was one of his chief elements of power. But he was preëminently Scotch in his practical understanding, a man of sound judgment, of executive force, who knew men and had a most vigorous and boundlessly tactful handling of them. In the realm of objective reality he had extraordinary clearness of discrimination and never blundered in his dealing with facts. He lacked intellectual subtlety, and in the speculative realm was not discriminating or profound. He dealt with the surface and commonplace aspects of things. He reflects much, moralizes much, upon life ; but his reflections are somewhat too obvious and sometimes almost platitudinous. He touches his moralizings into attractiveness by his vivid fancy, and his good sense never deserts him. Under all his pulpit pyrotechnics there is a vein of shrewd common sense which proves him the typical Scotchman. He could not to any very considerable extent instruct, and he had nothing particularly new to

say. He glorified the familiar and never took hold of
the depths of truth. The deeper places of the human
spirit he could not reach, save as now and then he
flashed his way into them by his sympathies and by his
pathos ; but he could paint what lies at the surface of
life and could make it attractive and worthy of eager
attention.

The Scotchman is essentially a realist. His philosophy is that of common sense, and he discloses it in his
literature, in his theology, and in his preaching, as in all
else. Guthrie had the realistic habit of his countrymen.
He was a man of genuine and generous sympathies,
which disclosed themselves in his domestic life, which
was one of rare affection and devotion, in his social intercourse, his pastoral care of souls, his philanthropic
endeavors, and in his preaching. He was an ideal
city pastor. He loved the rush and excitement and
human passion of city life, and he was peculiarly fitted
to mingle in its scenes of sin and sorrow as the bishop
of souls. He had not the æsthetic endowment of Norman McLeod. He " loved the garish scene." It furnished images for his rushing rhetoric. This discloses
his leading quality. He was a man of action, not of
reflection ; a man of " tasks," not of " visions." Because
he was a man of genuine sympathies, he loved the good
opinion and the good will of his fellows. He was too
sensible a man to be unmanned by flattery. He was
too genuine a man and too sound a Calvinist to regard
himself as entitled to human adulation. But he had a
good deal of that guileless *amour propre* that characterizes some of his countrymen, and is naturally fostered by the high esteem in which the Scottish minister

is held by the people. He had a very decided respect
for men of rank, and a very innocent relish of their personal friendship, which he was just a little inclined to
advertise. He once said of himself that he was half
inclined to believe that he was cut out for a nobleman.
If he had been gifted with more of Carlyle's stalwart
Scotch individualism, he would have despised all this.
But after all, this guileless self-love was the reflex of his
love for his fellow-men, and he even turned it to the
advantage of his ministry, as the late Dr. Joseph Parker
did in a more obtrusive manner and on a more exten-
sive scale, and it became a condition of the greater effectiveness in his dealing with men. With all his reverence
for rank he had a genuine love for all classes of men,
and was in an eminent degree the friend of the poor.
He was a man in earnest, and such a man can never
lose himself in the idolatries of the people. This moral
earnestness he exhibited in the pulpit, as elsewhere.
It is interesting to read of the "hush of expectation
on the upturned faces of the people as, entering from
a side door, the preacher is seen pressing with eager
steps through the crowd who fill the passage from the
vestry to the pulpit," and of the "swing of the broad
shoulders, the face bent forward, the look of earnestness
on the flushed countenance, all telling of a man who
feels that he has come forth on an important errand and
is straitened till it be accomplished." This combination
of physical, emotional, moral, and religious intensity, this
capacity to be wrought upon in all the elements of his
manhood, measurably by the power of the truth in his
own heart, more largely, perhaps, by the images of truth
that sprang from his exuberant fancy and by the human

beings of all classes that hung upon his lips, — this, in large measure, lets us into the secret of his influence over men.   It is a living man.   It is the subtle, occult, penetrating force of a vivacious, joyful, friendly, sympathetic human personality, alive all through.

2. The influence of Guthrie's pastoral and philanthropic activity upon his pulpit work must also be taken into account.   As we have seen, Guthrie was a man of extraordinary pastoral effectiveness, of general administrative ability, of philanthropic activity and ecclesiastical enterprise, and here lie the most permanent results of his work.   The Free church movement was especially indebted to him.   St. John's church, which, under his leadership, was among the first to commit itself to the Free church movement, was designed for the poor and was located in one of the poorest quarters of the city, near which he fixed his own residence.   In his congregation there were, indeed, some of the most intelligent and cultivated people of Edinburgh, whom he greatly interested and strongly influenced.   And it was a fortunate thing for him as a preacher that he was obliged to meet such people in his congregation.   But his audience was composed largely of plain people, and even of the very poor, and he did not fail to preach to them according to the measure of their intelligence.   He had begun his ministry with the effort to reach the common people, and he went to Edinburgh because he could do a larger work among them.   His early style of preaching was plain and homely, entirely lacking in the descriptive quality which subsequently characterized it, and the thought was somewhat familiar in its conscientious Scotch orthodoxy.   But he found himself in his efforts

to reach the common people. It is not an uncommon thing for preachers to find themselves in this free, unconventional, illustrative style of speech, and no better school for the culture of it could be found than the catechetical class where Guthrie found it. It was his persistent purpose to do his best under all conditions, and in this Guthrie's example and influence have been very salutary.

But the point in hand is that his preaching was pastoral in its character and that it was directly influenced and wholly conditioned by the manifest needs of his congregation. He learned from the members of his congregation, as he visited them in the parish, what most impressed them in his preaching, and made careful note of it. His experience in mercantile life has already been spoken of, and its influence upon his parish work. But it had also an indirect influence upon his pulpit work. His pastoral type of preaching took largely the evangelistic form, and he is a worthy example of the effective pastoral evangelist. He always sought to make an impression upon the conscience and heart to win men's allegiance to Christ, and to strengthen them in it. So strong in intent was the emotional interest and so strong in result the emotional impression, that the intellectual and even ethical interest were sometimes sacrificed to it. A substantial, permanent moral result he certainly had sincerely at heart; but so intent was he upon an immediate and vivid impression, that he must sometimes have failed of the desired effect, if indeed he did not sometimes lose sight of it. This is the defect of what we call sensational preaching, even of the better type. There is a disproportionate impression upon the imagination and the emotions. With respect to simplicity, directness, and deep, strong, moral purpose, the preaching of Guthrie does not impress us as that of Spurgeon does, and it may be questioned whether the results of his preaching were not meagre, as compared with those of Mr. Spurgeon's preaching, useful as he was in his evangelistic work. As an orator, capable of producing powerful, immediate impressions, Spurgeon is not his equal. But Guthrie plays with his rhetoric. In general the aim of the two men is the same. It is to present the gospel in such way that it will strike home at once. But the methods are very different and the results different. Spurgeon deals more largely with truth in immediate Biblical form. It is indeed colored by the crass literalism of the school in which he was trained. But the matter and the style are Biblical and the single aim is always manifest. Guthrie was, in his way, a Biblical preacher, as most Scottish preachers are, but his Biblical material is strongly colored by his rhetoric, and the thought often seems subordinate to the flamboyant style in which it appears. Guthrie is one of those preachers who is sure to draw the fire of the critic. And yet he was an effective evangelistic preacher.

But the point in hand here is that his work was conditioned by what he recognized as the needs of his hearers. The volume entitled " The City, its Sins and Sorrows " is one of the treasured results of his personal contact with suffering human life, necessitated by his work as the pastor of the poor. The three monographs in which he makes a plea for the ragged schools which he was instrumental in establishing in Edinburgh, that have been gathered into one volume, are another

2 B

product in literary form of his experiences with the lower classes in city life. These volumes disclose in a notable manner his power of pathos, in which the *London Times* declared him to be peerless among British preachers. This contact with the lower phases of life deepened his human sympathies and intensified his sense of the need of reaching the hearts of men through their imaginations. His life as a churchman also and the demands upon him for platform oratory, in which he exceeded all other Scottish preachers of his day, became tributary to his pulpit work. He was in fact essentially a platform orator, who carried the method of the platform into the pulpit. His work as a philanthropist led him in the same general direction. All became tributary to his effectiveness as a preacher. The cause of the poor, of temperance, of education, of missions, of needy ministers, of church extension, of ecclesiastical freedom, — all the great interests of mankind, no one of which was foreign to him, and to all of which, as he came into connection with them, he devoted himself with untiring zeal, found in him a most effective pulpit advocate. He was a faithful and trusted pastor, earnestly devoted to the "cure of souls," according to the best approved Scottish custom; a wise church leader, especially trusted during the last fifteen years of his pastoral life for his increasing breadth of vision, largeness of spirit, and practical tact; but always in an eminent degree the friend of the poor and suffering, wherever they were to be found, gathering the inspirations of his pathos from the scenes of distress with which he was constantly familiar. That any true preacher should fail to see that the persuasive power of the pulpit is dependent upon pastoral life in the cure of souls and in philanthropic devotion to the suffering, and that any one should be willing to surrender such a condition of power over the human soul, is amazing. To isolate the pulpit from the parish and from the larger world of needy human life, to withdraw from the struggling world into selfish isolation, or to devote one's self to philanthropy merely as a big administrative enterprise at a safe distance from suffering individual life, is to "cut the nerve" of pulpit power. The man who does this deserves to fail, as he will fail, and the church that tolerates it should perish. He is the best preacher in our day who is most familiar with human life. There never was a time in the history of the Christian pulpit when there was such a demand for close contact with human life as now. It was the strength and the glory of the Evangelical movement in Scotland, of which Guthrie was in some sort the most effective representative, that it took Christianity away from the realm of abstract thought and of literary dilettanteism into the depths of human life. Thomas Guthrie and Norman McLeod kept the fountains of human feeling constantly astir, and won much of that power to move men that was peculiar to them from familiar intercourse with the needy world.

3. The material and structural elements of Guthrie's preaching must enter into our estimate of it. In the material but not in the formal sense of the term he was a Biblical preacher. Biblical themes always furnish the basis of his discussion. Biblical topics entered to a considerable extent into the process of development. Biblical characters and incidents were largely used as illustrative material, citations of individual Biblical pas-

sages were not infrequent, and a Biblical tone pervaded the whole. But he was a topical rather than a textual or expository preacher. In interpreting the Scriptures he always selects the main topics of his passage for discussion, and instead of subjecting them to critical analysis and unfolding the thought of the writer, he seizes upon their practical aspects for the purpose of moral inculcation and incentive. He finds in the literary form of the passage a stimulus for his own imagination, and the entire discourse addresses itself to the fancy and the feeling of the hearer rather than to his power of reflection. The aim is to stimulate to moral action rather than to edify by enrichment of Christian knowledge. His method is the method of accommodation, and shows no results of modern Biblical scholarship. But Biblical discourses like those found in " The Gospel in Ezekiel," " Christ and the Inheritance of the Saints," and " The Parables " are full of valuable practical suggestions, are strong in moral incentive and brilliantly vivacious in rhetorical form. The substance of the sermon, however, is definitely influenced by his theological point of view, as will naturally be the case with any man who has any theology which he regards as worth while. Guthrie was not a theologian, yet he had his theology, and it lies in the background in all of his Biblical preaching. He holds, although in a moderate and reasonable way, the dogmatic point of view, from which it seems impossible for all Scottish preachers who have not been trained in modern methods of thinking to emancipate themselves. His preaching was wholesomely, and it must be acknowledged on the whole reasonably, evangelical, but it was such according to the

type of a moderate Scotch Calvinism.   It is a type of
theology with which the Scottish people are familiar
and which they like to hear.   They call it the simple
gospel, however remote in fact it may be from "the
simplicity that is in Christ," because they have been
educated in it and because it has a familiar sound.
Guthrie was a man of noble, catholic spirit, a man,
in fact, ahead of his time in tolerance and high-mindedness.   But he was not the man to break with traditional Scottish theology.   He had neither the equipment
nor the disposition for it.   It is his philanthropy, rather
than his theology, although the latter is of a sufficiently moderate type, that shows the trace of the
modern humanistic spirit and culture.   There is no evidence that the point of view held or the opinions pro-
pounded by Thomas Erskine or McLeod Campbell
ever touched him or had much meaning for him.   He is
not the man to part company with his hearers in any
event, and he is, moreover, manifestly persuaded that
Calvinism strikes the original note of the gospel.   There
is but little that is fresh in the substance of his thought.
It is essentially commonplace.   It is the fresh illustration of the truth, not fresh conception of it, that constitutes the attractiveness of his preaching.   Good work
this, indeed, for any man — this work of making familiar
truth interesting by the freshness of the form in which
it is presented, and the only work, very likely, in which
most men may expect to succeed.   But it is not the
most vital or quickening or spiritually helpful preaching.   There certainly are religious points of view that
bring God nearer to us, and that make Christianity
more real and more reasonable, but they belong to a

realm with which Dr. Guthrie was not familiar. Not infrequently he overpresses Scripture terms in the interest of his Calvinistic theology, wresting them only to get what he has put into them. To enforce the doctrine of total depravity he makes Paul teach that the "carnal mind" is nothing but "enmity against God," enmity is the very element of man's unregenerate life, — as love is the element of God's life. Defect in the spirit of obedience is fully developed enmity. In the same way he presses Scripture terms to make them teach the doctrine of a substitutionary atonement. His representations of future punishment are highly dramatic, and Scripture terms here, too, are overpressed in the interest of a sensational effectiveness. His world is always in moral peril, and he finds in the moral situation material for his dramatic representation. Human life, as redeemed in Christ, seems to have no such effect upon his imagination as do its tragic perils. Yet he treats most attractively and persuasively the love of God and the universality of the atonement, and in this he shows that at heart he had broken with the traditional Calvinism of his countrymen. It is this that draws upon his noblest sympathies and is the spring of his noblest pathos. The doctrines of grace are the centre of his teaching, and even under their defective forms of representation he succeeds in showing the heart of God in most winsome ways, and man's working relations with redemption are presented in the truly Evangelical spirit. He was a most diligent worker, although not a thorough student nor a reflective thinker, and his attainments were only in the line of general culture and knowledge. There is a lack of solid sub-

stance in his preaching.   There is more heat than
light.   His mind is objective and realistic.   He dwells
upon external relations and fails to enter deeply into the
inner life.   One suspects that he never reached the full
measure of his intellectual power.   He had seemingly
the possibility of manly strength, but he did not develop it.   His influence upon his fellow-men, however,
was great, and in his ecclesiastical and philanthropic
activities he has left a permanent impression upon
his age and country.   But he has left nothing behind
as a pulpit teacher that will be of permanent value.

As regards the technique of the sermon, it is to a
considerable extent emancipated from homiletic restraints.   It is off-hand and dashing in its freedom and
moves rapidly.   It makes a vivid impression, sometimes
a series of comparatively unrelated impressions.   The
introduction is always striking, and approaches the subject from afar.   The very first sentence is enigmatical
in its apparent unrelatedness.   The remote is always
interesting in so far as it stirs the mind into inquisitiveness and puts it upon the search for what is to follow.
The principle of gradual approach, therefore, along
lines of somewhat remotely related thought is a valuable
one.   But a remoteness that is far-fetched overworks
the principle.   There is a certain externality, almost a
suggestion of artificiality, in the relations of Guthrie's
thought.   There is a lack of organic quality in the
development of the sermon, and the very diction sometimes has a metallic ring.   Artificial combinations of
things remote, which suggest strained effort after striking effects, are not uncommon.   From the text, " The
tree is known by its fruit," he has a sermon entitled

"The True Test," and this is the introduction: "If there shall be no more salvation out of Christ on the day of judgment than was found on that day when the avenging waters pursued the shrieking crowd to the tops of the highest hills and washed off the last living man from the last dry spot of land, how important for us to know whether we are in Christ, united to Him, not in name and by profession only, but in deed and in truth! To try this we have a plain and infallible test in these words of our Lord, 'The tree is known by its fruit.' On this I remark, (1) It is possible to ascertain our real state and character," etc.   This certainly is far-fetched and inharmonious.   The dramatic reference to the Deluge is out of harmonious relation with the character of the text and with the thought of the sermon.   But it is in line with his dramatic instincts.   He has a prevailingly tragic conception of life, and likes to deal with its tragic aspects.   In the sermon above referred to his thought is fetched from a distance, and is brought into inharmonious relations, in order to start with something that is striking.   There is a certain rhetorical dash about this dramatic quality in which the sermons abound. There are elements of attractiveness and of power in it. If we had listened to the man, we should doubtless have been strongly impressed, despite defects of method, for it is the man that carries the sermon.   But to the critical reader there is a suggestion of artificiality about it. The sermon does not unfold itself from within, hence the thoughts seem to lie in a sort of external juxtaposition, rather than in close, inner organic relation.   It is suggestive of patchwork.   We think of the homiletic carpenter.   In his avoidance of all homiletic formality

he makes his text intimate his subject by frequent repe-
tition. He is not definite in his conception or statement
of his theme, and he sometimes discusses the wrong
theme. The development of the sermon is often confused and inconsequential, and he discusses topics that
are not covered by his theme and have no organic relation with the sermon. In all this there is abundant
homiletic freedom and an easy affectation of triumph
over homiletic restraint. But it is not highly successful. The brilliant rhetoric of the sermon indeed carries
it, but the sermon would have carried itself, and would
have carried the critical hearer, and especially the critical reader, more effectively under better restraints of
well-approved method. The sermon, most conscientiously wrought out indeed, was prepared for immediate
effect, and seemingly more attention was given to rhetorical form than to substance of thought or to method
of development.

4. We are led thus to consider Guthrie's graphic
style as perhaps the chief source of his pulpit power.
It reminds us of the style of French preachers with
whom he must have been at one time familiar. It was
seemingly impossible for Guthrie to say anything in a
plain, non-rhetorical manner. Even a French Parisian
could complain of his lack of colloquial simplicity, of a
certain " dress parade " quality, and of thought so objective as to fail to reach the inner life. He studied those
objects, scenes, and events that would furnish pictorial
and dramatic material for his style, — the ever moving
sea with its shipping, the city streets, the country land-
scape, the family, the home, the mother, the absent ones,
royalty, the poor, the toiler, the battlefield. Everything

was tributary to his illustrative style. From his accurate descriptions of the sea some one inferred that he must have been a sailor in early life. He had studied representations of it. In fact, he overdid the study. He gives too much attention to his illustrations. He overillustrates. His illustrations are gathered from a great variety of sources. They are heaped together and add nothing to the interpretation of the thought. They represent the thought in various forms, but weaken rather than strengthen the impression. "In preaching," he says, "mind the three Ps," — prove, paint, persuade. Speak to the mind, to the imagination, and to the heart and will. He did scant justice to the first. His strength was with the second. His painting was doubtless intended to be tributary to the work of proving and persuading. But the imagination received stronger impressions than the understanding, and, one suspects, stronger impressions than the will. He was certainly not a successful pulpit teacher. He meant to be a successful advocate and persuader, and doubtless he was. But he was above all a painter, and he knew himself as such. What another might do with the brush or the chisel he knew that he could do with the pen. He found that it is the pictorial style that vividly impresses the average hearer, and he resolved to cultivate it. In early years he gave no indication of what subsequently proved to be his distinguishing gift. His style, we are told, was "absolutely unadorned, stiff, and even formal." His first sermon was read from manuscript, but he resolved to abandon it thenceforth, and he adhered faithfully to his resolve. It was his opinion that "he who reads, instead of delivering, his sermon, looking his hearer fairly in the face, throws away a great advantage." It was a wise resolve. He preached memoriter. In order to succeed in this he was accustomed to strike out all that could not easily be remembered. It would embarrass him in his work of committing, and it would not, he thought, readily impress the hearer. Hence also his habit of vocalizing as he wrote, and of committing in silence. He never allowed himself to vocalize while committing. It would unfavorably affect the subsequent delivery of the sermon. One fancies that this habit influenced his style. The objects of thought, as they appear in his illustrations, are placed in external juxtaposition. In describing, for example, the process of physical decay he takes the different parts of the human body in order, so that he may the more easily remember his description, — the hair, the face, the arm, the lower limbs, then the body as a whole; and then in order follows a description of the failure of the powers of the soul. The same thing appears in his description of the changes of nature. He follows the order of the seasons, — spring with its songs of birds, summer with its flowers, autumn with its fruits and grains. So in his description of changes at the old birthplace. Here are new faces in the school, on the farm, in the pulpit, in the pews. So in his sketch of the changes which an atom of matter undergoes. This atom is detached from the rock by the frost, goes into the stream, the stream takes it into the valley, the stream subsides and leaves it on the bank, it goes then into a blade of grass, the grass dies and gives it to the flower, the moor-cock crops it (note the poetic moor-cock), the eagle catches the moor-cock and gets possession of our atom, the eagle dies and gives it to the pasture-land, the lamb now gets hold of it, some human being gets hold of it as he eats the lamb, and now at last it becomes the possession of some "hand that wields a sceptre, or the locks that lend grace to beauty, or the tongue that guides the counsels of a nation or proclaims salvation." Then he makes a move on the heavenly bodies. They change. The planets are now here, now there; now in the east and now in the west. They travel regularly in order that his thought may travel with them. And this whole line of move-ment, descriptive of change, ends in the pole star. This is the only steady thing in the entire description, and this is only a seeming of steadiness.

Now, what the pole star is only in seeming, that is God in reality. And so, after this whirling introductory dance, we have at last reached our theme. All this is doubtless an aid to the memory, but it is overdone. The style, also, is diffuse and repetitious. There is a lack of concentrated vigor. The substance of the sermon is rather thin, and the thought does not get ahead. There is, moreover, a certain artificial glitter of decoration. The illustrations are largely from the gayer scenes of nature and of life, or from whatever is most obtrusive or familiar. They sometimes suggest observation with conscious reference to the work of illustration, and they seem thrust on from without, rather than naturally sug-gested in the process of development. He compares, for example, the appearance of sameness in the midst of nature's changes to the spinning of a top which keeps it from falling. For this reason, that is, by rea-son of the far-fetched and artificial character of the illus-

trations, his preaching lacks in beauty of organic life.
There is too much external decoration. That canon of
artistic taste, and of ethical judgment as well, that the
details of a picture should all be selected with reference
to the central theme and that illustration should not be
so obtrusive that we lose sight of the thought illustrated,
was violated by Dr. Guthrie. The central thought is
sometimes obscured rather than illuminated, and the
central impression weakened rather than strengthened,
and so the sermon loses in real power. The impression
may be vivid, but it is not matched by mental and moral
strength. It is true that men of learning and culture,
as well as rank, listened to him with delight. Hugh
Miller was a regular attendant at his church; Lord Jeffrey had a sitting there; Sir William Hamilton regarded
him as the best preacher he ever heard, and, when reminded that he was deficient in logic, replied, " He has
the best sort of logic, there is but a step between his
premise and his conclusion." This surely is valuable
testimony as to his impressiveness as a preacher, and
his power to hold the interest of intelligent men, and
we can readily accept the judgment of the greatest of
English journals that he was the greatest pulpit orator in Great Britain and the greatest master of pathos
among English-speaking peoples. And we can see the
source and sort of impression. It was his great dramatic power, and it illustrates the unquestionable fact
that those who are bearing the great responsibilities of
life, who are struggling with its barriers and are crushed
by its burdens, need to be stirred and aroused and so
strengthened by the Christian preacher. The pictorial
and dramatic preacher will always have a hearing, and

from widely different classes. Just here was Guthrie's
helpfulness. He illustrates the defects, but also the virtues, of such preaching. Many incidents are recorded
illustrating his power over his audiences. Men were
literally swept from their seats as with a whirlwind of
dramatic power. They so far forgot themselves that
they would turn and shout their enthusiastic admiration
to the congregation. Preachers like Chrysostom and
Beecher often spoke to audiences that applauded them.
But Guthrie's dramatizing brought them to their feet,
and liberated their vocal organs. Behind all this dramatic intensity, however, there was a serious purpose.
There was a wise head and a manly heart there, and to
bring the gospel of redemption to needy men in direct
and vivid appeal was the preacher's aim.

It is idle to undertake, after all, to apply the tests of
cool intellectual criticism to such preaching. The dramatic gift is a great gift. It covers a multitude of defects. In fact, the problem of all preaching is how to
muster the resources of positive power sufficiently to
overbear or to neutralize the defects. Defects there
must be, but the power that can move men and can
bring them into allegiance to the Master of life can
afford to carry them. Guthrie will be remembered for
his power to move the souls of men, and his defects will
all be lost in the unquestionable excellency of his work
as preacher and philanthropist. To every man his work.
If a man can dramatize in the pulpit, and any man may
well covet to do it, let him assiduously but wisely cultivate his gift, for it may be made worthy of the end for
which men preach, and worthy of the truth that should
be preached with persuasive power to needy men.

CHAPTER IX

CHARLES HADDON SPURGEON

MR. SPURGEON was a characteristic product of English dissent. It is true that in his dogmatic provincialism, his exegetical crudeness, and his intolerance of the
modern spirit and method, which he never understood,
he was not at all up to the level of the best type of
nonconforming preaching. But in many of its strongest
and most effective qualities, he was a true child of Puritan dissent. In his independence of spirit, his manly
boldness, his sturdy common sense, his keen insight
into ordinary human nature, his love of Biblical truth,
his tact in catching and his ingenuity in expounding its
salient, practical features, his concrete habit of mind
and his skill in illustration, in his rhetorical realism and
oratorical directness and forcefulness, he was preëminent among its modern representatives. Let us turn,
then, first of all to the story of his public life and then
to his preaching.

I

THE BUILDING OF THE PURITAN PASTORAL EVANGELIST

The career of Spurgeon has for us all the interest
of a problem that awakens curiosity and challenges
explanation. He was doubtless the most impressive

and permanently successful evangelistic preacher of his age.   With relatively meagre preparatory general educa-tion, and with no technical training of the schools, he was able, before he was twenty-one years of age, to win and hold an audience of from eight to ten thousand people in the city of London.   For long periods of time in succession he was able to preach every day in the week, and continued for almost forty years to minister to the same ever enlarging congregation with apparently unabated interest and effectiveness, despite his physical infirmities and his parochial and extra-paro-chial administrative work.   Such a man is hardly less than a homiletic prodigy.   No man who is interested in effective evangelistic preaching should willingly fail to know something about so successful and useful a preacher, and no minister can well afford to ignore him or to refuse to avail himself of the incentive which a study of the man and of his work may secure.

In race descent Mr. Spurgeon was a Dutchman, by adoption an Englishman, in religious education and training a Quaker and Puritan combined, and he dis-closed many of the characteristics of all these sources. His remote progenitors were refugees in the period of persecution from the Netherlands, who fled to Essex County, England, where he was born in 1834.   In his physical personality he bears the mark of the Dutchman. He was of only medium height, but stocky and robust, with a countenance unexpressive in repose, but forceful in action.   His resemblance to Macaulay has often been noted.   One of his ancestors was a Quaker.   And here we have the sturdy independence, the dogged tenacity, and somewhat rude common sense of the Dutchman,

with something of the unworldliness, the brooding mysticism, the subjective piety, and the uncompromising
individualism of the Quaker, put into the hands of
English Puritanism for training. It was good soil to
cultivate, and the husbandry, according to its kind, was
good. That it fell into Puritan hands was thoroughly
appropriate. Puritan culture developed all this inborn
independence of spirit, common sense, Christian realism
and idealism combined, capacity for the invisible, sense
of the abiding presence of the Holy Spirit,—this unworldliness, outspokenness, and straightforwardness. His
grandfather was a Congregational minister with a Calvinistic nurture and a corresponding theology. He was
pastor of one church for fifty-three years, and was able
to bear the remarkable testimony that he had never
suffered an hour's unhappiness in his personal or professional relations with that church,—a testimony not
only to his own personal character and intellectual productiveness which his grandson shared, but to the loyalty of an English Congregational church, which in
all the changes of modern life has never been wholly
lost. With this sturdy man, who believed that Calvinism was the original gospel, who believed proportionately in the reality of a personal devil, and who,
like Luther, had many a tussle with him, the grandson
spent much of his time in early years. In a like atmosphere of religious realism he was nurtured in his father's
house, and, whatever its limitations, there can be no doubt
of the strength and value of this influence for his subsequent career as a preacher. His father, although a lay-
man and a business man, officiated as pastor of a
Congregational church. In this Dutch-English, Puritan

2 C

home, he was subject to a very positive religious régime, and attained very early to an unusual degree of moral and religious maturity. In undertaking to account for the interest he awakened in all classes of people, for the stir he made in the public mind whenever his presence was announced, and for his wide-reaching influence, it should be first of all remembered that he was a man of distinctive religious genius. With all his shrewd common sense, which served him so well, he belonged primarily to the realm of the invisible. He was a heavenly minded man, done up in rather rough, Dutch-Puritan style, and the prophecy of his coming religious usefulness had gone before him. The world is ready to listen to such a man, for the capacity for the ideal and invisible has never been lost from human nature, and it only awaits its embodiment in human form. Like most men of religious genius he was early inclined to isolation, loved his books and pictures it is said, was odd and individualistic, and had a strong sense of vocation. He became familiar with Bunyan, Baxter, and the English Bible, had a retentive memory, and stored what he read. A sort of premonition of his vocation was disclosed at the age of twelve, when he was accustomed to exercise his natural oratorical gifts in preaching to his brothers, sisters, and companions. This habit of giving vent to his thoughts and feelings, in connection with his reading of religious books, must have stirred the homiletic impulse within him. It contributed perhaps to that freedom and naturalness which subsequently characterized his preaching, and, awakening a sense of the ministerial calling, may have disclosed itself in his early assumption of the right to rebuke even his elders, when they seemed to him to be on the wrong track. His self-reliance and pluck, his hatred of all shams and shows and pretences and all forms of tyranny, and his intense love of freedom were an early disclosure. This independence, which passed into an amiable opinionatedness and self-will, was seen when, at the age of sixteen, after much pious meditation and, according to his measure, study, he became convinced that his inherited views of Christian baptism were erroneous, and he united with the Baptist church.

This same independence he disclosed in a most remarkable, and, it must be said, irrational manner, in declining his father's offer of aid in securing for him a college education. Till he was fifteen years old he attended school and, it is said, did his school tasks well. He was then appointed usher, or assistant teacher, in a private school at Newmarket, near Cambridge, where he continued for a year. The appointment to such a position near scholastic Cambridge, and the successful doing of his work, would indicate that he had acquired a fair preparatory education, and it would seem that he might have entered the College of the Nonconformists at Stepney, now Regent Park College, to which, during this year, his father for several hours one day strenuously, but in vain, urged him. There was a touch of fanaticism and superstition upon him. Like many men of untrained religious genius, he was subject to strong inward impressions, which objectified themselves, and he saw visions and heard voices. One day he had an appointment, at his father's instigation, with a college teacher to talk over the question of his entering college. By some miscarriage they failed to meet. This he construed as clearly providential, and then he seemed to hear a voice that said to him, of course in Scripture lan-guage that was familiar to him : " Seekest thou great things for thyself ?   Seek them not " (Jer. xlv. 5). And this decided the question.   It was the divine will that he should not be a college man.   This illustrates his susceptibility to impressions from Scripture.   He gets from it what the impression of the moment suggests, and this, without reference to the original, historic meaning of the passage, he interprets as divine guidance, even in regard to a vital question involving his whole future career.   Of this same college question he says later on, " I have all along had an aversion to college."   And later still, " I am more and more glad that I never went to college."   This discloses a singular narrowness of vision.   It is not sane.   But in the light of his career it can hardly be called discreditable.   From this it should not be inferred that he undervalued knowledge and in-tellectual training, that he lacked studious habits, that he undertook to substitute intuition or subjective im-pulse for knowledge won by hard work, or that he was an advocate of an unlearned ministry, which is indepen-dently endued with " Holy Ghost power."   He under-valued the college curriculum, but he always counselled his students to study hard, to win all the knowledge and to get all the training possible, and what he advocated he practised.   He distrusted the college as too closely affiliated with the movements of modern thought and life which might undermine the faith once delivered to the Puritan saints.   His early reading, as we have seen, was religious.   He gave himself to the Puritan writers, and perhaps no man of his day had a better knowledge

of them. His " Treasury of David " attests his laborious, conscientious, loving study of them. Pointing a
visitor one day to the works of Puritan theologians and
preachers, with which the shelves of his library were
loaded, he said, " I have preached them all." They
had indeed all become tributary to his extraordinary homiletic suggestiveness. But with other and various species
of literature he also increasingly familiarized himself.
He was an intelligent but rapid and omnivorous reader.
With works on geography, history, biography, poetry,
and general popular literature he was at home. With
all his devoutness, unworldliness, and single-hearted religious earnestness, he was no ascetic. For the sake of
his influence he preached and practised "total absti-
nence," but he smoked his cigar "to the glory of God."
He seems to have inherited the gift of humor. He had
the fun and frolic of his family and race, as well as
their common sense and business thrift and enterprise.
In striking contrast with the austerities of his Calvinistic theology is his jolly humor and his racy mother wit.
He always saw the humorous side of things, was an
admirable story-teller, a great punster, was loaded with
proverbs, and was himself a maker of wise sayings that
resembled proverbs. A volume of pithy sayings might
be extracted from his works, that would be as notable
in their way as Mr. Beecher's. His jovial disposition
and his racy humor disclose themselves in his lectures
to the students of his " Pastor's College," and they are
not inharmonious with the seriousness of the subjects
discussed. These lectures have not infrequently a touch
of coarseness, of "cock-sureness " and bumptiousness,
that is unpleasant, and their judgments are often super-

ficial; but they are well worth reading, not only for their pungent, striking, illustrative method of putting things, but for their sturdy common sense and their reality.

During the year when he was usher at Newmarket, after having united with the Baptist church and before he was sixteen years old, he began to preach. Children and adults in the rural districts about Cambridge, gathered in schoolhouses, constituted his first audiences. His success was such that, at the age of seventeen, he was chosen pastor of a small Baptist church at Waterbeach, not far from Cambridge. During this pastorate of almost two years the membership of his church doubled, every monthly communion service witnessing accessions to it. At that time the New Park Street Baptist church of London, an old church with an interesting history and a succession of able and learned men as pastors, was in search of a minister. His general reputation, rapidly won, for success in pulpit and pastorate, and particularly a Sunday-school address delivered by him at Cambridge, resulted in drawing the attention of the officers of this church to him, and in January of 1854, before he was yet twenty years old, he became its pastor. It was in a depleted condition numerically and financially, and seemed a forlorn hope. But the auditorium was soon crowded, and hundreds who had deserted the church returned. He preached almost daily, and he was in demand elsewhere in and about London, especially in connection with philanthropic and missionary movements. His sermons were always Biblical, but were such under close Calvinistic limitations, not to say fetters. He spoke in a free, simple, pithy, colloquial manner, as was always his wont, and the unconventional straightforwardness and reality of his speech were telling. His early structural method he subsequently characterized as one of "glorious confusion." It is not clear that the old Puritan preachers were doing much for him at this time, else he would have known the ingloriousness of such homiletic confusion. But he had the good sense to correct it, although his method always suggests the homiletic knack. "Now," he says, "I have a shelf in my head for everything, and whatever I read or hear, I know where to stow it away for use at the proper time." This idea of a "shelf" for his knowledge is not badly descriptive. It is perhaps more accurate than he realized. It suggests a storehouse, a well-arranged magazine of information. It was an orderly but somewhat external and formal method. The sermon lacks organic development. Thoughts are taken down as from a shelf and placed in juxtaposition. It is the work of a fertile but untrained mind. His sermons in the early years are full of illustrations wrought up from his reading in a somewhat formal and pedantic manner. But he constantly developed in intellectual sobriety. His preaching was always concrete and illustrative, but increasingly weighty in substance and fruitful in suggestion. He observed the thought, appropriated the method, as he caught the style, of the old Puritan preachers. In fact, it was the English Bible and the old Puritan writers and preachers, brought into contact with a fertile and ingeniously suggestive mind, that shaped his preaching. From the first year of his London ministry his sermons were published, have been gathered into nearly forty volumes, have gone wherever the English language is spoken, and many have been

translated into foreign tongues.   Crude in thought and
rough instruments of power they are, and will not live.
But in their earnestness, their reality, their pith and
pungency, they are doing well their short-lived work.
Accomplished German writers on homiletics speak in
high praise of them.   The Christian world has rarely
witnessed such an instance of homiletic productiveness.
During the first enlargement of his church building in
1854, when he was only twenty years old, he preached
in Exeter Hall and was the sensation of the hour.   This
may seem to illustrate what the Netherlanders, Spurgeon's ancestors, regarded as the volatile character of
the English people in Queen Elizabeth's age, a quality
that is not commonly attributed to them.   But it more
conclusively illustrates the genuine power of the young
preacher.   His church building was many times enlarged, till the Tabernacle stood as the monument of his
genius as a preacher, and the church that had grown to
large proportions was in all ways one of the most pros-
perous in England.   Here for a long succession of years,
not only the common people, but people of education
and intelligence and culture, were among his interested
and profited listeners.   Prominent preachers of the
Anglican church regarded him as the greatest of all
the preachers of nonconformity.   Mr. Gladstone knew
good preaching, and he had a high estimate of Mr.
Spurgeon, being seen not infrequently as an interested
listener at the Tabernacle.   John Ruskin knew good
English, and he highly estimated him as a master of
idiomatic English style, and for several years he held a
sitting in his church.   American preachers, like the late
Professor Park, himself a great preacher, but of a very

different school, listened to him with great admiration
and profound emotion. He visited Scotland many times
and the enthusiasm awakened by his preaching is said
to have more than matched the enthusiasm with which
their own Chalmers had stirred the sober-minded Scotch.
Even from conservative and highly respectable Oxford
came the testimony that there were " few of the immense
audiences that were privileged to listen to him that were
not astonished and delighted at the wonderful power
and ability with which he was so highly gifted." These
campaigns of oratorical conquest inclined him at one
time to the folly of abandoning his church and of entering
upon the career of a professional itinerant evangelist,
from which he was saved by the great wisdom of his
people in securing for him an audience room commensurate with his needs. Everything seemed tributary to
his success as a preacher, — not less the sneers, in his
early ministry, of the so-called cultivated classes and
the opposition of ecclesiastical enemies, than the favor
of the common people and the laudation of friends, — till
at last his hold upon the English people of all classes
and ecclesiastical connections became thoroughly fixed,
so that he was taken as a matter of course, and became
a recognized moral and religious force to be reckoned
with by all intelligent people.

The world knows the story of his career, and it knows
fairly well the agencies, processes, and personal qualities by which he won the confidence even of those who
at first sneered at him, and by which his influence was
constantly enlarged. His success was not an accident,
nor a mistake. It was not simply the sincerity of his
faith in what he preached, and the strength of his con-

viction, not his religious devotion, his genuine good
nature, his mother wit, his tact in dealing with men, his
fertility of suggestion, his productive imagination, his
great power of acquisition and retention, his pathos and
humor. We must also consider his great tenacity of
purpose in grappling with hard work. Few men have
combined his genius for preaching and for administration. And his career illustrates significantly the value
of pulpit power in the administration of large parochial
and philanthropic enterprises. Other preachers have
had the full measure of his power in reaching large
masses of the people from the pulpit, but few have ever
had anything like his early success, and but few his
measure of success in multiplying the sources of beneficent influence in the work of philanthropy. And as he
multiplied the agencies of personal power, he himself
also developed in weight and sobriety of thought, measurably outgrew the defects of his early training, and
counter-worked by his practical common sense the crudeness of his theology. His sympathies also constantly
enlarged, notwithstanding his limited theological horizon,
and his style, always picturesquely illustrative, increased
in dignity and strength. He contributed nothing to the
thought of the church. But as the watcher and winner
of souls he has touched powerfully the life of the church.
He will live, not in the theology he preached, but in the
lives he has lifted and in the institutions he has founded
and fostered.

II

THE PREACHING OF THE PURITAN PASTORAL EVANGELIST

Mr. Spurgeon was distinctively an evangelistic preacher. And it is as the representative of the popular effectiveness of this school of preachers that he has been selected for our consideration. His pastoral preaching indeed aims to instruct and edify in Christian knowledge and virtue, but, on the whole, it is better adapted to the work of stirring men to evangelistic and philanthropic effort. He speaks, indeed, in a way to the mind, for he is one of the clearest of preachers. But what he says passes straight and swift through the mind into feeling, conviction, and action, and it is his aim so to present the truth as to win faith in and allegiance to Christ. He was somewhat polemical in his preaching, especially in the early period. But there is no permanently valuable apologetic quality about it. He deals with the doctrines of grace according to the Calvinistic type, but they are adjusted to evangelistic impression, and he is in no adequate sense a doctrinal preacher. One would find himself misled if he were to rely upon him for a reasonable and discriminating statement of the most important Christian doctrines, and if he were of an independent, critical mind, he would be seriously disappointed. His statements of doctrine make more impression upon the imagination than upon the critical judgment. He handles a great amount of Biblical truth and in a very effective way. But in the largest and best sense he is not an expository preacher as Robertson is.

He deals with Scripture in such way that it catches the fancy, stirs an emotional interest, and doubtless secures practical results, but he conveys to the mind no clear and connected knowledge of Biblical truth. He deals with the ethical aspects of truth, and lays its moral demands forcefully upon the conscience, but he gives the critical hearer no adequate conception of the basis of moral obligation, no adequate Christian conception of the nature of moral law, no adequate vision of the highest good, no adequately discriminated statement as to what is distinctive in Christian duty, nor does he deal very largely with the different forms or spheres of Christian virtue. Like all evangelistic preachers, he deals mostly with the cardinal doctrines of grace and with the cardinal Christian virtues of faith and love; but those virtues that grow out of this soil in multitudinous Christian forms, as conditioned by the various relations of life, and are realized in the development of Christian character, he rarely touches. He cannot be called, therefore, in any adequate sense, an ethical preacher. He deals abundantly with Biblical biography and history, but it is all in the evangelistic interest and according to the evangelistic method. But his power as an evangelistic preacher cannot be doubted.

Premising, then, that Spurgeon must be estimated as such, and will stand the test of no other estimate, let us look at a few of the more prominent elements of his power, which may be helpful, noting incidentally such defects as may prove admonitory.

1. Beginning with what is most exterior, but with what has also a vital root, Mr. Spurgeon demonstrates the power of naturalness in the work of the preacher. It is

the prevailing opinion among Englishmen that his success was in no small measure due to the perfect simplicity, reality, straightforward directness, and unconventionality of his pulpit method.   All this is contrasted with the conventional type of preaching that prevails in the Established church.   This, of course, is only one phase of the question, and there is much that lies behind it and gives accent to it, but it is an important consideration. Preaching tends to become conventional, and the new man with a genius for preaching is needed to lead the way in a more spontaneous and natural method.   Spurgeon is just such a man.   But, although distinctly a man of homiletic genius, he is also a product of methods that prevail in the Free churches of England, and which are in strong contrast with those that prevail in the Established church. Anglican preaching, especially at the time when Mr. Spurgeon appeared, was of such sort as to render the success of such a man easily possible.   There is not much evangelistic preaching in the proper sense in the Anglican church, which in influence overshadows all other churches.   Its preaching is ecclesiastical and lacks freshness and vitality.   In Spurgeon's early days it lacked in rhetorical and oratorical power of a genuine sort, and was dull, monotonous, and conventional.   If in the evangelical branch the preacher handled the truth with more power of emotion and sentiment, this seemingly had degenerated largely into feeble sentimentality.

In the Free churches men have learned their art by practising it in a simple, straightforward manner.   In this way the talent for evangelistic preaching is cultivated in a most notable manner.   The Establishment

does not produce this type of preachers to any considerable extent. Men cannot preach before they take
orders, and Spurgeon had been preaching for several
years before the age at which the Anglican churchman
is permitted to take orders. Robertson belonged to the
Establishment, but he was more than an Anglican product, and his power was not that of the evangelistic
preacher. But for the Anglican church, such a man as
Spurgeon would be an impossibility. Prophetic gifts,
even when developed within the limits of its own ecclesiasticism, as in revolutionary periods has been the case,
have been discredited. The career of the Wesleys and
of Whitefield are proof. Doubtless there is better soil
and atmosphere for these gifts than formerly. But in
Spurgeon's early days they were unproductive. It is
the freedom of the dissenting churches that makes Mr.
Spurgeon possible. Here men begin early and find
themselves by grappling vigorously with the obstacles
of their calling. In the case of the commonplace man,
the result is, doubtless, often bad enough. Mediocrity
and cant have free range. But in the case of a man of
great native homiletic gifts, the result could not fail to
be the development of great preaching power. With
better training Mr. Spurgeon might have been bettered
as a preacher. But the training independently of the
actual work of preaching never could have accomplished
the desired result. At the time Mr. Spurgeon appeared,
there were a few conspicuous preachers in the Free
churches, but the average of excellence was not high.
It was, on the whole, easier for a man of mark to secure
a place of eminence in these churches than it would have
been later on, or than it would have been in this coun

try. Accordingly the success of Mr. Spurgeon, with his
supremely evangelistic spirit, especially with his fresh
gifts of speech, is the more easily explained. Possibly
he might not have secured in this country, that has produced such a preacher as Henry Ward Beecher, so eminent a position. But be that as it may, he had the right
environment, he had an easy field, and the requisite endowments, and the gifts of grace that are essential to
the great evangelistic preacher. Such a man was needed,
and he was sent as a leader in this type of preaching in
which his influence has been great and wide-reaching.

As already intimated, unlike some great preachers
of this school, he was not much indebted to his physical equipment. It was not, like that of Guthrie, a commanding presence. He was neither tall, nor comely,
nor particularly graceful. In facial expression he was
somewhat dull and unattractive. He was thick set, and
there was about him a suggestion of physical grossness.
He bore an expression of unfailing good nature, but the
countenance was not suggestive of eminent intellectual
or spiritual qualities. His dress was unprofessional, appropriate to the character, the tastes, and environment
of the man. He had a hearty and wholesome contempt of ministerial pomposity and of ecclesiastical
millinery. His movements were not wholly graceful,
like those of Guthrie. His voice, however, was exceedingly clear and distinct, had great compass, and was
capable of expressing great varieties of feeling. It
expressed the qualities of tenderness, severity, stateliness, and strength with great effectiveness. It had
hardly the richness of Beecher's voice, or the clarion
quality of Whitefield's, as it is reported to us. With

the exception of the voice, there was in Spurgeon very little that was impressive. Naturalness, however, spontaneous freedom, and simple straightforwardness were very marked. He was easy and self-possessed, and there was about him an air of moral sobriety and seriousness. He had no pulpit mannerisms. He stood erect, or, when reaching after his audience, bent over the desk in a wholly natural and not altogether ungraceful manner, and there was no appearance of conscious effort. He stood there in perfect simplicity and talked in a free, familiar, conversational manner, as if he were intent upon taking his audience into his confidence. It has been suggested that his preaching in this regard must have resembled that of our Lord. And there is ground for the suggestion, for the one word used by the evangelists in characterization of the preaching of Christ is the word "talk." He spoke to the people as one talking in a simple, colloquial manner, without oratorical effort. Even in his oratorical flights, Spurgeon never lost his naturalness. There was nothing of the intensity and businesslike aggressiveness of Mr. Moody. One questions for the moment whether the very limitations of his learning and the meagreness of his intellectual training may not have been tributary to this quality of naturalness. One is even puzzled transiently with the question whether in such bliss of ignorance, in which simplicity and spontaneity and freedom reign supreme, it were not "folly to be wise." Did not Mr. Spurgeon know himself better than any of his friends knew him, when he resolved not to go to college and chose to learn what he might only in his own conscious calling as a preacher? But after all such doubts lose sight of the fact that Mr. Spurgeon was a man of extraordinary native preaching gifts, and that these gifts simply triumphed measurably over his defects of education and culture. If genius can thus triumph over defects, it certainly can triumph over the supposed tendency of a larger knowledge and closer training to repress the native forces, or to "freeze the genial currents of the soul." If he was powerful in what we may regard as his relative ignorance and undiscipline, he would have been far more powerful in the right sort with better instruments at his command, and his influence might have been much more permanent. Education of the right sort can never hamper genius. Its natural and legitimate result should be to emancipate it from its limitations and deterrents. But one of the great lessons which Spurgeon's success as a preacher teaches is that nothing should be permitted to repress the freedom of the preacher. A literary or theological or homiletical training that should hamper a man, or in any sort or measure check the free expression of his energies, would be a curse. The problem for every preacher is how to train himself effectively in lines in which he can work most freely. Spurgeon thoroughly solved that problem in his early life. It does not take a man of homiletic genius like him very long to find out what he can do best and how best he can do it. Spurgeon attempted to do only what he could do naturally and with freedom. A man without his gifts may be longer in getting at the secret of his strength. But it will at last be discovered or the man will work as a slave.

2. Spurgeon's consciousness of vocation is an element of power in his evangelistic preaching that may well be

2 D

noted. He always disclosed and frequently asserted, especially in his early ministry, the consciousness of a divine call to do just the work he was doing. The failure of his ministry, in so far as he found failure in it, and in that of other men, he attributed to a lack or loss of assurance that God was behind them and was working through them. " I am as much called," he says, " to preach the gospel as Paul was," and who can doubt it ? In presenting the claims of the gospel, in appealing to men to accept the service of Christ, it surely is of unspeakable value to the preacher to feel that he has been called and sent to do that work, to feel that a message has been committed to him, and that in proclaiming it he is indeed an ambassador of God. It must increase a man's power tenfold. All great evangelists have felt this. Mr. Spurgeon's approach to his fellow-men was that of a man who was conscious of moral authority and power, and for this reason his speech was masterful. Note his lofty treatment of men whom he regards as in rebellion against God. In one of his early sermons [1] he speaks of the invitation to the tomb of the risen Lord as being given to Christian disciples only. Then he utters a word of admonition in most confident and authoritative fashion to all profane souls, to the sordid, the carnal, and the frivolous, and bids them away from the tomb. It is all done in such rhetorical fashion as not to offend seriously, but in the very venture there is clear trace of the consciousness of authority to deal with sinners as an ambassador of God. It must be acknowledged that it is done in a very impressive manner. In speaking to this class he always

[1] "The Tomb of Jesus," " Spurgeon the Modern Whitefield," No. XI.

manifests the same boldness and faithfulness. He
talks straight at men and is not afraid to probe their
consciences. To those who leave their own congregations to hear him as the latest sensation, he utters the
boldest and severest rebuke. There was great power
in this clear, direct, bold appeal. Of course the man
who does this successfully must have the ear of the
people, and must understand his ground. But surely
there will be no very successful evangelistic preaching
which is not in the right way and at the right time
direct, searching, bold, and uncompromising, striking at
the centre and dealing with sin as it should be dealt
with.

3. As involved in the consciousness of vocation, the
positiveness of Spurgeon's preaching is another element
of power in his evangelism. Needed everywhere in
our day in active Christian life, a positive faith is
supremely necessary in the pulpit, and above all in successful evangelistic preaching. Spurgeon's positiveness
disclosed itself in various ways, but preëminently in his
apparent absolute freedom from theological doubt.
To doubt the truth of the Roman Catholic faith, Newman regarded as a sin. Not the less sinful would Spurgeon regard any doubt of the truth of Calvinism. Is it
not found in God's Book? And who shall doubt what
God has said without sinning? He apparently had not
the slightest doubt that Calvinism was identical with
Christianity. He had not thoroughly mastered the Calvinistic system, and never apprehended its difficulties.
But he knew its prominent features. He took hold of
individual truths that appear in Calvinistic dress, and he
made practical use of them, in doing which he was con-

fessedly skilful and forceful.   He believed with all his
might.   Sometimes, indeed, his positiveness lapses into
discourtesy and even into a species of amiable impudence.
He undertook sometimes to demolish unbelief in sledge-
hammer fashion, as if it might be put down by the force
of his personal will.   He criticised his ministerial brethren who were many of them his peers in piety, and his
superiors in learning and in intellectual discrimination.
He wasted a good deal of energy in his early days in
undertaking to set the ministerial world right.

In later years, however, he saw his error, and became
more courteous and more catholic in his spirit.   He
thoroughly disliked Arminianism and pitied Arminians.
He was perfectly sure, and he was perfectly honest in
his conviction, that what he called the " Down Grade
Movement" was due to the abandonment by the churches
of the Calvinistic doctrines of grace.   Scepticism with
respect to the old doctrine of a substitutionary atonement, the inerrancy of the Scriptures, future eternal
punishment, and other doctrines, was surely the result
of abandoning the positive teachings of the church
creeds, even with respect to less important matters.   All
this had resulted, he was convinced, in a great decline
in the spiritual life of the church.   He accordingly with-
drew from the Baptist Union and organized a new con-
ference, whose basis was to be allegiance to the doctrines
of grace as interpreted by Calvinism, the doctrine of
immersion, and the mission of the ministry to win souls.
He was extreme in his theological positions.   He denied
that there was any adequate power in Christian experience to test the truth, and adhered to the doctrine of
an infallible Bible.   Man once had the power to discover

the truth; but he believed, as Newman did, that it had
been lost, and now we must all rest upon the external
Word of God. The doctrine of eternal punishment must
be accepted, despite its difficulties, because it is found
in the Bible. His conception of prayer was substantially that in it we go to God for what we need and
want, expecting that we shall always get it. It is going to the bank with a check, which God will honor
promptly. There is, therefore, no need of loafing about
the bank. Present your check, get what it calls for,
and leave. He held extreme and unreasonable views
of divine intervention in the support of the philanthropic
institutions which he had established. There are two
ways and only two — there can be no third that is successful. One is the method of implicit reliance upon
God; the other is reliance upon men. There is no middle course. To rely partly upon God and partly upon
men is always unsuccessful. He sometimes attacked
errors of which he knew but little, but with all the assurance of infallibility. All this was a weakness which he
partially recognized in later years. But, after all, it was
the defect of a strong quality. The positiveness and the
strength of the faith behind was a condition of power.
It is better to be intelligently positive, positive in knowledge and yet in charity, positive in a few things and not
cherish the foible of omniscience. But infinitely better
be positive even in ignorance and mistake than double-
minded and vacillating. No pulpit can be a place of
power unless there be strong positive faith and conviction there. If Spurgeon's positiveness leads him sometimes to magnify himself, if there is a certain *naïveté* in
his occasional references to himself in the pulpit, it is

only a part of the strength of his individuality, and he made this innocent self-consciousness tributary to his power as a preacher. For people are interested in what centres in so notable a personality. His positiveness and force of individuality, which was somewhat rude by reason of his defective training and culture, led him sometimes almost into irreverence. Some of his prayers in the early part of his ministry were well-nigh shocking. He doubtless intended to shock the commonplace respectability of the formal religionists about him. His familiarity with the quaint old Puritan divines encouraged him in this, for he at first followed what is bad as well as what is good in them. He was sometimes as rude and sensational as Rowland Hill, with the difference that he lived in the latter half of the nineteenth rather than of the eighteenth century. He was an inveterate punster and carried the punning habit into the pulpit, which may have been tolerable, if at all, only in view of his manifestly sincere desire to reach and benefit his fellow-men, and in view of his youth and immaturity and consequent failure to take fully into account the dignity that is demanded of the Christian preacher.

It may seem unfair to dwell upon these early defects. But the sole object in so doing is to indicate that they are a manifestation in rude form of the positiveness, the individuality, and the force of his character, to accentuate the fact that the success of his career was despite rather than because of these defects, and that the manifest earnestness and sincerity of the man carried them. These faults he measurably overcame in his later ministry. And it must be acknowledged that the courage, the directness, the plainness, with which he sought to

impress the claims of the gospel upon men, his powerful denunciations of sin, his faithful warnings against its
ruin, his complete emancipation from the fear of man,
his refusal to be brought into bondage to any man or
class of men, the prophetic freedom with which he proclaimed all that his convictions cherished as true — it
must be acknowledged that all this is most admirable,
and that it is in large measure the secret of his influence
over men.

4. The value for effective evangelistic preaching of
a working knowledge of the Bible is copiously illustrated
by Mr. Spurgeon. It cannot be said that he had anything more than a superficial knowledge of it as a literary product. Of Biblical criticism he knew nothing
adequately, and he was an unreliable expositor. In
fact, he was not in any proper sense an expository
preacher. He never dealt with the Bible in such way
as to convey to the mind, as Robertson did, a clear and
connected knowledge of Biblical truth. He uses the
Bible in such way as will catch the fancy, stir the emotions, and secure practical results. Incentive and edification, as he would understand it, was his aim. He had
much skill in getting Biblical truth into working use.
His exegesis is often grotesque. But he is ingenious in
his use of Biblical material. He illustrates the value
of a generous use of the imagination in deducing fruitful thought from the Scriptures. He was master of the
old Puritan method of Biblical suggestion. It is a relic
of, but an improvement upon, the old allegorical method.
He develops his subject textually for the most part,
and the evangelistic aim is apparent throughout. As an
illustration, take his treatment of John iii. 16. It is the

Biblical and evangelistic method of getting his thought before his hearers. " I want to make you see how great that love is by five different particulars." And this is the textual outline of the sermon whose title and theme are " The Immeasurable Love ": 1. By observing first the gift (" He gave "); *a.* what, *b.* how, *c.* when. 2. The plan of salvation (" whosoever believeth, etc."); *a.* mental assent to the doctrine of substitution, *b.* personal acceptance of it, *c.* personal trust in a personal Saviour as such substitute. 3. Those for whom this salvation is provided (" whosoever believeth "). 4. Deliverance, the negative result (" shall not perish "). 5. The positive result (" shall have eternal life ").

One will hardly fail to see what a great variety of truths are embraced within the limits of the one complex truth of the text, and one must also be impressed with the possibilities of the textual method of preaching. But the critical hearer or reader will note the difference between the Biblical suggestiveness of practical use and the theology that is imported from without into it, as illustrated by his attempt to expound the doctrine of faith and of the atonement. " Faith is a firm and cordial assent to the truth that God did send his Son . . . to stand in the room and stead of guilty men . . . so that he bore the punishment due to our transgressions." It is not only a mental assent to the truth of substitution, but a " personal acceptance " of it. It is primarily mental acceptance of a certain truth. Elsewhere, however, he seems to have in mind the fact rather than the truth of the atonement. Still, as he conceives it, the atonement is the fact of substitution. By personal transgression one appropriates Adam's sin and makes

it his own.   By faith, as above conceived, one appropriates Christ's righteousness and his atonement and
makes them his own.   Punished for appropriating the
sin of another, saved by appropriating the righteousness
and the satisfaction of another.   All this is an importation of technical theology into a simple textual development, and the success of the sermon is not at all
dependent upon the conceptions involved.   The confusion of thought, too, is not the result of simple Biblical
exposition, but of a theological importation.   The appropriation of a truth is confounded with personal acceptance of a fact.   And the appropriation of Christ's
righteousness is confounded with the appropriation of
his atonement.   Stress is laid upon mental assent,
which is not a Biblical conception.   This, also, is a
theological importation.

Now, all this for purposes of correct theological thinking is not valuable.   For discriminating and sceptical
minds it might be positively mischievous.   But to the
undiscriminating mind he succeeds in conveying, even
by his confused and contradictory imported theological
form, an important working truth, and the critical but
friendly mind will read behind his form of statement an
inner truth of salvation.   And so it is in general with
his preaching.   The success of the sermon does not
depend on the hearer's acceptance of the preacher's
theological statements, which are imported from his
Calvinistic creed.   There is always a residuum of
practical working truth, — truth that enters through the
lower doorways of the soul and touches the heart without informing the mind.   His felicitous use of the text
is an interesting feature of his Biblical preaching.   The

text is kept constantly before the mind. He has the skill of the old Puritan preachers in repeating his text, or parts of it, in a great variety of connections throughout the sermon, so as to keep it constantly before the mind, bringing it into relation with a great variety of thoughts, thus throwing new light upon it, or securing new significance for it, and making it the more impressive. It thus speaks for itself in many relations and becomes the more cogent rhetorically. One notes readily, also, that his mind is completely saturated with Biblical diction. And this gives a certain elevation to his style, with all its rugged homeliness. Biblical expressions are found on almost every page, and it is hardly worth while to linger with citations from them. But they impart, not only an element of dignity to his style, as well as clearness and simplicity, but of beauty as well, and often the touch of pathos. The choicest elements of beauty in his style, and for so plain a preacher they are not infrequent, are the product of his familiarity with Biblical diction. His rhetoric has been nurtured from these sources, and by Christian hymns, and especially by the old Puritan writers. They impart a graceful, rhythmic movement to his sentences. They will be found in abundance in the sermon above referred to. Thus Biblical diction contributes not only to the plain and homely qualities of his style, especially to the Saxon element in his vocabulary, but to its rhythmic grace. And one fancies that his use of figurative language, in which the metaphor, apostrophe, and interrogation abound and which contribute to the qualities of style above mentioned, was the result, to a considerable extent, of his familiarity with the language of the Bible.

5. Mr. Spurgeon illustrates the effectiveness of a
skilful use of the *ad hominem* method in the handling
of evangelistic truth.   He appeals with a good deal
of tact to men's common observations and experiences,
to their feelings, prepossessions, and interests, and to that
quick perception of analogies which seems to be the
gift of the popular mind.   The use of striking contrast
is one of the features of this *ad hominem* method of
appeal.   To endeavor to greaten the truth to the apprehension and in the estimate of the hearer by contrast
is one of the favorite methods of evangelistic, as it is of
apologetic, preachers.   Mr. Moody was facile in his use
of it, and in it we seem to see Spurgeon's influence.
It was a favorite method of the Puritan preachers, from
whom it was caught and domesticated, but modified, by Mr.
Spurgeon.   It is a characteristic method of many popular
textual preachers like the late Dr. Joseph Parker.   It
was a familiar device of the Rev. William Jay, and in
him it is an echo of the old Puritan voice.   The Welsh
preachers have a knack at it.   It is easily overdone, and
demands judicious handling.   In fact, it is easily brought
into contempt.   Its suggestions may easily be specious
and even false, for it is not an appeal to the higher
intelligence or to the critical judgments, but to the faulty
experiences, to the hasty imaginings, even to the preju-
dices and emotional, and perhaps selfish, interests of
men.   Christian apologetics has often used this principle
of contrast in a speciously *ad hominem* manner.   It may
be used, indeed, in a perfectly legitimate and very effective manner; but if based on false assumptions, it becomes shallow and irrational and inconclusive.   The
contrast, for example, between the assumed ignorance

and weakness of the apostles and disciples of Christ and the greatness of their achievements has often been used for the purpose of heightening our impression of the supernatural power of Christianity, and often very inconclusively.

Robert Hall finds an argument for the supernatural character of the atonement in the assumed fact that it is out of all relation with ordinary human experience. The contrast between Christianity and the religions of nature, for the purpose of magnifying the former, is sometimes used inconclusively.   All this has been over-worked, and we are finding a better method.   The contrast between God's methods and man's methods, between what God does and what we should be likely to do, between God's estimates and human estimates, is an expository method in very common use in the pulpit. We find it in Mr. Spurgeon's sermon on "The Im-measurable Love."   These are the contrasts: The gift was *God's Son.   We* have no such son to give.   No man could save *his own life* by giving up his *own son*, but God *saves us* by giving up His *Son's life.   He* gave His Son to *exile* and *hardship*, not as we might do in sending our children into missionary life to *end it gloriously. When* God gave is contrasted with our giving.   *He* gave from *eternity*, hence is *constantly giving*.   Not as we give — *suddenly* and *spasmodically*.   The value of this method judiciously and skilfully used is evident.   Its defects, too, are obvious.   The example just cited from Spurgeon is in general unobjectionable and is fairly effective, although not very weighty.   But we sometimes find examples that are objectionable because shallow and specious.   For instance, his argument for the perseverance of saints in the sermon above cited. "Whosoever believeth shall not perish;" well, the penitent has believed, and so become a Christian. He "shall not perish." Therefore he will not go back. If he should cease to be a believer, he would perish. But it is said that he shall not perish. Since this is so, it is clear that he will continue to believe. Again, the believer is a member of Christ. Christ cannot lose one of his own members. You cannot drown me by keeping my foot under water. You must get my head under. Thus Christ, the head, must be destroyed before the believer can perish. This is clever, but specious. It is not argument, but *ad captandum* appeal.

But it must be acknowledged that he often handles this method with much mental and moral sobriety, and with great force and persuasiveness. He exalts common sense with great success in the affairs of religion, summoning men to the use of the same faculties in religion that they use in everyday life. He not only interests but he instructs men by presenting what is familiar to them, by illustrating what is obscure in the use of what is common and well known. He heightens the significance of the truth by showing it, not only in its resemblances, but in its contrasts.

6. The power of pathos in the proclamation of the gospel is well illustrated by Mr. Spurgeon. He was not the master of pathos perhaps to the extent that Dr. Thomas Guthrie was. After hearing him preach, Guthrie expressed the opinion that Spurgeon was deficient in pathos. But this must be regarded as an inadequate estimate. He did not affect pathos in his preaching to the extent that Guthrie did. He espe-

cially did not lay such stress upon it, and it may be questioned if his use of it be not much more simple and spontaneous. He drew to a considerable extent from pathetic texts, and even in his handling of ordinary texts he can readily find the pathos that lies in their suggestiveness, thus disclosing the power of Biblical truths to evoke pathetic expression. His knowledge of the familiar scenes of common life, of what lies nearest the average human heart, his familiarity with scenes of suffering and sorrow and sin, which cultivated a naturally tender heart, all this, in connection with his lack of training in abstract thought and facility in concrete expression, favored the culture of pathos and inclined him to seek for and to make use of the material of pathos, which is so abundant in the Scriptures. A heart that is truly human, that loves what touches the nature that is common to us all and makes us kin, that knows the sin and shares the sorrows of men, that has felt the love of Christ, that is familiar with Biblical literature and with the poetry of the church and with the lives of God's saints, — these are for the preacher some of the sources of pathos. He who would be an effective evangelistic preacher will get far out and far down into real life, far into the sins and sufferings of men, will know the human heart, and above all the heart of Christ as disclosed in His life of condescension and sacrifice.

Some of Spurgeon's early sermons are especially interesting, not only in their homiletic ingenuity, but in their pathos. The sermon on the tomb of Jesus, above referred to, from the text, "Come, see the place where the Lord lay," may furnish an example. The resurrec-

tion of Christ would not naturally suggest the possibilities of pathetic treatment. But in the case before
us it appears abundantly. Pathos mingled with a certain dramatic forcefulness abounds here. It is the
textual development and is as follows: The invitation:
" Come." Reasons why we should heed the invitation
and come to Jesus' tomb. The reasons are naturally
suggested by the scenes themselves which the tomb
of the crucified furnishes.

The attention arrested: " See the place where the
Lord lay." If we come, what shall we see? We shall
see this and that, all sketched with true feeling and
with true pathetic suggestion.

Emotion excited: With what feelings should we come
and what should we learn? All this is a very simple
and natural use of association for the purpose of interesting our feelings and moving our affections and
awakening the soul's devotion to Christ. There are
some rather crude things here which belong to the
early period of his ministry. But the sermon is a suggestive and helpful one, and there is a store of comfort
in it for the heart of the simple believer.

Of Spurgeon's great value to the cause of Christianity
and to the Christian church and to the cause of general
philanthropy there can be no doubt, and especially of
his value as an inspiration and in many respects even as
a model for any man who would know how to preach
evangelistically, and who would covet the wisdom and
the grace and the unspeakable joy and priceless reward
of him who wins the allegiance of men to Jesus Christ.
It is preaching that strongly takes hold of the human
heart, conscience, and will. If one will subordinate his

critical faculties, and permit himself to be borne along on the current of the preacher's earnest feeling and consecrated purpose, and will hold himself in responsive attitude toward him, he will be strongly interested and impressed by it. No well-educated and well-trained man is likely to be misled by Mr. Spurgeon's defects, and it is precisely such a man that will derive most profit from him, because it will be a judicious appropriation of his merits. Any preacher who will analyze his product, and get at its sources of power, who will let himself be instructed and quickened by it, who will take the best of it, in the inspiration and in the method of it, and pass it over into his own line of work, using it in such way as is agreeable with his own personal peculiarities, will not fail to become a successful evangelistic preacher, a result greatly to be desired in the interest of an effective Christian pulpit in our day. Modern critical habits are not likely to permit any educated man to indulge in an extravagant homiletic use of Scripture. And for any man who is in danger of a too formal and critical and unsuggestive pulpit use of Scripture, Mr. Spurgeon may be very helpful.

INDEX

Allen, Prof. A. V. G., " Life and Letters of Phillips Brooks," 195; cited, 207, 221.

Anselm, Archbishop, Bushnell on " Cur Deus Homo," 151.

Apologia, Newman's, cited, 253, 262, 263, 266, 267, 274, 275, 281, 282, 286, 298.

Arbirlot, parish of, Guthrie's first pastorate, 356, 357.

Aristotle, Robertson student of, 63.

Aristotle's Ethics, Schleiermacher student of, 11.

Arnold, Dr. Thomas, 61, 259, 260; broad churchman, 261; Newman's opposition to, 274; exacting classical standard, 313, 320.

Augustine, St., 150, 304; polemical preaching of, 327.

Barby, Moravian school at, 5, 8.

Barrow, Dr. Isaac, Beecher a student of, 112, 126; an apologetic preacher, 322.

Beecher, Rev. Henry Ward, compared with Schleiermacher, 42, 129; with Robertson, 98, 106; with Spurgeon, 104, 399; with Luther, 100; with Newman, 140; with Bushnell, 105, 106, 111, 115, 130; with Brooks, 112, 130; a typical American, 99, 100, 106; representative American preacher, 100, 101; individualistic quality in preaching, 101-115; address before New York and Brooklyn Association, 109, 110; student of English preachers, 112, 126; intellectual qualities of productiveness, thoroughness, range, and catholicity, 115-136; compared with other American orators, 119;

theological beliefs, 134-135; gifts of expression, "the Shakespeare of the pulpit," 136-142.

Berlin, Schleiermacher's connection with, 12, 13, 14, 15, 22, 39.

Berlin University, Hegel colleague of Schleiermacher at, 2; when and by whom established, 15.

Blair, Rev. Hugh, studied and translated by Schleiermacher, 11.

Book of Genesis, Robertson's lectures on, 77.

Books of Samuel, Robertson's lectures on, 77.

Brechin, birthplace of Guthrie, 351, 352.

Brighton ministry, Robertson's, 60, 70, 76, 88.

Brighton, working-men of, 53, 76, 84.

British Critic, Newman's editorship of, 316; Mozley's contribution to, 316.

Brooks, Bishop Phillips, compared with Beecher, 196, 209; with Bushnell, 196, 199, 204, 209, 226, 228, 232, 239, 245; with Emerson, 216; with Guthrie, 202, 243; with Liddon, 209; with Lincoln, 207; with Mozley, 209, 239; with Newman, 197, 205, 209, 246; with Robertson, 197, 204, 209, 216, 222, 225, 228, 232, 238, 239; with Schleiermacher, 203, 204, 216; sermons cited, 243, 244, 246, 247; Puritan ancestry and ecclesiastical influences, 195-196; broad churchman, 197-198; college life, interest in literature and history, 198--199; interest in the lives of great men, Mohammed, Luther, Cromwell, and Carlyle, Harvard humanities, choice of ministry, 200; Divinity